D1319791

The Creativity of God

World, Eucharist, Reason

We have, as a theological community, generally lost a language
in which to speak of the createdness of the world. As a
consequence, our discourses of reason cannot bridge the way
we know God and the way we know the world. Therefore,
argues Oliver Davies, a primary task of contemporary theology
is the regeneration of a Christian account of the world as
sacramental, leading to the formation of a Christian
conception of reason and a new Christocentric understanding
of the real. Both the Johannine tradition of creation through
the Word and a Eucharistic semiotics of Christ as the
embodied, sacrificial and creative speech of God serve the
project of a repairal of Christian cosmology. The world itself is
viewed as a creative text authored by God, of which we as
interpreters are an integral part. This is a wide-ranging and
convincing book that makes an important contribution to
modern theology.

OLIVER DAVIES is Professor of Christian Doctrine at
King's College London. He is also a visiting fellow at the
Centre for the Study of Christianity and Culture at Regent's
Park College, University of Oxford. He is the author of *A
Theology of Compassion* (2001) and has co-edited, with Denys
Turner, *Silence and the Word* (2002).

Cambridge Studies in Christian Doctrine

Edited by
Professor COLIN GUNTON, *King's College London*
Professor DANIEL W. HARDY, *University of Cambridge*

Cambridge Studies in Christian Doctrine is an important series which aims to engage critically with the traditional doctrines of Christianity, and at the same time to locate and make sense of them within a secular context. Without losing sight of the authority of scripture and the traditions of the Church, the books in this series subject pertinent dogmas and credal statements to careful scrutiny, analysing them in light of the insights of both church and society, and thereby practise theology in the fullest sense of the word.

Titles published in the series

The Creativity of God

World, Eucharist, Reason

OLIVER DAVIES

PUBLISHED BY THE PRESS SYNDICATE OF THE UNIVERSITY OF CAMBRIDGE
The Pitt Building, Trumpington Street, Cambridge, United Kingdom

CAMBRIDGE UNIVERSITY PRESS
The Edinburgh Building, Cambridge CB2 2RU, UK
40 West 20th Street, New York, NY 10011-4211, USA
477 Williamstown Road, Port Melbourne, VIC 3207, Australia
Ruiz de Alarcón 13, 28014 Madrid, Spain
Dock House, The Waterfront, Cape Town 8001, South Africa

http://www.cambridge.org

First published 2004

Printed in the United Kingdom at the University Press, Cambridge

Typefaces Lexicon No. 2 9/13 pt. and Lexicon No. 1   *System* LᴬTᴇX 2ε   [TB]

A catalogue record for this book is available from the British Library

Library of Congress cataloguing in publication data

Davies, Oliver, 1956–
The creativity of God: world, Eucharist, reason / Oliver Davies.
    p.   cm. (Cambridge Studies in Christian doctrine; 12)
Includes bibliographical references and index.
ISBN 0 521 83117 2 (hardback) ISBN 0 521 53845 9 (paperback)
1. Philosophical theology.   2. Creation.   3. Lord's Supper.   4. Reason.
I. Title.   II. Series.
BT40.D385   2004
231.7–dc22   2003065448 CIP

ISBN 0 521 83117 2 hardback
ISBN 0 521 53845 9 paperback

For Joyce and Isaac

Was in Deiner Sprache das Seyn ist, möchte ich lieber das Wort nennen.

What is termed 'being' in your language, I would prefer to call 'word'.
Johann Georg Hamann, *Letter to F. H. Jacobi*

Contents

Acknowledgements

Many books which have been long in the gestation are indebted in countless ways to more individuals than can easily be named. This book is no exception. I have a particular and very personal indebtedness to friends and scholars who have contributed hugely to the progress of this book at the Universities of Virginia and of Cambridge. Amongst these I should name Peter Ochs and David Ford; but there are many others whose input has been of great value, as well as those whose contribution is unknown either to themselves or to me. I must give special thanks also to the series editors, Daniel Hardy and Colin Gunton, for their invaluable support. I believe that this book picks up themes in the recent work of Colin Gunton, whose untimely death has been such a loss for the theological community. I must thank also Father Gregory Kant and Deacon Chris Morash of the Church of the Incarnation in Charlottesville, Virginia, who welcomed myself and my family into the vibrant sacramental life of the parish at a critical period in the formation of the Eucharistic theology that will be found in these pages. My thanks are due also to Paul Fiddes for our many 'Berlin' conversations, and I wish to thank Gavin Flood for his enduring support, engagement and friendship. I am grateful to the Arts and Humanities Research Board for a grant which facilitated the writing of this book. The book is dedicated to Joyce, my mother, and to Isaac, my 'first-born'.

Introduction
The cosmological imperative

πάντα δι' αὐτοῦ ἐγένετο, καὶ χωρὶς αὐτοῦ
ἐγένετο οὐδὲ ἕν.

All things came into being through him, and without him
not one thing came into being.

      John 1:3

The Christian doctrine that God is creator is as much a claim about the nature of the world in which we live as it is about the world's origins or the shape and destiny of the self. And yet theologies addressing the theme of the creation in the modern period tend to focus primarily upon the creatureliness of the self, developed in terms of a theological anthropology, on the one hand and upon the world as product of divine action on the other. What is missing is a concern with the nature of the world as created, and the relation of the world as created with God, by virtue of its nature as world.[1] In the attempt to reconcile the traditional ways in which we speak about God with the ways in which science teaches us to talk about the world, contemporary discussions of science and theology have moved beyond the argument from design, seeking also to explore points of agreement between scientific and theological method and between a scientific

---

[1]. Stephen Toulmin drew attention to this deficit in his *The Return to Cosmology: Postmodern Science and the Theology of Nature* (Berkeley: University of California Press, 1982). The integration of science, cosmology and theology (together with ethics) has recently been attempted by Nancey Murphy and George F. R. Ellis in their *On the Moral Nature of the Universe* (Minneapolis: Fortress Press, 1996). See also Kathryn Tanner, *God and Creation in Christian Theology: Tyranny or Empowerment?* (Oxford: Blackwell, 1988); Dan Hardy, 'Christ and Creation', in *idem, God's Ways with the World* (Edinburgh: T. & T. Clark, 1996), pp. 114–31 and 'Creation and Eschatology', in *God's Ways*, pp. 151–70; Colin Gunton, *Christ and Creation* (Carlisle: Paternoster Press and Grand Rapids: Eerdmans, 1992) and *The Triune Creator* (Edinburgh: Edinburgh University Press, 1998).

and a theological understanding of the world.[2] In some cases there are certainly traces of an investigation of the world as created but these are inevitably closely tied to the data and insights of science. Whether viewed from the perspective of scientists interested in a theology of creation, or from the perspective of theologians who are concerned with the operation of divine causality within the world, modern theology, which is to say, post-medieval theology, shows an extensive deficit in its engagement with the *createdness* of the world.

There are many different ways of accounting for this state of affairs, which is the product of fundamental and complex changes in science and culture during the sixteenth and seventeenth centuries. But it may be helpful to point to two distinct uses of the term 'explanation' and to the rise of one at the expense of the other. The first use derives from Baconian science and is normative in science today. To explain is to understand the causes of something. It therefore offers a way of predicting, even of replicating, the phenomenon concerned. For Francis Bacon similarly, to know the essence of something is to know how it is made.[3] Amos Funkenstein has referred to this as 'ergetic', or technological knowledge.[4] Science from this perspective offers explanatory models for understanding why the world is as it is and is not other. But there is a second usage of 'explanation', which is akin to what Stephen Toulmin has described as a system-theory account of explanation, which renders an individual event intelligible by placing it within a broader scheme of things, based upon 'the principle of regularity'.[5] Explanation in this sense serves to establish the broader coherence of a set of beliefs by drawing more and more data within its scope. This is a kind of thinking which we do all the time, as

2. On scientific arguments for the dynamic openness of the world, and thus its availability to divine power, see for instance A. R. Peacocke, *Creation and the World of Science* (Oxford and New York: Oxford University Press, 1979), pp. 104–11 and 209–11 and *Paths from Science towards God* (Oxford: Oneworld Publications, 2001). See also John Polkinghorne, *Science and Providence* (London: SPCK, 1989), *Reason and Reality* (London: SPCK, 1991) and his more recent edited volume *The Work of Love. Creation as Kenosis* (London: SPCK, 2001).

3. Francis Bacon, *Novum Organum*, Book II, Section 5 (*Works*, vol. I, pp. 230–1).

4. Amos Funkenstein, *Theology and the Scientific Imagination: from the Middle Ages to the Seventeenth Century* (Princeton: Princeton University Press, 1986), pp. 12 and 290–327.

5. Stephen Toulmin, *Foresight and Understanding* (New York: Harper and Row, 1963), p. 39. Toulmin borrows this term from Copernicus' *Commentariolus* by which Copernicus intended to make a clear distinction between scientific explanation as *prediction* and scientific explanation as *understanding*. Toulmin points out that some efficient predictive systems, such as mathematical models for the movements of tides or of planets, for instance, have scant claim to be based on an understanding of the events they predict, whereas other successful scientific theories, such as Darwinianism, cannot be said to have any significant predictive value (in terms, that is, of the precise characteristics of new species that may evolve). See Toulmin, *Foresight*, pp. 18–43.

Quine has demonstrated, and it is indicative of the way in which a particular set of beliefs which we implicitly or explicitly hold to be true expands to fill the shape of our world.[6] We cannot be agnostic about everything for which we hold no firm evidence or of which we have no grounded
understanding. Indeed, 'scientism' or a materialistic world-view which
sits heavily on our society is itself a product of explanation in this second
sense. The binding nature of scientific verification within the laboratory
cannot be extended into more general questions about human reality or
about the meaning and nature of the world without a substantial increase
in subjectivism, which itself seriously conflicts with the scientific method.
Most scientistic accounts of the world are shot through with a variety of
materialistic and reductionist ideologies and subjectivities, only partially
concealed.

Perhaps a better way of describing explanation in this second, systems-
theory sense is as the production, deepening and extension of 'meaning',
or what Werner Jeanrond has termed 'macro-hermeneutics'.[7] It is through
the generation of meaning that we come to be at home in the world. It
might be judged important, then, that the Christian community should
have to hand an account or accounts of the meaning and intelligibility of
the world as *created*. But the contours of contemporary faith are such that
while we may believe ourselves to be the creatures of God, and the world to
have its origins in the creativity of the divine will, we are making thereby
little more than a claim regarding the proprietorship of the world, which
is to say that the world belongs to God. Hence we are answerable to God
for the ways in which we deal with it, against a secular view of the autonomy of the human. It is therefore almost purely political in its application. It is possible also that the contemporary importance of the claim that
God created the world is a tacit acknowledgement on the part of the Christian community of the centrality which explanation in our first sense, as
tracing the cause of a thing, has taken on in our culture. It might therefore represent an attempt to contest secularism on its own epistemological
ground: by arguing that God is the ultimate *cause* and that those who know
and understand the ways of God have most authority when it comes to pro-
nouncing on ultimate causes.[8] But if this is the case, then it is clear that the
emphasis among theologians on explanation in the first sense is at the cost

6. W. V. Quine, *Pursuit of Truth* (Cambridge, Mass.: Harvard University Press, 1990).
7. Werner Jeanrond, *Theological Hermeneutics* (New York: Crossroad, 1991), p. 4.
8. I would myself share Thomas Aquinas' scepticism whether human beings can ever grasp
the meaning of a truly divine and total act of creation (see *Summa theologiae* (*ST*) I, q. 45).

of explanation in the second sense, with the consequence that those who hold to a theology of creation (amongst whom of course we should also include Jews and Muslims) are significantly under-resourced with respect to grasping the meaning or intelligibility of the world specifically as created.

The first thesis of this book is that successive attempts to accommodate theology to modes of scientific reasoning, for all their legitimacy, may have distracted the theological community from a generous and creative exploration of the *meaning* of the world; and thus, in turn, have led to an inadequate reception of the theology of creation. Some might suggest that such a project is not necessary in itself. After all, the outstanding Christian theologians of modern times have managed perfectly well without it and a concern with the parameters of human existence, as we find in such foundational works as Schleiermacher's *Lectures on Religion*, Kierkegaard's *Philosophical Fragments*, Bonhoeffer's *Act and Being* or Rahner's *Spirit in the World* seem effectively to have taken the place of accounts of the nature of the world. But there is nevertheless one critical difference between the cultural and intellectual contexts of the period from the early nineteenth to the mid twentieth century and our own day. Over the last two decades we have seen an abundance of literature which has served to recontextualise scientific and technological thinking. This is not necessarily to be equated with what some might feel to be an uncompromising relativism, such as we find in Paul Feyerabend or Richard Rorty, but it can also be found in the careful detailing by philosophers of science of the ways in which science is shaped by its economic and social contexts.[9] We are more aware of the proper parameters of scientific reasoning than was the case in previous generations, and it is in this sense that we can take Michel de Certeau's observation that 'reason is placed in question by its own history'.[10] I am not advocating here the undermining of reason as such, however, but rather the recognition that there is a plurality of reasonings, just as we now more generally accept, and experience in our everyday lives, the existence of a plurality of knowledges. Those reasonings are in one way or another tradition-based. They exist only within a framework of specific terminologies and histories, and those that practise them must in some degree be formed within a community that reasons in the same way.

9. Stephen Toulmin, *Cosmopolis: the Hidden Agenda of Modernity* (New York: Free Press, 1990) and Nancey Murphy, *Theology in the Age of Scientific Reasoning* (Ithaca: Cornell University Press, 1990).

10. Michel de Certeau, 'The Black Sun of Language: Foucault', in *idem*, *Heterologies. Discourse on the Other* (Minneapolis: University of Minnesota Press, 1986), pp. 171–84 (here p. 179).

The second thesis of this book has the following form. Firstly, if reason itself is fundamentally the interface between ourselves and the world, then the way that we reason, our understanding of rationality itself, will extensively determine the ways in which we perceive and experience the world. Secondly, if the createdness of the world as content is effaced for us, then the powers and faculties that define the self as a centre of perception, feeling and consciousness in the world are also implicitly allocated to the domain of the non-creationist, which is to say, the secular. Sentience is a form of passivity: the self's own condition as ordered to its objects. Where those objects are predominantly determined as *quanta*, as precisely measurable space-time entities whose causal interactions are quantifiable as fields of force, then the human faculties themselves are ordered to the processes of quantification. It is this that underlies the privileging of technological reason and the dominance of what we might call a 'closed', or reductionist rationalism within our culture.

From the perspective of religion, and our communion with God, by far the most important consequence of this state of affairs is the disjunction between our sense of the divine and our ordinary perceptual experience. The vocabulary we use about ordinary perception and our knowledge of the world can be extraordinarily precise, but when we speak about knowing God, we refer to 'mysticism', 'spirituality' or 'religious experience', all of which are highly indeterminate, or indeed evasive, about which human faculties are in play. To some extent, of course, this is explicable as an acknowledgement that God is not an object and cannot be known as objects in the world are known. But it is indicative also of the deeper problematic which flows from the fact that the world is not known *as created* in our ordinary perceptions. Our knowledge of God is thereby not set in any kind of relation at all with our ordinary knowing, neither one of consummation nor of contradiction, despite the fact that according to the Christian doctrine of the creation, the world which we ordinarily know belongs to God and is of God's making.

Here the contrast with a pre-modern world-view is helpful. Since the createdness of the world was visible in its nature as world, in the medieval synthesis, the human faculties which were ordered to that world retained an openness from within to the knowledge of God the Creator. What we would today term 'religious experience' was understood in the pre-modern cosmos to be already implied in and intrinsic to ordinary cognition. It was figured either as the final stage in the ascent of the mind to God, drawn by the intrinsic momentum of a divine creativity at work in the world, or as the radical negation of ordinary knowledge, that is, as 'unknowing' which is darkness from excess of light, or indeed as a combination of both.[11] The movement of negation denoted by the latter is not simply 'tagged on' to ordinary experience, nor is it a free-floating 'experience of negation', but it is rather a conceptual advance of a radically corrective nature which restores what we have inexactly termed ordinary knowing back to its foundation in an originary divine causality. 'Not knowing' becomes a necessary mode of knowing because the world on which all knowing is predicated is itself mysterious, bearing the marks of divine createdness within it. In other words, the lack of a coherent theological cosmology today has the consequence that our intimacy with God is set outside our intimacy with the world, and neither is fully integrated into the concept of createdness as revealing the deepest nature of the world in which – as creatures – we live.

It is the pre-modern cosmos, with its carnivalistic combinations of the theological and proto-scientific, which offers one of the best examples of an understanding of human reason as created and shaped in its depths by the createdness of the world. The pre-modern however is definitively a place to which we can never return. It was during the 'unmaking of the Christian cosmos' (in W. G. Randles' phrase[12]) from the sixteenth century onwards that the Christian Church suffered some of the most damaging and traumatic intellectual defeats in its history. This cosmology was predicated not only upon what proved over time to be a false understanding of the nature of the universe but also upon a concept of reasoning which identified *scientia* with authority or received traditions. It was a system of thinking which, being deductionist, operated with axioms which could not be questioned, and for which the foundations of knowledge rested ultimately upon a belief in the content and form of divine action that we would today consider to lie outside the realm of faith. Looking back upon that pre-modern world can easily become a futile exercise in a certain kind of cultural nostalgia. But it can also afford valuable insights into imaginative possibilities which have disappeared almost entirely from our own society. The first point to be noted is that – for all their indebtedness to Neoplatonism and Aristotelianism – the pre-modern models of the world were also an attempt to accommodate and listen to a number of scriptural passages which assert the cosmic dimensions of Christ as God's creative

---

11. See the section on Bonaventure's *Itinerarium mentis in deum* at pp. 36–42 below.
12. W. G. L. Randles, *The Unmaking of the Medieval Christian Cosmos, 1500–1760* (Aldershot: Ashgate, 1999).

and universal Word. The Old Testament repeatedly stresses the role of the divine presence who animates the world, whether as the Spirit or the Wisdom of God.[13] In the New Testament, the Gospel of John begins with the affirmation that it is the Word of God through whom 'all things came into being' (Jn 1:1–3), and in the letter to the Colossians we read that Christ is 'the image of the invisible God, the firstborn of all creation; for in him all things in heaven and earth were created, things visible and invisible, whether thrones or dominions or rulers or powers – all things have been created through him and for him' (1:15–16). Hebrews begins with a creationist hymn to Christ who 'sustains all things by his powerful word' (1:2–4), and in 1 Corinthians Jesus Christ is the one 'through whom are all things and through whom we exist' (8:6). In the Gospel of Matthew (11:19; 12:42) and again in 1 Corinthians in particular (1:18–31), deep associations are established between the creationist Wisdom tradition and the person of Christ.[14] As Colin Gunton pointed out, faith in Christ actually implies belief in him as the one through whom we and the world were made.[15] Our failure to think through what these passages might mean for our understanding of the world is a failure also of our Christology and our soteriology. It is a failure to grasp the meaning of the creation in its deepest *coherence*, as being the thematic key not only to the way the world is, but also to what and how we are, and to what God has given us of himself to hold and to understand.

Although possibly somewhat esoteric in character, semiotics, which is the science of signs, offers a succinct and formal account of the structure of meaning, and thus can offer us valuable insights into the relation between self and world. Pre-modern semiotics, in its fullest and most sophisticated developments, constituted what we can call today a 'triadic', or 'pragmatic', mode of reasoning. Stated simply, this was predicated upon the view that the world was created, and that the world's createdness included not only the human self but also the space or relation between self and world, which is the sphere of perception, feeling, imagining and reasoning. Its triadic form flowed from the intrinsic relatedness of self and world on the grounds of a common relation to the Creator God. It was thus a kind of reasoning which is consistent with and posited by a

---

13. See Psalm 33:6: 'By the word of the Lord the heavens were made, and all their host by the breath of his mouth.' See also Prov. 3:19: 'The Lord by wisdom founded the earth; by understanding he established the heavens.'
14. See also Eph. 1 for cosmological Christology.
15. Gunton, *The Triune Creator*, pp. 14–40.

theology of creation in its Jewish, Christian or Islamic form. Meaning, or reality, or world are formed within the coincidence of three elements: signs which signify, 'things' or *realia* which are signified and the people or interpreters for whom the signs refer. This is a kind of semiotics, or logic, which is particularly associated in the modern period with the work of the American pragmatist Charles Sanders Peirce, but it was already characteristic in the complex theological form of the work of those early theologians, including Origen, Augustine, Thomas and Bonaventure, who were operating within a creationist view of the world.[16] That type of reasoning, formulated within a thoroughgoing theology of creation, contrasts with the kinds of reasoning which emerged from the sixteenth century onwards and which show a dyadic, or binary, structure. In dyadic reasoning the human interpreter is not banished from the act of meaning but is in the service of Reason and its entourage which already sets out certain preconceived principles of knowing and thus of the world that is known. The reification of 'reason' as a *mathesis universalis* obscures the fact that what we really mean by reason (noun) are human beings who reason (verb): reasoning is actually an activity carried on by individual subjects at specific times and places. From a Christian perspective those individuals, and their communities, are God's free creatures alive in God's created world. Within such a context, reasoning has to be rethought, therefore, since it is now predicated upon a much more radical conception of the extent to which humans participate in the formation of reality itself. Reality is not a difficult script to be read, or a complex equation (or at least not that alone), requiring highly specialised skills and knowledge. It is not something that we either 'get right or wrong'. It is more fundamentally a place of invitation, a hosting by the divine creativity which takes ourselves to be integral to the performance of the infinite fecundity and goodness of God which is at the root of the world and its meaning.

The present volume represents an attempt to integrate the cosmological passages of Scripture into the contemporary theological mind. Its concern therefore lies with an inquiry into the nature of the world, viewed from a Christological perspective, and with thematics which spring from this, including the nature of the 'real' and the human faculties of reasoning and perception which are ordered to it. It attempts an integrated

---

16. It is Peter Ochs who has so importantly drawn our attention to the alignment between a pre-modern scriptural hermeneutic (in this case a rabbinic one) and contemporary pragmatics. See his groundbreaking study *Peirce, Pragmatism and the Logic of Scripture* (Cambridge: Cambridge University Press, 1998).

account of the self in the world, based upon a reading of the cosmological scriptural passages, and employing elements of contemporary philosophical thought which seem most suited to the development and articulation of a biblical theology of createdness.

In the first two chapters of the book, under the titles 'The architecture of createdness' and 'The metaphysics of createdness', I present a brief outline of the pre-modern cosmos firstly in terms of natural science and astronomy and secondly in terms of metaphysics, semiotics and historical reason. It is only through such an engagement with theological and proto-scientific systems from the past that we are able to grasp today what it means to live in a theophanic cosmos, in which the createdness of the world is powerfully accented. Everything in our own culture militates against such an understanding. In no sense, of course, am I advocating a return to a pre-modern world-view, in which proto-science and theology combined in ways that are unthinkable for us today. But nevertheless we can find instruction here as to the *possibility* of a theological account of the world's createdness. We can see also the immense effects of such a theology on an understanding of the self and of our relation to the world. The third chapter, 'Cosmological fragments', surveys the break-up of the classical synthesis with the rise of modern natural science, as exemplified in the work of Copernicus and Francis Bacon, and sets out some of the early attempts to reinstitute an integral cosmology. The intention here is to observe some of the principal strategies for recreating a sense of humanity's integration into the whole at the outset of the modern period. In the work of Winckelmann, this occurs through an appreciation of art, while in Jacobi we can see 'cosmic' transformations of the intellect. Winckelmann anticipates the 'aesthetic turn', therefore, and a modern transcendental epistemology of the 'sublime', while Jacobi points forward to the religious subjectivity of Schleiermacher and eventually to the tradition of 'religious experience'. Hamann is also included at this stage since we can see in his work a vigorous attempt to retrieve a theological cosmology through a distinctively Hebrew, language-centred and scriptural account of the world. Hamann therefore plays a key role in mediating something of the classical figurations of cosmic createdness in terms which derive closely from Scripture and yet which are free of their proto-scientific and essentialist dimensions.

In chapters 4, 5 and 6, I aim to set out a contemporary account of cosmic createdness through a close reading of scriptural passages which concern the speaking of God. The focus here lies upon a scriptural account of the nature of language itself, and of the way in which human language is contained within and acts as a reflex of divine speech. This is a distinctively biblical view of language and it is one which contrasts with the classical conceptions of language which we otherwise inherit today. The primary locus of language, by this biblical account, is the divine speech itself, which is both revelatory and *creative* in the most originary sense that word can convey. The world comes about by virtue of the divine speaking. What we find here, therefore, is an intimate connection between speech and presence, which is to say, the presence of the Speaker, or God, the one who is addressed, and the world that is spoken about. All three form a unity. But presence, according to this model, is enfolded *within* language and is not extraneous to it. That presence, given with language, and the originary act of divine speaking, is also foundationally plural: each element coexists with the others and cannot be thought outside the context of the others. This plurality is central to the nature of the world, in which language is social, and there is a circularity about the ways in which we speak about the world and the way in which reality comes to meet us in our ordinary experience. A plural, multivocal world is also one which is open to and at times gripped by the divine speaking which, in the Gospel of Jesus Christ, is shown to be triadic. Culture is deeply determinative of the way we act and shape the world. But it is a plurality which is itself grounded in the nature of the divine speaking. The Gospel narrative of Jesus Christ shows that God's speech is in fact Trinitarian. We learn from this disclosure that the multivocity of the originary divine speaking is itself kenotic and compassionate, since – in the revelation which is through the Son and in the Spirit – God speaks with us and not with Godself alone. God must therefore come down to our level, as it were, becoming himself part of the world that is structured according to God's own breathing and speaking.

The second element in this middle section of the book is the use of a theory of the text in order to conceptualise the relation between the divine speaking and the world. The world stands to the divine originary breath/speaking as a written text does to the voice of its author(s). This parallel has a double value. In the first place it offers a model of the coinherence of God and the world which reproduces many aspects of the medieval system of analogy without, however, employing the Aristotelian model of causality which postulates a similarity between cause and effect. And secondly, while a theory of the cosmic text is not explicitly present in Scripture, it is deeply consonant with a scriptural account of the world. Texts, like bodies, are voice-bearing, and when the author entrusts their voice to a text, it undergoes a kind of alienation as the content of the speech passes from an intimate, oral medium to one that is objectified in the visibility of the written word. The text itself thus becomes a modality of embodiedness: a voice-bearing *corpus* of deferred, or replicated, presence. The author now knows that from now on their voice can only be received through an extensive act of interpretation. The authorial voice remains in the text, to be heard and understood, but only indirectly and through the interpretative imagination of others. The world is much like this in its relation to God. It demands to be understood and known by a community of human interpreters. Most fundamentally, the divine voice (and will) can be and frequently is entirely misunderstood and abused by its human interpreters. The divine voice, or breath, which is entrusted to the text of the world becomes estranged within the medium of the text. It is this that leads to the second cycle of divine creativity, which is the repristination of the text of the world. In this section of the book, I develop a pneumatology which understands the Holy Spirit to be the continuing presence of the divine breath/voice in the world – the world-text's memory of its origin in God – and the Son to be the redemptive and sacrificial sounding again of the divine speaking *within* the text, as the retrieval of the world-text back into the flux of originary Trinitarian speech.

The third section of the book is concerned with the model of reality which emerges from the Eucharistic celebration, itself a making present of the redemptive sacrifice of God. The words of institution, which form part of the Passion narrative, represent the point at which Christ's body merged with the world and the divine voice was heard again, anticipating the resurrection and ascension. Intrinsic to our own liturgical participation in that moment, which was the moment in which Jesus – as the Word of God – entered the divine logic of Scripture, is the communication of the world as the body or self-communication of God, to and within the worshipping community. In the Real Presence of the Eucharist, the universality of Christ as root of the physical universe is made sacramentally present to the liturgical community. In ways that are unfathomable to us, we discover the world to be the embrace of God, and thus find our own bodily existence to be refigured and ourselves to be set in a new relation with the world. In the penultimate chapter I explore the contours of this new sense of embodiment in the light of a transformative encounter with Christ as the body of the world. And in the final chapter, I reflect upon the kind of reasoning which is generated by this new condition of being in the world, focusing in particular upon pragmatic reasoning which recognises the extent to which we are ourselves implicated in the real. I seek to develop an account of pragmatic reasoning from within an exegesis of the transfiguration pericope, in the belief that it is this kind of reasoning which implicitly bears the contours of a theology of creation and thus, in its higher intensifications, carries with it a movement of sanctification and glorification.

This volume as a whole, then, sets out to offer a repairal or healing of the concept of reasoning through reinvestigating the cognitive relation between humanity and the world, which is to say, the functioning of the human faculties within the world of God's making. It is an attempt to make sense of those scriptural passages which affirm the cosmic character of Christ as source, root and ultimate *meaning* of the world. This is inevitably a heuristic project; it is not one that can be demonstrated or coercively argued. Rather, the kind of 'explanation' at work here is one which appeals to a sense of the order of things and to Christian experience of the world in its deepest aspects, which is conceived in freedom. It is an imaginative exercise as much as a discursive and analytical one. And the imagination will inevitably have a crucial role where issues concerning the nature of the world as such are in play. We cannot conceive of the world's fullness except in terms of horizons and leaps of understanding as we move from the particular and known to what might be, to what lies at the limits of the conceivable. It is this power of extension which is the proper function and play of the imagination. Of all our faculties, it is the imagination which most seems to grant a creative space, or possibility, to the self as we live out our lives in the world. It is in this sense, therefore, that this book seeks freely to engage the theological imagination of the reader, offering a new alignment, or recontextualisation, of our ways of reasoning, and thus perhaps liberating new possibilities of making sense of God's world, and of finding our rightful place within it.

An archaeology of createdness

The architecture of createdness

La gloria di colui che tutto move
per l'universo penetra e risplende
In una parte più e meno altrove.

The glory of him who moves all things
Penetrates the universe and shines
In one part more and in another less.

Dante, *Paradiso*, canto I

The project of constructing a new theology of the createdness of the world can usefully begin with a reflection on world-views from the past which achieved this same aim, though in ways deeply alien to us today. But the cosmological sense-world is constructed of diverse impulses and ideas in a complex unity of sense-inputs, presuppositions, ideas and imagination. The reconstruction of an implicit cosmology in the pre-modern period is a particularly demanding task, therefore, which entails the analysis of fields as diverse as astronomy, the arts, metaphysics, semiotics and epistemology, all of which can be said to interact in distinctive ways in the formation of what we might call 'the sense of a world'. In the following chapter, two different cosmological structures will emerge. The first is cosmology *by extension*, which placed heaven in the heavens, at a point far removed from the earth, but in a field of extension that was continuous with it. This is perhaps most difficult for us to understand today though it was, arguably, the most foundational aspect in the formation of medieval perception with its ideologies of heaven as site of our highest values and ultimate destiny. The second is cosmology by *participation*. This is the hierarchical universe whereby transcendental, eternal realities become manifest within the empirical domain, by virtue of its 'symbolic' character, where the notion of symbol carries a metaphysical charge which is again unfamiliar to us today. Presupposed here is the belief that heaven is potentially present everywhere, since – as the highest stratum of existence – it is implicated at all the lower levels which can under certain circumstances become transparent to it. This capacity of the sense-world to undergo transformation has deep consequences also for the ways in which the pre-modern world understood the nature of the human mind which engages with and is permeated by that sense-reality. It is that theme which I shall take up in chapter 2.

Heaven in the heavens

The idea of heaven is pervasively present in medieval thought and culture.[1] A pre-modern cosmology in its formal aspect was the product of two competing groups: Christian theologians and natural philosophers.[2] The concern of the theologians lay with expounding the meaning of the 'two heavens', the second of which – the firmament – divided the waters which were above the firmament from those which were below (Gen. 1:6–7). Their further concern lay with the relation between an incorporeal God and a corporeal universe and with the final dwelling place of the Blessed, that is with heaven as the seat of God. Natural philosophers on the other hand applied the principles of classical science, as mediated through Neoplatonic and – from the late twelfth century onwards – Aristotelian texts, to an understanding of the shape and functions of the universe. Two problematics showed the interaction of these schools. The first concerned heliocentrism, which combined questions of mechanics and physics with theological concerns about the place of humanity in the universe, while a second, which was the issue of the location of the Empyrean (or dwelling place of the Blessed), combined general astronomy with questions to do with the character of the life of the saints in heaven. This latter theme seems remote to us today and it has received relatively little scholarly attention, but it represented a nodal point of cosmological thinking in the pre-modern world.

1. See Jan Swango Emerson and Hugo Feiss, eds., *Imagining Heaven in the Middle Ages: a Body of Essays* (New York and London: Garland Publishing, 2000) and Colleen McDannell and Bernard Lang, eds., *Heaven. A History* (2nd edn, New Haven: Yale University Press, 2001).
2. W. G. L. Randles, *The Unmaking of the Medieval Christian Cosmos, 1500–1760* (Aldershot: Ashgate, 1999), pp. 1–8. These two groups were later joined by the early astronomers who were beginning to measure the movements of the heavenly bodies in new ways.

The need to combine Scripture with 'science' was already apparent in the influential, fourth-century text known as the pseudo-Clementine *Recognitiones*. Here the firmament is identified as being 'solid ice, hard as crystal' which took up all the space between the earth and the first heaven.[3] This closely followed the account in Genesis (the 'water below the firmament' of Genesis becoming ice or crystal) and established a tradition which was to be followed by a number of influential early medieval theologians, including the Venerable Bede and Raban Maur.[4] A significant problem with this model lay in combining the solidity of the firmament with the movement of the planets, and it would later be modified by a return to the separate, rotating crystalline spheres of the Ptolemaic universe. A second model marking a synthesis between scriptural and classical accounts was devised by Basil the Great (329–79) and set out in his *Homilies on the Hexaemeron*. In contrast with the pseudo-Clementine firmament of continuous ice or crystal, Basil proposed that the continuous element was 'humid air' and that the firmament separated the lower part, of clouds, from a higher, more refined realm of purified air.[5] Basil's position proved to be an important anticipation of an idea which later gained ground in Europe with the influence of Aristotle's *On the Heavens*, in which Aristotle advanced the concept of the 'fifth element'.[6] As the 'primary body of all', it is quite unlike earth, air, fire or water; it is 'eternal, suffers neither growth nor diminution, but is ageless, unalterable and impassive'.[7] Only one kind of motion, or change, is native to it, which is that of a perfectly circular movement; it has no linear motion. Albert the Great cited the possibility that the fifth element extended from the moon as far as the outer circle or Empyrean. Thomas Aquinas affirmed that the heavens were composed of Aristotle's 'fifth element' in his *Commentary on the Sentences*, although he avoided stating any particular view in the *Summa Theologiae*.[8] From the thirteenth century onwards, the Aristotelian 'aether' came progressively to be seen as the rarified substance of which the planets themselves were composed and which constituted the medium through which they moved.

3. *Die Pseudoklementinen*, vol. II: *Rekognitionen in Rufins Übersetzung*, ed. Bernhard Rehm (Berlin: Akademie-Verlag, 1965). The text survives in Rufinus' Latin translation.
4. Randles, *Medieval Christian Cosmos*, pp. 2–3.
5. Ibid., pp. 3–5.
6. Pierre Duhem, *Le système du monde*, vol. I (Paris: A. Hermann, 1913), pp. 198–205.
7. *On the Heavens*, I, 3, 270b (W. K. C. Guthrie, trans., *Aristotle on the Heavens* (Cambridge, Mass.: Harvard University Press, 1960), p. 23).
8. *ST* I, q. 68, a. 1.

Aristotle's 'fifth element' was also to play a vital role in the developing conception of the Empyrean as the eternal dwelling-place of the Blessed.[9] Basil the Great was the first specifically to link the first heaven of Genesis tradition with the dwelling of the saints, and the advent of Aristotelianism provided a new framework for reflection upon the nature of this heaven and the character of the life of the saints. Aristotle's aether functioned as a 'place' and provided a space for 'substantial entities', though this entailed something of an enigma, since God could not be contained in any place. The collision of the Aristotelian principle that everything has its natural place in the cosmos, which dictates its natural movement, with the theological principle of the incorporeality of the Godhead (the contemplation of whom is the bliss of the Blessed in heaven) led to diverse strategies of reconciliation. Albert the Great, for instance, added an eleventh heaven, above the Empyrean, for the Trinity and, from the period of Thomas Bradwardine (*c.* 1290–1349), God was held to occupy 'an infinite imaginary space' beyond the spheres. But if the Empyrean was a body and a place, in the Aristotelian sense, then it was reasonable to ask what kind of life was possible for the saints in their own resurrected bodies. This kind of question is generally left to one side by modern Christian theologians, who may feel that the mysterious character of the body of glory and of heaven precludes too precise an inquiry. But the medievals, with their mix of theology and physics, asked very specific and detailed questions about the operation of the senses in the Empyrean, in the belief that the farthest reaches of the universe still exhibited the same kind of spacial characteristics as were evident on earth.

Albert the Great first surveyed the operation of the five senses in the Empyrean, tackling the problem of how sight might be possible in a space of unparalleled brilliance, and how people might be able to speak in 'indivisible and impassible' air.[10] In the Empyrean, odours would be the product not of corruption, as was the case according to Aristotelian principles, but would be transmitted as a 'sensible species', and the saints would still possess the power of taste, even if they were not called upon to use it. Finally, the faculty of touch would be maintained but only through the

---

9. The Christians first met the term in Neoplatonist texts (*Historisches Wörterbuch der Philosophie*, vol. II, pp. 478–9).
10. Randles points in particular to *Summa Theologiae Pars Secunda*, tract. XI, qu. 52, mem. II (*Opera Omnia*, ed. A. Borgnet (Paris, 1895), vol. XXXII, p. 555). Medieval views on the operations of the senses in the Empyrean are surveyed by Randles in *Medieval Christian Cosmos*, pp. 12–31.

spiritual senses and not by direct action upon the body. Writing in his *Commentary on the Sentences*, Thomas Aquinas similarly surveyed the senses, drawing upon Albert's work, and concluded regarding vision (in Randles' summary) that 'the brightness of a body in the state of glory does not adversely affect the transparency of the pupil of the eye because the state of glory does not abolish nature'.[11] The Spanish Franciscan Alphonso de Tostado de Rivera Madrigal (1401–54/55) was perhaps the most physicalist in his thinking about the conditions of life of the saints in the Empyrean. In his account 'paradise is a place in the widest sense of the word inside the denseness of the orb of the Empyrean and it is neither vacuous, nor full of air, but it is the heavenly body itself in the dense mass of which are the souls of the Blessed'. The resurrected saints 'will be inside the Empyrean … within the mass of the substance of the heavenly orb, exactly as a man would be inside a stone or inside a wall'.[12]

Within a century the notion of the Empyrean began to wane, however. It was rejected by the Protestants as being a scholastic construct, and the new astronomy had no place for it. When Copernicus published his groundbreaking work *De revolutionibus orbium caelestium* in 1543, he took no account of the biblical universe. The Empyrean remained an important element in Catholic theology, however, until the mid seventeenth century. The Flemish Jesuit Leonard Lessius (1554–1623) strongly maintained the impossibility of adequately conceiving of the Empyrean, with its saintly hierarchies, outside an Aristotelian understanding of space and, perhaps borrowing the phrase 'some sort of celestial air' (*auram quamdam caelestam*) from Kepler, advocated a fluid and airy interior to the Empyrean in which the senses of the saints could function freely.[13] The Portuguese Jesuit Sebastião Barradas (1543–1615) on the other hand argued that all the senses of the saints would function normally within the solid Empyrean 'by miracle'. Their bodies would be naked but radiant with different colours – green, gold, white and blue. And the Blessed would have their own houses, all transparent but some more luxurious than others, as befitting rank. The Baroque character of Barradas' vision is evident, and Gabriel Henao described it as 'pious and florid' in his *Empyreologia*. Henao, who was otherwise so inclined to literalism and to traditional teaching on the Empyrean, added that the allusion to dwellings should be taken

---

11. Randles, *Medieval Christian Cosmos*, p. 24. A key text in Thomas is the *Commentum in quattuor libros sententiarum*, IV, dist. 44, q. 2, 1 d.
12. Quoted in Randles, *Medieval Christian Cosmos*, pp. 28–9.
13. Ibid., pp. 138–9.

'metaphorically', implicitly acknowledging that some discussions of the Empyrean which had previously been an attempt to explain, understand and educate were now becoming emotive descriptions aimed at spiritual improvement.[14]

The universe as outlined by Aristotle in his treatise *On the Heavens* resonated positively with the Christian world-view in several important ways. In the first place, it was predicated on principles that had been worked out with respect to the world of ordinary perceptions; to that extent it understood the cosmic in terms of the earth. This was to assert an anthropocentric view of the universe which conformed with the cosmic centrality of humanity according to the Christian religion. Aristotle's conviction that the earth was an immobile object at the centre of the universe gave a primacy also to the earth, as the place in which the cosmic events of salvation history took place. Much would be made in the sixteenth and seventeenth centuries about the verses at Joshua 10:12–14 in which God caused the 'sun to stand still in the sky', since this seemed inconsistent with the new heliocentrism which challenged the Christian and Aristotelian claim that humanity and the earth were situated at the centre of the universe. The human image of the cosmos was sustained also by the extension into the spheres of the Aristotelian concept of body and space: the one being ordered to the other. Although Aristotle's fifth element, aether, was set apart from the other elements in terms of its properties, it was still recognisably an element in which substances could have local existence. Aristotle dismissed the possibility that the heavenly bodies might be suspended in a void on the grounds that motion through a void is not possible. The extension of the fifth element to the Empyrean enabled Christian theologians to focus their concern on the nature of the existence of the saints in heaven, a matter which, though it may seem 'otiose' to us to today, as Randles points out, makes perfect sense where conceptions central to both theology and physics overlap.[15] Finally Aristotle also offered a finite world, in which all matter was contained within the limits

---

14. Gabriel Henao published his *Empyreologia seu philosophia christiana de empyreo caelo* in 1652, over a hundred years after the appearance of Copernicus' *De revolutionibus orbium caelestium* (1543). In two substantial volumes Henao, a Spanish Jesuit, summarised arguments from previous centuries concerning, for instance, the density of the 'air' breathed by the saints in the Empyrean that formed the outermost, or uppermost, ring of the universe (how this compared with the thin air of high mountains), whether they could actually walk outside the Empyrean, on its convex surface, and whether God and Christ were located in the same physical place as the saints (see Randles, *Medieval Christian Cosmos*, pp. 140–1).

15. Randles, *Medieval Christian Cosmos*, p. 31.

of the universe. However vast the projected distances and masses, the Aristotelian universe was one which did not know the embarrassment of infinity.

Heaven on earth

The application of Aristotelian principles to the cosmos as a whole set up a continuum of experience between earth and the farthest reaches of the universe and legitimated an imaginative appropriation of space into the concerns of human society and religion. In effect, it projected the human body into the farthest reaches of space. But at the same time, we find in the pre-modern period a conviction that heaven is not only located at an identifiable point in the physical universe, in the farthest circle of the stars, but that the heavenly is also visible on earth, within the contours of our everyday empirical perceptions.[16] Liturgy is one of the foremost examples of this, and it is one with which we are familiar today. The liturgical cycle ensures that the passage of 'ordinary' time is constantly overtaken by eschatological, or what we might even call 'cosmic' time. The Christian notion of time as an anticipation, reception and proleptical celebration of the fullness of messianic presence is reinforced by liturgy as the centre to which temporal progression constantly refers. But in the pre-modern world, music, with its links to the arts and to mathematics, and architecture, were also powerfully expressive of the celestial realities on earth.

Music

Three Platonic themes are of particular importance for the theology of medieval music. The first is found in a passage from the *Timaeus* in which Plato argues that proportion or harmony is the very principle of the cosmos itself.[17] Even the spheres make a harmonious sound as they move through the heavens.[18] The second is a passage from the *Republic* where Plato maintains that the study of music-mathematics gives access to the inner realities of the cosmos.[19] And the third is the belief that music can have

16. See Emerson and Feiss, eds., *Imagining Heaven*, for a survey of the relevant sources.
17. *Timaeus*, 35–6.
18. *Republic*, X, 617a–b.
19. *Republic*, VII, 531a–d. See also Book VI of Augustine's *De musica*, where he explicates music as a direct route from the 'material to the immaterial' (ii.2; but see also i.1, and xiii.38–xvii.58). A new edition of Augustine's *De musica*, Book VI, has recently appeared by Martin Jacobsson (*Aurelius Augustinus. De musica liber VI*, Acta Universitatis Stockholmiensis, Studia Latina Stockholmiensia 47, Stockholm: Almqvist & Wiksell International, 2002).

an ennobling and formative effect on the human soul.[20] All three of these principles play through a text on music which can be dated to the early sixth century and which was to exercise a great influence down the centuries. Boethius' *De institutione musica*, which formed part of his *Quadrivium* or introduction to the arithmetical sciences, divides the study of music into three aspects.[21] The first is the cosmic music which is produced by the movement of the spheres. Although we cannot in fact hear this music, Boethius insists that 'it is nevertheless impossible that the extreme speed of movement of such vast bodies should produce absolutely no sound at all'.[22] Music is the principle of the harmony of the cosmos, so it is in the intrinsic consonance of the elements and the seasons that we perceive this particular kind of fundamental musical form. Boethius' second type of music is internal to humankind and is again the principle of order and harmony which in this case governs the relation between soul and body. It is on account of this that 'music is so naturally united with us that we cannot be free from it even if we wished to be so'.[23] We are thus deeply affected by the character of the music we hear, and can be formed in our moral nature by the qualities of music.[24] The third kind is music produced by stringed, percussive and wind instruments, and it is this to which Boethius dedicates the rest of his discussion.

Although the books from Boethius' treatise, in which he is likely to have discussed 'cosmic' and 'human' harmonies drawing upon Ptolemy's *Harmonica*, do not survive, the 'speculative' dimensions of music as the principle of order and harmony which underlies all things were not lost from view in later discussions of 'practical' music.[25] The principal reason for this was the understanding of music itself as a science of ratios and proportions. Music represented the most immediate access to the systems of numbers and calculations which constitute the underlying order of the world. The study of music, therefore, with its close proximity to mathematics, was an ideal prelude to the study of philosophy, as Aristotle had

---

20. *Republic*, III, 401d–402a.

21. For a general discussion of Boethius' work on music and the mix of Aristotelian and Platonic sources in its composition, see Leo Schrade, 'Music in the Philosophy of Boethius', *The Musical Quarterly* 33 (1947), 188–200.

22. Book I, Chapter 2.

23. Book I, Chapter 1.

24. David S. Chamberlain gives a fuller and richer exposition of the moral force of music in Boethius' Consolation of Philosophy in his 'Philosophy of Music in the Consolation of Boethius', *Speculum* 45 (1970), 80–97.

25. Henry Chadwick, *Boethius. The Consolations of Music, Logic, Theology and Philosophy* (Oxford: Clarendon Press, 1981), pp. 81–3.

noted, and to the ultimate and highest meanings of the universe.[26] Even with respect to the work of a thirteenth-century scholastic theologian such as Richard Grosseteste, the argument has been made that 'music was absolutely essential for understanding the basic concepts that formed a foundation for all the disciplines'.[27] The performance of music, then, as a social art was the practical expression of an understanding of the underlying order of things which 'tuned' the human soul to the deeper realities, themselves numerical in form, as it inspired the listeners and raised their souls to contemplation of the highest things.

A further insight into the meaning of music in the medieval world comes from the writings of the Benedictine Abbess, Hildegard of Bingen (1098–1179), who was herself one of the most creative of medieval composers. Following an interdict placed upon the practice of singing in the daily worship of her community, Hildegard wrote a letter to the prelates of Mainz in which she vigorously defended the role of music in the formation of the human spirit. Music, she argued, embodies the innocence of humanity before the Fall so that 'in Adam's voice, before he fell, there was the sound of every harmony and the sweetness of the whole art of music'. Indeed, had Adam remained 'in the condition in which he was formed, human frailty could never endure the power and the resonance of that voice'.[28] Hildegard reminds the clerics that the devil had been greatly perturbed when he 'heard that men and women had begun to sing through divine inspiration, and that they would be transformed through this to remembering the sweetness of the songs in the heavenly land'.[29] Music here is identified with a pre-lapsarian state and is particularly associated with heaven so that the performance of music is a direct participation on earth in the heavenly reality.

It is in Hildegard too that we find an imaginative synthesis of the cosmological theology of John 1:3 with the classical conception of harmony as the measure of the cosmic order. In her *Liber divinorum operum* she equates the sounding of the Word with the very life of creatures:

> The Word sounded and brought all creatures into being. In this way the Word and God are one. As the Word sounded, he called to himself all of creation which had been predestined and established in eternity.

---

26. Cf. *Metaphysics*, XIII, 1078a31–1078b6.

27. Nancy van Deusen, *Theology and Music at the Early University* (Leiden: E. J. Brill, 1995), p. 206.

28. Hildegard von Bingen, 'Hildegardis ad praelatos Moguntinensis', in L. van Acker, ed., *Hildegardis Bingensis Epistolarium, Pars Prima I–XC* (Turnholt: Brepols, 1991), pp. 61–6.

29. Ibid.

> His resonance awakened everything to life ... Now when the Word of
> God sounded, this Word appeared in every creature and this sound was
> life in every creature.[30]

This represents a bold advocacy of sound as the foundation of divine creativity, whereby the world is ordered in its own particularity and yet is
constructed from within the divine nature. In contrast with emanationist
theologies of light, or of the idea, the life of creatures is identified in this
passage with the sound-word-voice that proceeds from a divine speaker
and which in a dialectical combination of immanence and transcendence
both remains distinct from and identical with its source.

Architecture

One of the functions of music is to unite the two distinct trajectories of
the medieval world-image, that is, cosmology by extension and by participation. The 'music of the spheres' belongs to the passage of the heavenly
bodies through the aether, while music performed on earth is a participation in the heavenly cycle of praise. The element of light performs a similar
function. Light is the first principle of the created universe: it is the intelligibility of things. But light is also seen as the effulgence of the uncreated
light – and Christ himself as the first 'radiance'. It is the interplay of these
two distinct perspectives developed in terms of architecture that comes to
the fore in a treatise written by Abbot Suger following the reconstruction
of central parts of the Church of St Denis in 1144. The *Libellus de consecratione
ecclesiae S. Dionysii* contains two striking passages. The first is a celebration
of light associated with the rebuilding of the choir in the new Gothic style:

> Once the new rear part is joined to the part in front,
> The church shines with its middle part brightened.
> For bright is that which is brightly coupled with the bright,
> And bright is the noble edifice which is pervaded by the new light;
> Which stands enlarged in our time ...[31]

The 'new light' (*lux nova*) is simultaneously the light of Christ and his
New Dispensation and is the greater dispersal of light achieved by the new
choir in Gothic style to replace the duller Carolingian apse.[32] An important

---

30. *Liber divinorum operum*, IV, 105.
31. Quoted from *Abbot Suger on the Abbey Church of St-Denis and its Art Treasures*, ed., trans. and
annotated by Erwin Panofsky (2nd edn by Gerda Panofsky-Soergel, Princeton: Princeton
University Press, 1979), pp. 50–1.
32. Panofsky, *Abbot Suger*, p. 22.

influence upon Abbot Suger was the *Celestial Hierarchy* of Pseudo-Denys, whose works were preserved in the abbey, on the grounds of mistaken historical assumptions regarding the saint and the abbey's dedication. Pseudo-Denys articulated a symbolic system predicated in no small part on a cosmic hierarchy of light, which fell or cascaded from the heavens to earth, animating and spiritualising all things. In the *Celestial Hierarchy*, where he considers the orders of supernatural beings, he defines 'hierarchy' in the following terms:

> A hierarchy bears in itself the mark of God. Hierarchy causes its members to be images of God in all respects, to be clear and spotless mirrors reflecting the glow of primordial light and indeed of God himself. It ensures that when its members have received this full and divine splendour, they can then pass on this light generously and in accordance with God's will to beings further down the scale.[33]

This light-metaphysics or metaphysics of hierarchy also supported a programme of symbolic interpretation which constituted a return through material things to the source of all in heaven. And it is this programme which appears in Abbot Suger's explication of the meaning of the gilded bronze reliefs of the Passion and 'Resurrection or Ascension' of Christ which adorned the doors of the central west portal:

> Whoever thou art, if thou seekest to extol the glory of these doors,
> Marvel not at the gold and the expense but at the craftsmanship of the work.
> Bright is the noble work; but being nobly bright, the work
> Should brighten the minds so that they may travel, through the true lights [of the eyes],
> To the True Light where Christ is the true door.
> In what manner it be inherent in this world the golden door defines:
> The dull mind rises to truth through that which is material
> And, in seeing light, is resurrected from its former submersion.[34]

Cosmic phenomenology

The pre-modern cosmos as outlined in the preceding sections represents a construction of the world which is radically distinct from anything we know today. What for us is metaphor ('heaven above') was for our ancestors

---

33. *The Celestial Hierarchy*, 165A (trans. Colm Luibheid, *Pseudo-Dionysius. The Complete Works*, New York: Paulist Press, 1987), p. 154.
34. Panofsky, *Abbot Suger*, pp. 46–9.

a matter of deliberate and literal belief. Science and theology combined in a way that is unthinkable for us today, since science itself drew for its authority upon the sources of revealed Christianity. It is important at this stage therefore that we employ an analysis, which I am calling 'cosmic phenomenology', to lay bare the deep structures of pre-modern perception and thus to make possible a thoroughgoing contrast with our own.

The analysis begins with an important distinction between two concepts that are related but separate: the invisible as that which cannot ever be seen (and which I shall call the *invisible*) and the invisible as that which can be seen but which does not for the moment present itself to sight (which I call the *unseen*). The unseen is nevertheless visible, therefore, while the invisible is always unseen. The unseen is a crucial component in ordinary perception, according to Merleau-Ponty, since much of what we 'see' contains a strong component of the unseen. In his classic study *The Phenomenology of Perception*, Merleau-Ponty argued that our field of vision is always limited by the three-dimensionality of the objects we see. When we perceive a cube, for instance, we see the sides which present to us and we construct the sides which are hidden from us. But we construct them in such a way that they appear to be integral to our perception of the cube: it is not that we imagine the cube to be without the sides which are concealed from us, rather we integrate them – as imagined or remembered – into the overall image of the object as presented to us in the surfaces that we can see. Husserl first noted this process and called it 'apperception', but Merleau-Ponty developed it as a principal feature of the way in which we perceive unified objects in a three-dimensional world.

The unseen features in a second way which is equally important in the process of constructing the world. Objects which are outside the present range of our perceptions can still be present to us as either remembered or imagined forms. We do not cease to believe in the continuing existence of objects which we no longer see. Memory and imagination combine in the persistence of objects which, while in themselves visible, are no longer seen. According to the passage of time, more and more of our 'world' is constituted of such reconstructed images; more and more is *unseen*. But we gain images too of objects and places which we have never seen. Here the dynamic is not memory but is rather our ability to construct from what we have perceived the forms of things that we have not perceived. From the elements of the 'seen' world, we build new unseen ones by practices of the imagination. The world of imaginative literature, or travel writing, is of course a primary form of this kind of perceiving.

But there is a third kind of 'seeing' which can be described as distinctively 'cosmic'. Such a seeing applies outside any immediate, empirical frame of reference; and it is here that we note a significant difference between pre-modern perceptions and our own. The framing reality of the empirical world, for the medieval, lay in the remote heavens above, by virtue of extension, and in the hierarchical structure of the world order, by virtue of participation. The former belonged to the category of what I am calling the *unseen*: it is not generally the object of our senses, on account of the great distance dividing earth from the Empyrean, but it might conceivably be so. Also, the heavenly realities become visible in the symbolic nature of the world that does form a natural part of our everyday perceptions: in light, sound, space and time. This is not the same as seeing such realities *tout court*, but it did allow a glimpse of what such a seeing might be like. The interior of the church, filled with the sounds, colours and perfumes of heaven, allowed the congregation to understand something of the visibility of the heavenly realms, located beyond the stars. This principle of the unseen unlocks a further significant difference between the pre-modern and the modern cosmos. In his later work Merleau-Ponty advanced the view that the human subject is herself located within what he called the 'elements' of 'flesh' and 'language' (likening them in fact to the 'earth, air, fire and water' of medieval cosmology). For Husserl, following the Cartesian tradition, the subject somehow stood outside the domain of the physical, observing it from a privileged space. But for Merleau-Ponty, the awareness of the self is only exercised within the domain of the physical, as 'flesh', in which the subject knows herself to be visible to others as they are visible to her. Thus human self-awareness is positioned within a field of perception which itself encompasses the subject: she knows that the very hand by which she feels the world can be felt by others. The organs of her perception can necessarily themselves become the object of others' perceptions. Merleau-Ponty's model of what he called 'reversibility' is that we ourselves are part of the world that we perceive, and the fact that we can stand over against others as a subject to an object means that we too can become an object of others' perceptions. Being known as we ourselves know, is part of the *at homeness* of the self in the world.

We can say therefore that the traditional cosmos was one in which the unseen was nevertheless potentially visible and, as such, offered purchase to the human imagination as a place in which human subjects might themselves – in theory if not in practice – both see and be seen by the invisible powers who lay behind the realm of empirical perception. But for us today, the realms that control the fabric of the perceivable world are conceived not as entities, essences or presences, but rather as *forces*; and forces cannot be visualised as contents. We can get no visible or indeed sense-based purchase upon these, for forces are to be *measured* and are perceptible in their effects alone. In our terminology, they are *invisible* and not *unseen*. From the perspective of a phenomenology of perception therefore, the constructive aspect, or unseen, is in the modern world limited to the first two types outlined here: the construction of three-dimensional objects within space and the bringing to mind of objects not actually present. We do not conceive of the realms that circumscribe the empirical as being in any sense comparable to or an extension of the empirical forms of the unseen, and the deep, explanatory causes of the universe resist imaginative reproduction. In other words, this third kind of perception, or 'cosmic' seeing, is impossible for us today. If the sense of cosmic 'at homeness' was a guiding principle of medieval cosmology and metaphysics, and if it articulated a profound sense of the central role of humanity in the very structure of God's world, then it is this that sets apart the pre-modern from the modern sense of world. For the contemporary man and woman, the conviction that we are at home in the cosmos has to be articulated in the face of the apparent isolation of the human race, the seeming absence of spiritual companions, the historical contingency of our origins and the precariousness of our fate.

2

The metaphysics of createdness

Sola autem natura rationalis creata habet immediatum ordinem ad
Deum. Quia ceterae creaturae non attingunt ad aliquid
universale ... natura autem rationalis, inquantum cognoscit
universalem boni et entis rationem, habet immediatum ordinem ad
universale essendi principium.

The rational created nature alone is immediately ordered to God, for
the other creatures do not attain something universal ... But the
rational creature, insofar as it knows the universal *ratio* of good and
being, is immediately ordered to the universal principle of being.
Thomas Aquinas, *Summa Theologiae*

In the previous chapter I reviewed the structure of a pre-modern sense of
embodiment. It is this primary cosmological perspective which provides
the context for an analysis of the pre-modern self, thinking, feeling and
perceiving in a world very different from our own. The argument that I am
advancing throughout this book is that the way we reason is intimately
bound in with our understanding of the world, and our pre-conceptual
sense of being in the world. In this chapter I address the philosophical conceptualisation of the world which was achieved in the theory of the transcendentals. The theory of the transcendentals affirmed the primacy of being, the good and the true, as rooted in the divine causality itself, together
with their equivalence or 'convertibility'. It therefore turned on the belief
that the world is fundamentally united and is so on account of the common relation of all that exists with the Creator God. It is the divine act
of creation which unites the world as *creatum*. The transcendentals are the
conceptual expression of this unity and they reflect, in a thematised way,
the sense of the material world as a single extended field of Aristotelian

space. In the view of Jan Aertsen, it was the theory of the transcendentals, as an account of mind and world, which formed the distinctive ground of medieval philosophy and unified it as an intellectual movement.[1] The discussion here will focus on the way in which the theory of the transcendentals forms a context and background for the development of an account of mind which places God, and the knowledge of God, with all its complexities, at the centre of human reasoning. I shall begin with Thomas Aquinas, at whose hands the interplay between the transcendentals and reason received its most elaborate development. Bonaventure also deployed the theory of the transcendentals in his classic mystical treatise, *Itinerarium mentis in deum* ('The Journey of the Mind into God'), in order to establish an intimate connection between divine knowing and our ordinary knowledge of the world.

The second section concerns semiotics and the hermeneutics of Origen and Augustine. Semiotics is a form of reflexive reasoning which gives a more general account of the nature of understanding than is the case in formal logic, theory of knowledge or philosophy of perception. It typically has a concern with the nature of the sign – or language – and its relation with both the world and the self. The semiotics which emerges here is pervasively triadic and pragmatic, which is to say that both authors operate with a conviction that the human interpreter is intrinsic to the act of signifying. For Origen and Augustine, reality itself is constructed along hermeneutical lines and is grounded in a form of Trinitarian exegesis. For both the Greek and the Latin author, semiotics is an inquiry which begins with Scripture and the meaning of Scripture, but since Scripture itself serves as the key to an understanding of the world, semiotics is also inevitably concerned with questions to do with the meaning of the world.

Transcendentals and reason

The roots of the theory of the transcendentals can already be found in classical authors, especially Plato and Aristotle, but its history in Christian theology conventionally begins with the treatise *Summa de bono* (*c.* 1225–28) of Philip the Chancellor, continuing in the Franciscan authors of the *Summa theologica* (*c.* 1245) (generally ascribed to Alexander of Hales), and in the work of the Dominican Albert the Great (1206/7–1280).[2]

---

1. Jan A. Aertsen, *Medieval Philosophy and the Transcendentals* (Leiden: E. J. Brill, 1996), pp. 1–2.
2. Ibid., pp. 1–24.

Thomas makes extensive reference to the theory of the transcendentals throughout his work but specifically discusses them in only three texts, all written between 1250 and 1259. Taken together these offer a deeply coherent theory of the transcendentals, though with some significant variations.[3]

Thomas Aquinas

In the first *quaestio* of the series *On Truth* (*De veritate*, 1.1), Thomas refers to six transcendentals (*ens*, *unum*, *bonum*, *verum*, *res* and *aliquid*) which are primary and cannot be resolved into something prior.[4] The problem which inheres in the nature of transcendentals is how to formulate their unity and difference with respect to each other, given the need to treat being, and therefore its equivalents, not as a genus but as the common property of all. If the transcendental terms are truly primary, then they must be equivalent, but if they do not differ from each other in any respect, then they are tautological. Thomas expands Philip the Chancellor's understanding of their 'convertibility', whereby they are equivalent where they refer, that is, where they are applied to *supposita* ('objects'), but are to be distinguished in terms of their *ratio* ('concept' or 'definition'). The transcendentals thus represent modal explications of being which add something to being but only in terms of understanding. Thomas follows Alexander of Hales in making a distinction between being in itself (*in se*) and being in relation (*in ordine ad aliud*). To the former belongs the positive notion of a 'thing' or *res* which is the content of every object which makes it different from anything else. The terms *ens* and *res* can be distinguished in their *ratio* since the former refers to the fact that something exists while the latter refers to what it is. Thomas follows Philip the Chancellor in maintaining that *unum* adds negatively to being in itself the quality of indivision, as *ens indivisum*. Truth and goodness develop the theme of conceptual relation. It is in the nature of a transcendental to apply throughout all categories, so the transcendentals of relation have to apply to all things. This has the consequence that something must exist which is itself in relation with all that is and which can therefore become the site of the manifestation of the transcendentals from the perspective of their being 'in relation'. Thomas identifies this with the human mind, which, following

---

3. I am particularly indebted to Aertsen's penetrating study for much in the discussion which follows.

4. But in *De veritate*, 21.1 he refers only to being, one, the good and the true. In his *Disputationes Metaphysicae* (3.2.3–6) of 1597 Suarez included *res* within *ens* and *aliquid* within *unum*.

Aristotle, 'is in a sense all things'.[5] The human self is thus at the centre of Thomas' development of truth and goodness as the transcendental properties of all that is. The dominant motif here is *convenientia*, or 'conformity' between the two chief faculties of the human mind and the world. Where entities conform to the human intellect, that relation grounds truth, and where they conform to the will, that relation is the ground of goodness.[6]

According to the general structure of Thomas' theory of the transcendentals, being or *ens* is the first object of the intellect: it is being which is most proximate to the human mind and is its first conception. All the categories and genera of things simply serve to give denomination or definition by contracting *ens* into specific entities with specific properties. The transcendentals, in contrast, run through all the categories; they are transcendental not on account of being beyond the categories but because they are included within all the categories.[7] As such, they are the most sublime *content* of the world, and represent the closest intimacy between God and the world. In the 'Prologue to the Commentary on Pseudo-Denys' *On the Divine Names*' Thomas specifically rejects the Platonic theory of participation, whereby entities can be said to participate in 'separate species of things', such that any individual horse participates in a separately existing horse-nature.[8] But at the same time he affirms the principle of participation in the case of the *communissima*, such as 'good, one and being'. As the most abstract and common properties of things, the transcendentals are closer to the divine nature and are 'called good or one or being by derivation from this first'.[9] The sense that the transcendentals are the visible signs of the createdness of the world by virtue of their particular proximity to the divine nature, which is the cause of all things, is further developed in discussions of the individual transcendental properties. The being of entities is the 'most universal' and most indeterminate of all; in Jan Aertsen's

---

5. *De anima*, III, 8, 431b21.

6. In the discussion at *De veritate*, 21.1 Thomas replaces the notion of 'conformity' as the principle which governs truth and goodness with that of 'perfectibility'. Every entity constitutes a combination of the species and the act of being by which that entity subsists in the species. The species perfects the human intellect while the act of being perfects the will.

7. See Ludwig Honnefelder, 'Der zweite Anfang der Metaphysik. Voraussetzungen, Ansätze und Folgen der Wiederbegründung der Metaphysik im 13./14. Jahrhundert', in J. P. Beckmann et al., eds., *Philosophie im Mittelalter. Entwicklungslinien und Paradigmen* (Hamburg: Meiner, 1987), pp. 165–86. See also A. Zimmermann, *Ontologie oder Metaphysik? Die Diskussion über den Gegenstand der Metaphysik im 13. und 14. Jahrhundert* (Leiden and Cologne: E. J. Brill, 1965).

8. *In librum Beati Dionysii De divinis nominibus expositio*, prol.

9. Ibid. Cf. *Quodlibet*, II, 2.1.

phrase, it is 'the most proper name, because it is in virtue of its universality the least improper'.[10] But it is also 'the perfection of all perfections', which is the ground of all other properties.[11] In a discussion from *On Truth*, God emerges as 'truth itself' since the ultimate ground of truth is the adequation between the thing and the divine intellect.[12] In the case of the good, God alone is goodness in the truest sense, since goodness is a property of the actual, and only God subsists in pure actuality.[13]

The doctrine of the transcendentals stands at the heart of Thomas' account of the createdness of the world, but at the same time there is an unmistakable sense that Thomas is reluctant to draw any too direct or overly systematic relation between the transcendentals as they exist for the human mind in the world and their existence in God.[14] What we see here is a tendency to emphasise the immediacy with which the createdness of the world presents itself to us together with a dialectical tension regarding our capacity to make sense of it *in our own terms*. This same tension is apparent in Thomas' more extensive analysis of *ens*, or 'being', as the 'first' of the transcendentals, and as 'that which the intellect first conceives as most known and in which all other concepts are resolved'.[15] Expressed in terms of Thomas' metaphysical realism, *ens* offers a direct and unmediated apprehension of the way things are. The world simply presents itself to the mind with an immediacy which is incontrovertible and which, according to this view, grounds the mind in the reality of the objective order. In one very important sense, therefore, the immediate or proper object of the human intellect is the actuality, or act of being, of an individual entity, as we encounter it in the real world, which is at the same time God's world. But the human act of reflection which parallels the immediacy of our apprehension of the being or actuality of objects in the world is a highly dialectical one. Thomas describes the study of metaphysics as the 'highest of all the sciences' since it deals with ultimate issues of causality and of the

---

10. *ST* Ia, q. 13, a. 11 and Aertsen, *Medieval Philosophy*, p. 366.
11. *De potentia* 7.2 ad 9.
12. *De veritate*, 1.7.
13. *Summa contra Gentiles*, I, 37.
14. In *De veritate*, 1.4, sed contra (5), Thomas follows Philip the Chancellor by linking 'entity', 'truth' and 'goodness' with the threefold causality of God, as efficient, formal and final cause of the creation respectively. And, as Norman Kretzmann has argued, the conceptuality of the transcendentals is applied on a number of occasions in Thomas' discussion of the appropriations of the Persons of the Trinity (see his 'Trinity and Transcendentals', in R. Feenstra and C. Plantinga, eds., *Trinity, Incarnation and Atonement* (Indiana: University of Notre Dame Press, 1989), pp. 79–109. The key text on the transcendentals as 'divine names' is found at *In I Sent.*, d. 8, q. 1, a. 3c). But these speculations are relatively few and far between.
15. *De veritate*, 1.1.

greatest intelligibility and abstraction.[16] It is the natural desire to know and to attain to the highest possible knowledge which impels us to formal reflection upon existence as such, or 'being *qua* being', in the science of metaphysics. But that reflection is subject to the same rules of reasoning as any other science, and here it is useful to refer to a passage in the Commentary on Boethius' *The Trinity* in which Thomas outlines the formal structure of analytical thought. The point at issue is the distinction between that mode of thinking called *ratio*, or 'reasoning', which is the discursive facility of the mind which moves from one point to another in a debate, and the mode designated as *intellectus*, meaning a direct 'comprehension' or 'understanding'. The former stands to the latter 'as movement to rest or acquisition to possession'.[17] The intellect 'considers first unified and simple truth, and in it grasps its knowledge of a whole multitude of truths, as God, by comprehending his own essence, knows all things'.[18] The labours of reason, or *ratio*, on the other hand are discursive, partial and compound.

The natural movement of reason is that of a reduction which falls into two kinds. The first is reduction *secundum rem*, that is, according to the natural order, 'as when demonstration is made through causes or extrinsic effects'. The final goal of this reduction is attained 'when one has arrived at the supreme and simplest causes, which are separated substances', which is to say, God. But the mind can also undertake a reduction which is *secundum rationem*, or according to concept. In this case, the mind proceeds by 'intrinsic causes' which is to say, it moves from particulars to universals, which are simpler and more abstract. The final knowledge which this kind of reduction brings is that of the most abstract and simplest principle of all: 'being' and 'the things which are attributes of being inasmuch as it is being'.[19] This passage is important for the background it gives to Thomas' discussion of metaphysics in the 'Prologue to his Commentary on Aristotle's *Metaphysics*'. There he stresses that the proper subject of metaphysics is *ens commune*, or 'common being', and that God, as the cause of being, is not as such the subject of the science. Metaphysics is the most foundational of the sciences and thus regulative of all the others because it alone deals with what is 'most common', 'most intelligible' and therefore

---

16. *In Met. Proemium.*
17. *ST* 1a, q. 79, a. 8. The background to this distinction lies of course in Aristotle's *Posterior Analytics*, II, 19, 99b–100b.
18. *Expositio super librum Boethii De trinitate*, q. 6, a. 1.
19. Ibid.

'certain', and with a subject – *ens commune* – whose cause is the ultimate origin of things. But playing through these and other texts is the clear recognition, which is axiomatic for Thomas, that the inquiry into being represented by metaphysics can only identify existence as the effect of a cause. Neither the reduction *secundum rem* as an enquiry into extrinsic causes, leading to God as Creator, nor the reduction *secundum rationem* as an enquiry into intrinsic causes, leading to universal being, can penetrate into the *nature* of the cause itself, which is God. In the transcendentals, and in being as such, God is present as Creator. But to be present as Creator, is at the same time irreducibly a form of absence. Thomas' position appears to be that in and through the world, the human faculties of knowing and loving are ordered to the divine Creator. They are not ordered in their own worldly terms, however, but in ways that are dictated by the nature of our world *as created*. The world is present to the human mind, with an immediacy to which Thomas repeatedly draws us back, but it also points beyond itself to a creator, with whom we are united 'as to something unknown'.[20]

In his discussion of the role of reason in Thomas' work, Denys Turner has captured this dialectic with particular force. Turner argues that according to medieval conceptions of cognition, the human mind exists in the tension between 'reason' as the discursive faculty of knowing and 'intellect' as insight or understanding. Intellect proximates humanity to the direct knowing of the angels, while reason reflects our embodied state. As noted above, intellect is the state of 'rest', which represents the attainment of understanding, while reason is restless and discursive: it is that modality of the mind which strives to make connections and to understand. While some more Augustinian systems of thinking hold out the possibility that we can enjoy a direct cognition of intellect, Thomas contrasts reason and intellect more directly in a dialectical interplay such that reason can only operate by the light of intellect but can never know the intellect as such. As we struggle to make sense of the world, as created, reason is brought to an encounter with its own limits. What lies beyond that limit becomes, in Turner's phrase, a 'demonstrated unknowability'.[21] It is not the evocation of mystery as such nor the collapse of reason through exhaustion which Thomas has in mind here but rather the culmination

---

20. Quoted by Denys Turner in his study of the role of reason in Thomas Aquinas (forthcoming, Cambridge University Press).
21. Ibid.

of the rational process. We apprehend the world through reason, and the world leads on to God, from whom comes the very light of intellect by which we understand. But as we are led to try to understand God, reason is confronted with a causality, or creativity, which *it knows it cannot understand*. As Turner states it, 'in that "unknowing" lies reason's self-transcendence as intellect. And the act by which it thus self-transcends is proof of the existence of God.'[22] In other words, the creativity of God which is everywhere implied in the created world, to which the created world in all ways points, is itself immediately present to the mind but in a way that transcends our capacity to grasp it. The human mind necessarily must engage with the divine creativity, as this is the world's ultimate meaning, but it cannot do so as a created power; for 'to create' is, as Thomas reminds us, a wholly divine act.[23] Human reasoning is therefore perpetually caught between its necessary *telos* in God, who is the source of the world, and its own limited capacities as created. It is this dialectical tension which lays the basis for faith, when *scientia*, which is the principle of authentic knowledge of the empirical world, is overtaken by the divine self-disclosure as revelation. At that point the foundational axioms without which there can be no authentic human knowing are to be identified with the data of revelation, and God himself becomes our teacher.[24] But even faith is no release from the dialectical structure of thinking in the presence of God. In his discussion of the relation between faith and understanding, Thomas defines faith as an imperfect understanding of those things which surpass natural reason, but one nevertheless which allows us to affirm them with certainty in the knowledge that 'whatever the outward appearances may be, they do not contradict the truth'.[25]

Bonaventure

The same problematics of the relation between human thinking and God concern Bonaventure in his 'Journey of the Mind into God' as concerned Thomas Aquinas. Standing within a more robustly Augustinian tradition, Bonaventure has less of a sense of the autonomy of reason than does Thomas, but he shares with Thomas the belief that God is the ground of human thinking and perception and yet also stands radically beyond it so

---

22. Ibid.
23. *ST* Ia, q. 45, a. 5.
24. John I. Jenkins, *Knowledge and Faith in Thomas Aquinas* (Cambridge: Cambridge University Press, 1997).
25. *ST* IIa IIae, q. 8, a. 2.

that no ordinary processes of reasoning can grasp the divine reality. The chief way in which Bonaventure explores this dialectic is through his concept of the hierarchalisation of the intellect whereby the human mind itself mirrors in the structures which are internal to its operation the cosmic layering of the universe. The form of the *Itinerarium* follows that of the vision of a six-winged seraph which came to St Francis on Mount La Verna, on the occasion when he received the stigmata. Allocating each stage to one of the seraph's six wings, Bonaventure sets out the journey to God as an ascent through the six powers of the soul, each of which has its correlate in the objective order. These faculties are the 'senses, imagination, reason, understanding, intelligence, and the summit of the mind or spark of conscience'.[26] The cosmological dimensions of this personal evolution can be felt throughout the work; they are present in the metaphor of the journey and the powerful images of 'passing over' (*transire*) which play throughout the text, setting up a rhythm of space and movement. The journey itself, by which 'we ascend from the lowest to the highest, from the exterior to the interior, from the temporal to the eternal', is set out in metaphorical terms, but against the background of a world-view which locates heaven at a point above the stars and which envisages spiritual intelligences as inhabiting the spheres and causing the movement of the heavenly bodies.[27]

For Bonaventure the mystical journey begins with sense perception and the physicality of created things, and he describes 'the universe itself' as 'a ladder by which we can ascend into God'.[28] Created things manifest to us 'the power, wisdom and goodness of God' in three distinct ways. Firstly they show the 'origin, process and end' of the world and secondly allow us to discern the existence of what is perfect, spiritual and eternal from the perception of what is imperfect, material and changeable.[29] The third way concerns the physical properties of objects in the world as these are perceived by the senses. Bonaventure identifies seven aspects to physical existence, or 'properties of creatures', which in his view manifest God's goodness, wisdom and power.[30] The first is *origin*, which suggests creation from nothingness, while the others relate to the three-dimensional characteristics of objects. Whether expressed as 'length, width and depth', as

---

26. *Itinerarium mentis in deum*, 1, 6 (Cousins, p. 62).
27. Ibid.
28. Ibid., 2 (Cousins, p. 60).
29. Ibid., 12–13 (Cousins, p. 64).
30. Ibid., 14 (Cousins, p. 65).

'number', or the 'efficiency of the operations', the *magnitude* and *multitude* of objects manifest 'the immensity of the power, wisdom and goodness of the triune God'.[31] The *beauty* and *fullness* of things (where the latter denotes the activity of the form which shapes matter) also communicate these same divine properties, again combining the static physical dimensions of objects with their dynamic effects. The *activity* and finally *order* of objects are similarly expressive of the divine nature, and the latter aligns the 'book of creation', the 'book of Scripture' and the 'body (*corpus*) of the Church' as analogical sites of divine order.[32]

Bonaventure's interest in the structure of ordinary perception is continued in Chapter II in his discussion of 'apprehension', or how the three classes of objects that constitute the sense-world (i.e. those that generate, those that are generated and those that govern the whole as spirits) enter the human self through the five senses. This process has three parts. The first is apprehension, or cognition itself, whereby – in accordance with the Aristotelian model – the likeness of the object is produced in the medium or particular sense, from where it progresses to the sense organ itself and thus to the 'apprehensive faculty'.[33] This act of perception then sets up a feeling of pleasure based upon different kinds of harmony or proportion between the object and its source, or between the object and its human recipient, leading in turn to an act of judgement. Judgement is the process whereby we enquire into why the perception of the object is pleasurable or desirable for us and 'find that the reason lies in the proportion of harmony'.[34] Judgement is at the same time an act of abstraction from the particularities of time and place, and is thus 'unchangeable, unlimited, endless and completely spiritual'.[35] By apprehension, pleasure and judgement, therefore, the whole of the external world, both material and spiritual, enters into the human self. Bonaventure subsequently adds a Christological-cosmological dimension to his analysis of sense perception as a manifestation of the divine creativity. One source of the pleasure or wholesomeness which comes to us from the perception of an object derives from the harmony of the likeness produced in our minds with the external form which is its source. The ultimate exemplar of this is the identity of the Son with the Father within the Trinity. It follows therefore that '[i]f

31. Ibid.
32. Ibid.
33. Ibid., II, 4 (Cousins, p. 71).
34. Ibid., II, 6 (Cousins, p. 72).
35. Ibid.

all things that can be known generate a likeness of themselves, they manifestly proclaim that in them as in mirrors we can see the eternal generation of the Word, the Image and Son, eternally emanating from God the Father'.[36] And in judgement too there is a participation with the divine since the reason of judgement, being unchangeable and unlimited, is also eternal and is 'either God or in God'. It is the case therefore that '[i]f everything which we judge with certainty we judge by such a reason, then it is clear that [God] himself is the reason of all things and the infallible rule and light of truth, in which all things shine forth infallibly, indelibly, indubitably, irrefutably, indisputably, unchangeably, boundlessly, endlessly, indivisibly and intellectually'.[37]

In Chapter III Bonaventure proceeds to a 'higher' and 'more internal' stage of the journey as he considers the way in which the Augustinian triad of memory, intelligence and will, which are constitutive of the human mind-self, or *mens*, are illumined by, or participate in, the transcendental properties of being, truth and goodness. Bonaventure states that '[u]nless we know what being *per se* is, we cannot fully know the definition of any particular substance'.[38] Nor can we know what being *per se* is unless we also know 'its properties, which are: one, true and good'.[39] With an enviable unity of purpose, Bonaventure unequivocally attributes our knowledge of 'being *per se*' to a direct divine communication, without which we could not know the imperfect being of entities in the world. He affirms also that when it makes true judgements, 'our intellect is joined to Eternal Truth itself since it can grasp no truth with certitude if it is not taught by this Truth'.[40] And when our will exercises choice between varying goods, it can only do so since 'the notion of the highest good is necessarily imprinted in everyone who deliberates'.[41] Taken together, these transcendental operations of the human mind constitute the image of God in us and their unified activity makes it – following Augustine in *On the Trinity* – 'a likeness so present to itself and having God so present that the soul actually grasps him and potentially "is capable of possessing him and of being a partaker in him"'.[42]

36. Ibid., 7 (Cousins, p. 73).
37. Ibid., 9 (Cousins, p. 73).
38. Ibid., III, 3 (Cousins, p. 81).
39. 'cum suis conditionibus' (ibid.).
40. Ibid. (Cousins, p. 83).
41. Ibid., 4 (Cousins, p. 83). The word for 'imprinted' here is *impresa*, which follows the Arab tradition of direct divine communication which we find in Avicenna (cf. *Metaphysics*, I, 5).
42. *Itinerarium*, III, 2 (Cousins, p. 81); the Augustine quote is from *De trinitate*, XIV, c. 8, n. 11.

The dialectic of Bonaventure's system comes through in the increasingly Christological shape of his cosmological thinking in the later chapters. In Chapter IV Bonaventure links the purification of the human soul, which is essential for the vision of the divine power and presence in created things, with the theological virtues. Faith is defined as faith in 'the uncreated Word and splendor of the Father', hope is hope to receive the 'inspired Word' and love is of the 'Word incarnate';[43] only in this way, through the theological virtues which are grounded in the Christian dispensation, can the image of God in us, which is the participation of the faculties of the self in the divine nature, be perfected. Moreover each of the theological virtues is linked with different spiritual senses as exemplified in traditional and intensely Christological readings of the Song of Songs. The Christological and incarnational dimensions of the soul's journey into God are made evident in Bonaventure's belief that the soul itself undergoes a process of 'hierarchalisation', through its increased internalisation and abstraction. This appears not only in its reformation as divine image and in its purification, illumination and perfection, but also in the discovery that the nine orders of angels are reflected in the structure of its own being, in terms of the ecclesial virtues associated with human nature, human endeavour and divine grace.[44] The attainment of these virtues marks the soul's entry into the heavenly Jerusalem where it is able to discern in the nine orders of angels the presence of 'God, who dwells in them and performs all their operations'.[45]

In Chapters V and VI Bonaventure explores the transcendentals of being and goodness as properties of God, again not hesitating to tie the transcendental properties of the created order closely with the divine attributes. Indeed, in his discussion of being as a name of God, Bonaventure again vigorously affirms his belief that we can only know imperfect being through perfect being and that therefore the divine being impresses itself upon us at the foundation of our cognition of the world:

> [i]f therefore non-being can be understood only through being and being in potency only through being in act, and if being signifies the pure act of being, then being is what first comes into the intellect and this being is pure act. But this is not particular being, which is limited because mixed with potency; nor is it analogous being because that has

43. *Itinerarium*, IV, 3 (Cousins, p. 89).
44. Ibid., 4 (Cousins, p. 90).
45. Ibid.

only a minimum of actuality because it only has a minimum of being. It remains that the being in question must be divine Being.[46]

Being reveals to us God's 'essential unity', and is linked with the Exodus narrative from the Old Testament where God declares himself to be He Who Is. The divine goodness, on the other hand, is made known to us in the divine 'emanations', which is to say in the Trinitarian missions, and is therefore particularly associated with the New Testament. By looking upon what has been revealed to us concerning the divine nature in Scripture, we can attain the fifth and sixth stages of our ascent into God and can contemplate the divine nature.

Chapter VII gives an account of the final state of the soul not in terms of a seventh stage however, to be set alongside the previous stages, but in terms of a dissolution of the hierarchy of the stages. The predominant motif of this chapter is the integration of the soul into the saving death of Christ, as a way of transcending both the world and the self. Christ himself becomes the 'way' and the 'door', the 'ladder' and the 'vehicle', and entry into his death is attended by a cessation of our ordinary intellectual powers, signalled by metaphors of 'silence' and 'superluminous darkness'.[47] We can read this complex final movement in different ways, but one of the consequences of this shift towards an incarnational motif is that it integrates the ascent into God with the recognition of God's descent into our world. Thus Bonaventure finally anchors his mystical metaphysics in the incarnational agency of God, combining the abstraction, essentialisation and internalisation of the Neoplatonist framework with the image and sense-based metaphoricity of incarnational theology. In the person of Christ, height and depth, inwardness and exteriority, immateriality and materiality are all integrated and united, and Christ himself effectively becomes – in Bonaventure's account of cosmology – a living embodiment of the hierarchical principle by which we are illumined and redeemed.

According to Bonaventure therefore, human reasoning needs to be seen within a cosmological context which has at its core the relationality between the microcosm and the macrocosm. The human mind mirrors within itself the Christological structure of the world, which is the ultimate meaning of the world, and is itself innately ordered to that cosmic reality. Human thinking then is necessarily dynamic as the structure of the world itself leads the mind up and through the materiality

46. Ibid., V, 3 (Cousins, p. 96).
47. Ibid., VII, 1 (Cousins, p. 111).

of sense-impressions into the internal and essential reality of abstracts and universals, and then to the supreme realities of the Trinity. This 'hierarchalisation' of the human mind is its realisation as God's creature, and it leads to the transfiguration of the mind, through a superluminous darkness and divine unknowing, which is the final destiny of human cognition.

Semiotics

As noted in the Introduction, semiotics as the science of signs is a particularly succinct way of conveying the structure of meaning. Semiotics is present everywhere in Aquinas and Bonaventure, but it is in the work of their predecessors Origen and Augustine that we find the most complete statements regarding what we might call a Christian scriptural semiotics.

Origen

Origen looked to Scripture itself for an account of what Scripture is and how it is to be read. In passages such as 1 Corinthians 10:1–11 and Galatians 4:21–31, he believed that he could identify a process of reading and understanding that was internal to Scripture itself and hence normative for those who accepted its divine origins. In the former passage Paul himself reads passages from Exodus and Numbers concerning the wanderings of Israel in the desert as 'examples', or *tupoi*, for us today (v. 6). Their idolatry, and subsequent punishment, was a sign to us that we should not test Christ in the same way: 'These things happened to them to serve as an example (*tupikōs*), and they were written down to instruct us, on whom the ends of the ages have come' (v. 11). In the passage from Galatians, Paul understands Hagar and Sarah, Abraham's concubine and wife, to represent the Old and New Covenants respectively. Hagar corresponds to the present Jerusalem while Sarah is 'the Jerusalem above'. On this occasion, their symbolic meaning is described as an 'allegory' (*allēgoroumena*). Origen's interpretation of these two passages is closely linked to his understanding of semiotics as such. The language of 'types' and 'allegories' form part of Origen's conceptualisation of the way in which the reading of signs constitutes a task that is at once interpretative and eschatological.[48] We are

---

48. See John David Dawson, *Christian Figural Reading and the Fashioning of Identity* (Berkeley: University of California Press, 2002) for a persuasive argument that allegory in Origen generally takes a figural form and thus maintains a continuity between Old Testament and New in terms of divine action.

not to read the Old Testament purely in its own terms, as static imagery, but are to read it, as Paul does, in the light of the messianic realisations of the New Covenant. To fail to do this is to fall victim to a crude 'idolatry'. In the same way we are not to read either the New or Old Testament from only a literal perspective but are to seek there the 'hidden treasures' that represent a higher, and divine, order of meaning.

But this advance into a higher order of interpretation is intensified again by Origen's view that the Gospel itself exists on two levels: drawing upon Revelation 14:6, Origen holds that it is simultaneously a 'temporal' and an 'eternal Gospel'. Although in themselves one, the existence of these two faces of the Gospel reflects our own inability to comprehend the divine self-communication in its purity. We are forced to rest upon the earthly or fleshly Gospel, with its material signs, as a point of access to the eternal or heavenly Gospel, which is the truth as it exists before God and in the presence of the saints.[49] The human mind, which rises from Old Testament signs to the mediated meanings of the temporal Gospel and finally to the truth of the eternal Gospel, is itself substantially changed in the process. Having received a participation in the divine Logos through the creation, the mind – in its 'logos-like' characteristics – becomes conformed to the divine, creative Wisdom. As Origen likes to point out, Christians can only read Scripture in the right way by virtue of their possession of the 'mind of Christ' (1 Cor. 2:16).[50]

The Origenist view of Scripture is one which placed the interpretative act, as a modality of both human and divine knowing, at the centre of Christian identity. The deep structure of that act was one which in turn was informed by a systemic cross-fertilisation between Incarnation, Scripture, Church and World. The logic of the first formed the coherence of each of the following three, and all together formed an analogical unity which set up a rich interplay between the different orders of existence. At times that analogy takes on a distinctly corporal character, as Scripture, Church and World are imaged as 'body', as if participating in the primal body of the incarnate Christ. But more fundamentally they are organised together as domains or levels of *interpretation*, where semiotics entails a coordination, even conformity, between the human mind that interprets, the interpreted sign given by divine grace, and the divine generative order itself which finds its fullest expression in the language and image of Wisdom.

49. *On First Principles*, IV, 25.
50. *Comm. Jn*, Book X, Chapter 27; *Comm. Mt.*, Book XIV, Chapter 11.

In Book I of his Commentary on John, Origen developed his argument that *Sophia*, or Wisdom, is prior to all the other names, or 'titles' of Christ. In an exegesis of 'In the beginning (*archē*) was the Word (*logos*)' (Jn 1:1), Origen laid down the principle that *archē* here signifies 'Wisdom' and that as site or place of the 'logos', it is clearly prior to and distinct from it.[51] Wisdom designates the nature of Christ as the one who understands the manifold and generative 'speculations' of the Godhead which are identified with primal creation. 'Logos', on the other hand, designates Christ in so far as he *makes known* to us the 'secret things of His Father'.[52] This distinction between generation and revelation is further strengthened by Origen's attribution of 'power' specifically to Wisdom. He repeatedly points to 1 Corinthians 1:18–31, where Christ is linked with the divine power and wisdom, and to the Wisdom of Solomon, which speaks of Wisdom as the breath of the power of God.[53] Origen's identification of Wisdom with the *energeia* of God draws out the extent to which Christ as Wisdom is not only the final term of our knowledge, as the highest mystery, but is also the generative ground of the creation, and the dynamic principle of our own return to that ground through the exegesis of the created order in the light of its ultimate origin and end.

Origen's use of the term *epinoia* shows the central role of Wisdom in his understanding of both Scripture and world, and the analogical resonances of these two spheres. The word *epinoia* is often translated as 'title' in order to designate the various names of Christ that are supported by exegetical tradition. These include, for example, 'Wisdom', 'Logos', 'Shepherd', 'Way', 'Truth', 'Light', 'Rod', 'Flower', 'Stone', 'High Priest', 'Servant', 'Sword'. *Epinoia* itself suggests an act of construction, or interpretation, and it is consonant with the practice of exegesis. The variety of the names of Christ does not reflect the diversity of his person, which is a unified personhood, but is a consequence of our own inability to grasp him in his most essential aspects: that is, as Wisdom who is the divine creativity. We fail to grasp him precisely as unified divine person within the Blessed Trinity who has become incarnate among us. Therefore the Christ figure, who is the 'supreme mystery' and 'hidden treasure' of Scripture and who – as Wisdom – is the divine fecundity that is present in all created things, comes to us finally as a sign to be understood. Himself the

51. *Comm. Jn*, Book I, Chapter 22. See the discussion of the *epinoiai* by Henri Crouzel, in his study *Origen* (Edinburgh: T. & T. Clark, 1989), pp. 189–92.
52. *On First Principles*, Book I, Chapter 2, §2–3; *Comm. Jn*, Book I, Chapters 22 and 42.
53. *On First Principles*, Book I, Chapter 2, §4–12; *Comm. Jn*, Book I, Chapter 23.

measure of all signs, Christ yields himself as a sign to us and as a task of interpretation.

In Origen's view, the world is structured according to semiotic processes of understanding and interpretation which mark the intersection of human and divine. The primal self-giving of God creates the ground of a semiosis in which – as creatures – human beings can participate in the divine creativity which consumes their humanity and initiates them into a new form of divine awareness. The debt to a Platonic conception of the world as modelled on an intelligible and unchanging reality is self-evident. But there is nevertheless a great divide between the world as envisaged by Origen and the cosmos of the Platonists. That distinction is bound up with the sense that Christ himself – as Wisdom – interprets the Father in power and that this semiosis is coterminous with the possibility of creation itself. Interpretation is not the mark of our fallenness therefore, as a kind of *doxa*, or imperfect knowing, but is rather the shape of our participation in the primal dynamic of divine self-giving. It is by the divine creativity that we learn to see beyond the sign to what it represents, and thus are able to progress back to the divine source, in a movement which Origen denotes as a simultaneity of knowledge and love.

Augustine

Many of these same themes run through the work of Augustine, though they appear in a significantly different register. In general, the mature Augustine places more emphasis upon our fallen condition and upon our complete dependence on God for illumination in a world where truth is veiled and interpretation inexact. Augustine has a less exuberant sense than Origen of our participation in the divine exegesis of Christ, but is motivated rather by a belief in the radical inadequacy of our own native powers of comprehension and a pervasive awareness of God's liberating gift to us in Jesus Christ. The Johannine description of Jesus as 'the light of the world' (Jn 1:9) is a central text for Augustine's reflections on knowledge, signs and the world. Augustine's development of a Christian semiotics is rooted not only in his own background as rhetorician, but also in his own spiritual biography. Augustine firstly developed textual strategies of allegorisation for countering the literalistic claims of the Manichees and then, following his reading of the Platonists, integrated a Platonic hierarchalism into a Christian scriptural faith. The effect was a far greater emphasis upon the literal sense of Scripture than we find in Origen with a commitment to history and to the created world as the ultimate semiosis of the divine creativity.

In his discussions of the nature of the sign, particularly in the early *De magistro* and the late *De trinitate*, the ground of semiotics is found in the person of Christ. In the former case, in what R. A. Markus has described as a somewhat 'sophistical' discussion, Christ emerges as the one through whom we gain knowledge of the unity of the sign (language) and the world and thus enter into meaning.[54] Things in the world cannot of themselves be known without signs, while the meaning of signs can only be given by 'seeing' their relation to things in the world; it is only through Christ, the 'teacher within', who is himself 'the inner truth', that we can gain entry into the world as a meaningful unity of *signum* and *res*.[55] In the *De trinitate*, the discussion is set within the context of an analysis of the Trinitarian vestiges which characterise the operations of the human mind. Here it is 'the word which shines within', in contrast to 'the word which sounds without', which suggests a Christological framework. The internal word is disembodied – and belongs to no language – but finds fleshly expression in the particularity of the word that is uttered. The function of the latter is to communicate the interior word, and so it is constituted as a sign which points to the intelligible reality of the interior word which is unspoken and unutterable in itself. This seems close to Augustine's incarnational theology, and although *De trinitate* seems unclear on the relation between the interior word and objects in the world, it is reasonable to assume that a kind of exemplarism is in play here. The interior word represents the divine illumination in the human mind which is a participatory awareness of the things as they exist in the divine mind. It is this, a participative knowledge of things as they exist in truth, within the divine Logos, which grounds true human knowledge of the world, and makes the signs that we utter truthful representations of the real order.[56]

In both *De magistro* and *De trinitate*, Augustine views human knowledge under the aspect of subjectivity, that is, from the perspective of the one

---

54. R. A. Markus, *Signs and Meanings* (Liverpool: Liverpool University Press, 1996), p. 81.

55. *De magistro*, XI, 38.

56. Bavaud has a discussion of those passages in which Augustine applies the Stoic 'word within' and 'word without' within an incarnational framework (G. Bavaud, 'Un thème augustinien: le mystère de l'Incarnation à la lumière de la distinction entre le verbe intérieur et le verbe proféré', *Revue des Etudes Augustiniennes* 9 (1963), 95–101). He points out that Augustine does not follow Tertullian and the Apologists in the application of this Stoic formula to Gen. 1 and the act of creation.

who knows. But in *De doctrina christiana* and, more importantly, his several commentaries on Genesis, the focus of his attention lies in the exterior aspect of the act, and in the nature of the world itself. In the former work, Augustine already clarifies his position on the relation between Scripture and history. One of the functions of his emphasis upon the literal sense of Scripture is that this allows him to read the biblical signs as literal signs which point to events in history, thus transposing the primary act of interpretation away from the text to the world itself, in its historical manifestations. Such textual signs, or *signa translata* as Augustine called them, can be received by the reader in an entirely literal mode while at the same time they point to events in the real world which called for a radical and Spirit-filled act of interpretation. The thrust of this semiosis was to show that Christ himself was the true meaning of history, and that the demonstration of this was the true meaning of Scripture.

In an exegesis of Vulgate Psalm 103 which occurs in both the *Enarrationes* and the *Confessiones*, Augustine understood the phrase 'like a skin it is stretched out' (v. 2) to refer to 'the heavens shall be folded together like a book' of Isaiah 34:4 and thus to be an allusion to the Scriptures which are 'your wonderful harmonious words which you have imposed on us through mortal men'.[57] Scripture stands over the creation, and creation itself is a scriptural semiotic, as appears from the many passages in which Augustine speaks of the way in which created things point to their creator. In *De civitate dei* he speaks of the 'eloquence of events' which point to divine action in the world.[58] In the *Confessiones* this is tempered with the realisation that the transcendental properties of things are not as they are in God: "So, it was you, Lord, who made them: you who are beautiful, for they are beautiful; you who are good, for they are good; you who exist, for they exist too. Yet they are not beautiful, they are not good, they do not exist, in the same way as you, their Creator."[59] And in the *Tractates on the Gospel of John*, Augustine draws out the fallen human condition more forcefully:

> 'The world was made through him, and the world knew him not.' Did the skies not know their creator? Or did the angels not know their creator, or did the stars not know their creator whom the demons acknowledge? All things everywhere bore witness. But who did not

57. *Confess.*, XIII.15.16. See also *Enarr. in Ps.*, 103.1.8.
58. *Civ. Dei*, 11.18.
59. *Confess.*, XI.4.6.

know? Those who are called the world from their love of the world. For in the act of loving we dwell with our heart.[60]

Our own subjective state is an essential precondition for our capacity to understand the true meaning of the world as God's creation which is transcendentally open to him. As Augustine elaborates in *De doctrina christiana*, we can either 'enjoy' (*frui*) the world in God and thus grasp it in its ground in him, or 'use' it (*uti*) according to our own limited and self-centred purposes. The world, like signs in general, constitute for Augustine an opportunity to be transformed by the grace of God, which is given with the sign. We can respond positively to the ways in which God speaks with us through signs, in what Augustine calls *admonitiones* which are 'events, usually insignificant, through which God's providential care for man takes effect'.[61] This serves to remind us that it is through signs and creatures that God summons us to the highest and most spiritual love.

Conclusion

In these brief summaries of the architecture, metaphysics and semiotics of the medieval cosmos we have seen something of the extent to which humanity itself took a central place in cosmological reflection. The twin axes of creation and covenant determined the application of 'science' in the service of a vision of reality as both gift and challenge to humankind. The problem of meaning is central to these perspectives, though not in the way it is for us, with our questioning as to what *constitutes* meaning, under the weight of a pervasive scepticism. Rather what we find here is a prior acceptance of the createdness of the world and a concern with the right understanding of the world, as the domain of God's creativity. The medieval mind understood itself to be an integral, and indeed key, part of the structure of the world, as created, and our creatureliness was exercised within the context of the faculties of mind, body and spirit which engaged with the world, through perception, understanding and feeling.

---

60. Tractate 2, 11, 2 (*The Fathers of the Church*, Washington DC: Catholic University of America Press, no. 78, trans. John W. Rettig, 1988), p. 69.
61. Frederick van Fleteren, 'Principles of Augustine's Hermeneutic: an Overview', in Frederick van Fleteren and Joseph C. Schnaubelt, eds., *Augustine. Biblical Exegete* (New York: Peter Lang, 2001), pp. 1–32 (here 6–7). See also Frederick van Fleteren, 'Augustine's Ascent of the Soul in Book VII of the Confessions: a Reconsideration', *Augustinian Studies* 5 (1974), 29–72 (especially 36–41). Nicholas Wolterstorff begins his stimulating work *Divine Discourse* (Cambridge: Cambridge University Press, 1995) by pointing to the extraordinary and long-neglected significance of Augustine's 'admonitions' for an understanding of the type of divine speech in Christianity.

That engagement was itself extensively dialectical, since the perceived world which presented itself with an uncontested immediacy to the human senses and mind also made present the unfathomable creativity of God. It was this dialectical exchange between self and world which became the domain in which the creativity of God could itself be received and made manifest from *within* the world, by human beings whose powers of will and knowledge made them creatures in God's image.

3
Cosmological fragments

Schöne Welt, wo bist du? Kehre wieder,
Holdes Blütenalter der Natur!
Ach, nur in dem Feeland der Lieder
Lebt noch deine fabelhafte Spur.
Ausgestorben trauert das Gefilde,
Keine Gottheit zeigt sich meinem Blicke,
Ach, von jenem lebenswarmen Bilde
Blieb der Schatten nur zurück.

Lovely world, where are you? Come back now,
Nature's gorgeous prime!
Only in the faery land of songs
Does your fabled trace live on.
The fields are now grey; they grieve,
And no god meets my gaze.
From that image, living and warm,
Only the shadow remains.
          Friedrich Schiller, *Die Götter Griechenlands*

We make no assumptions, in general, about the createdness of the world, nor do we understand, in the main, our own faculties to be intrinsically ordered to the divine Creator. The world-view of our own day is radically different from that outlined in the preceding chapters. But the transition from the one to the other was only gradual, taking place over centuries, and is not easily traced. It would be wrong, for instance, to think that the new rationalism of the seventeenth century was inherently atheistic or even hostile to Christianity in its traditional forms. And yet it was in this period that the seeds were sown of the enormous revolution which was to redefine Christianity and its intellectual contexts, and which continues to the present day. In this chapter I shall survey firstly some of the critical moments in the decline of the traditional cosmos before turning to a number of thinkers in whose work we can discern the beginnings of a reclaiming of the cosmological dimension within a new and recognisably modern environment.

Fragmentation

Copernicus and astronomy

The appearance in 1543 of *De revolutionibus orbium caelestium* by Copernicus marked a watershed in the conceptualisation of the physical universe, despite the fact that in many ways Copernicus still belonged to the medieval past. The heliocentrism he espoused was based upon the belief that the centre of the universe was located at the exact central geometric point of the numerous circular movements which, by his calculation, described the movements of the spheres. This was not in fact coincident with the position of the sun, which he believed only to be near to the centre of universe. In other words, his – false – belief in the perfectly circular movements of the earth and the planets dictated his heliocentrism (it was Kepler who half a century later showed that these movements were not in fact circular but elliptical).[1] Although there are many aspects to Copernicus' system which challenge Aristotelianism, not least the real motion of the earth and the subordination of physics to the data of astronomy, it would be wrong to represent *De revolutionibus* as a radically new departure in the history of astronomy in terms of its data. As Edward Grant has pointed out, the question of the diurnal axial movement of the earth had already been openly discussed in particular by John Buridan and Nicholas Oresme; Copernicus refers to many of the same classical texts as do the scholastics.[2] The revolutionary aspect of the work was an achievement of what Koyré has called 'pure intellectual intuition'.[3] Copernicus' letter of dedication to Pope Paul III, which replaced the original introduction to the text, communicates what clearly is a radically new *perspective*. In that letter

---

1. See Alexander Koyré, *The Astronomical Revolution*, trans. R. E. W. Maddison (Paris: Hermann, 1973), pp. 59–66 and 265–79. The perfect circularity of the celestial orbs goes back to the *Timaeus* 44d and 62d.
2. Edward Grant, *Planets, Stars and Orbs. The Medieval Cosmos, 1200–1687* (Cambridge: Cambridge University Press, 1996), pp. 647–50.
3. Koyré, *The Astronomical Revolution*, p. 54.

Copernicus stated the rights of science and the obligation of the cosmologist to see the true representation of cosmic reality. These views contrast strongly with the position adopted in the unsigned preface to the first printed edition which was written by Andreas Osiander, a Lutheran pastor and friend of Copernicus. Osiander believed in the traditional principle of *salvare apparentias* or 'saving the phenomena', which excused the astronomer from giving an account of the underlying causes of the planetary movements, confining his work to the prediction of such movements. His preface articulated the position that since one theory could not be shown to be more correct than another, it was not the hypotheses which were of most significance in *De revolutionibus* but its computational accuracy.

Osiander's intention was to deflect criticism from Aristotelian and ecclesiastical quarters, but Copernicus remained adamantly opposed to such scientific relativism.[4] What we see in Copernicus' work, in effect, is the recognition that the explanatory force of arguments is greater where they are more closely tied to observation and that simpler explanations are more persuasive than complex ones. Copernicus' cosmology, with its simplicity and elegance, represented a more 'systematic and ordered picture of the Universe' than had existed before.[5] Copernicus' importance, then, is that in his work a whole series of non-Aristotelian insights regarding the world came together in the form of a new paradigm.[6] We have to see his own conviction as to the rightness of his view of the world as being itself part of the emergence of that paradigm, based – at least ideally – upon data rather than preconceptions and being persuasive by virtue of its simpler and more comprehensive explanatory power. The Copernican system gained influence only slowly, however, and was consistently read in terms of 'saving the appearances'.[7] As Stephen Gaukroger notes, it was only when it was wedded to new accounts of the material nature of the universe as distinct from its shape, that the Copernican theory began to act as a revolutionary catalyst for the new thinking.[8]

Bacon and natural science

The evolution in natural philosophy during the early modern period was again a widespread phenomenon which took place gradually over a

---

4. Ibid., pp. 34–42.
5. Ibid., pp. 53–4.
6. Thomas S. Kuhn, *The Copernican Revolution* (Cambridge, Mass.: Harvard University Press, 1957).
7. Hans Blumenberg, *The Genesis of the Copernican World* (Cambridge, Mass.: MIT Press, 1987).
8. Stephen Gaukroger, *Francis Bacon and the Transformation of Early Modern Philosophy* (Cambridge: Cambridge University Press, 2001), pp. 166–75.

considerable period of time. But just as Copernicus can be taken as representative of the great changes in astronomy in the sixteenth and seventeenth centuries, a survey of the work of Francis Bacon shows the kinds of evolution in thought which laid the ground for a modern view of science and a materialist cosmology. Bacon (1561–1626) was born into a noble family and rose to become Lord Chancellor under James I. The fundamental insights associated with Baconianism concern the nature of knowledge and specifically of scientific inquiry. Bacon argued powerfully against the scholastic tendencies of his own day, proposing that reliable knowledge was predicated not upon the wisdom of the ancients but was rather cumulative. In other words, the history of thought represented progress rather than a fall from a previous Golden Age: 'truth is rightly called the daughter of time, not the daughter of authority'.[9] Scientific knowledge was also social in that it grew from the pooling of the resources of researchers. Bacon was against an excessive respect for authorities or indeed for individuals of genius, preferring a collaborative model of scientists working together ideally under the auspices of the state. Bacon is noted in particular for his critique of the 'Idols of thought', respectively those of the 'tribe', the 'cave', the 'marketplace' and the 'theatre', which he set out most extensively in Book I of the *Novum Organum*. These cover predispositions to cognitive error ranging from assumptions about the presence of order in the natural world ('tribe'), to personal idiosyncracies of thought ('cave'), misconceptions through language-use ('marketplace') and false philosophical training ('theatre'). The corrective to such human failings in the main is 'eliminative induction', by which Bacon meant a kind of abstractive reasoning which proceeds from empirical observation to the discernment of universal laws and the intrinsic properties of things. The latter are conceived in a purely material way, in stark contrast to Aristotelianism with its emphasis upon 'natures' and intelligible forms. In a significant passage from the *Novum Organum* he offers a new and radical definition of the forms:

> When I speak of Forms, I mean nothing more than those laws and determinations of absolute actuality, which govern and constitute any given nature, as heat, light, weight, in every kind of matter and subject that is susceptible of them. Thus the Form of Heat or the Form of Light is the same thing as the Law of Heat and the Law of Light.[10]

---

9. *Novum Organum*, Book I, Section 84 (*The Works of Francis Bacon*, ed. James Spedding, Robert Leslie and Douglas Denning Heath (London, 1857–74), vol. I, p. 190; quoted in Gaukroger, *Francis Bacon*, pp. 105–6).
10. *Novum Organum*, Book II, Section 17 (*Works*, vol. I, pp. 257–8) (quoted in Gaukroger, *Francis Bacon*, p. 140).

Bacon is strongly corpuscularian in his advocacy of the material composition of things as the key to their properties and behaviour and proposes that 'everything relating to bodies and virtues in nature should be set forth (as far as possible) numbered, weighed, measured, defined'.[11] Natural philosophy defined as the study of materiality is to be preferred to metaphysics and even to mathematics or mechanics as a way of accessing the reality that underlies appearances.[12]

Bacon did not present his natural philosophy in opposition to Christian faith; he remained true to his Puritan background. In fact, he deployed elements of faith as a theological substrate to his system. The development of the powers of 'eliminative induction' is equated with a purification of the mind and a return to a pre-lapsarian state of unity with the world. The account in Genesis 2:19–20 of how Adam named the creatures represents for Bacon, and others, an original state of pure knowledge of the world and the descent therefrom is the history of human corruption and error. More generally, Gaukroger has discerned in Bacon a motivation to replace the traditional image of the moral philosopher as 'sage' and guardian of society's values with that of the natural philosopher. The latter is an example to society in general in that he (Bacon thinks in exclusively male terms) manifests the distinctly moral qualities of 'self-control' and mastery of the passions. It is the natural philosopher also who is in a position to change the human condition for the better; the theme of a return to pre-lapsarian knowledge and unity with the world is attended also by the theme of humanity's God-given dominion over the world. The new knowledge is a knowledge of the fundamental material constitution of things in which reside also the principles of causality. To understand something is therefore to know how it is made and is to be in a position to make it oneself. In a play on alchemy Bacon tells us that if we come to an understanding of the 'Forms' or properties which together go to make up gold, then we shall ourselves be in a position to manufacture it.[13] Another way of stating this is that Bacon understands knowledge to be a 'maker's knowledge', to use Pérez-Ramos' phrase, and thus to be a form of human

11. *Parasceve ad Historiam Naturalem et Experimentalem* (*Works*, vol. I, p. 400) (quoted in Gaukroger, *Francis Bacon*, p. 142).
12. There is a hint, however, that Bacon continues the ancient tradition of privileging the role of sight in the acquisition of knowledge – which is paradoxically also a Platonic one – since he stresses the fact that atoms, the all-important constituent parts of matter are *visible* in their effects of 'stretching, contraction, dilation, distension' (Gaukroger, *Francis Bacon*, p. 135). Following the development of the microscope, later Baconians will extend this visibility to the level of the atom itself (Catherine Wilson, *The Visible World: Early Modern Philosophy and the Invention of the Microscope*, Princeton: Princeton University Press, 1995).
13. *Novum Organum*, Book II, Section 5 (*Works*, vol. I, pp. 230–1).

imitation of the powers of the divine.[14] Something of this can be felt also in Bacon's conviction that it is potentially within the powers of the natural philosopher to eradicate disease and to overcome the aging process.[15]

Bacon, like Copernicus, exhibits features of the old age as well as the new (he rejected Copernicus' heliocentrism, for instance, but lacked the experimentalism which was to come in later with the influence of Desaguliers through the Royal Society)[16], but we can discern elements in his thought that are identifiably in harmony with and almost certainly productive of modern conceptions of knowledge and of the world. If such changes were afoot during the sixteenth and seventeenth centuries in the areas of astronomy and natural philosophy, then so too in metaphysics and philosophy more generally. David Hume delivered a powerful attack on the principles of natural theology and belief in the createdness of the world, in his *Dialogues on Natural Religion*. One of his main arguments was against the position of William Palgrave, who used the analogy of the inference of a watchmaker from the existence of a watch for his argument that God the Creator could be inferred from the existence of the world. Hume made the telling point that the world is not at all like an object in the world and that the order of the world might result from the nature of matter rather than from the intentionality of a divine maker. It is in Hume's reflections on the nature of causality also that we find a significant contrast with pre-modern positions. For Thomas Aquinas and the medievals (and the Fathers before them), it was axiomatic that effects bore some likeness to their causes so that the effect of every cause is similar to itself.[17] Against this, Hume held in his *Enquiry Concerning Human Understanding* that like causes have like effects. In an age in which causality itself was understood to be material and mechanical, being based on the play of forces, the notion that the effect *participates* in some sense in its cause, mediated through a hierarchical structure of natures and essences, became wholly redundant.

The detachment of metaphysics from its traditional base in theology proceeded apace in this period. The Nominalists characteristically shifted the emphasis away from objective universals to the individual existent, but

---

14. See Antonio Pérez-Ramos, *Francis Bacon's Idea of Science and the Maker's Knowledge Tradition* (Oxford: Clarendon Press; New York: Oxford University Press, 1988).

15. See *Historia Vitae et Mortis* (*Works*, vol. II). Bacon's pragmatic belief that 'true' knowledge is 'useful' or 'productive' knowledge is also relevant here; see Gaukroger, *Francis Bacon*, pp. 155–9.

16. Larry Stewart, *The Rise of Public Science: Rhetoric, Technology and Natural Philosophy in Newtonian Britain, 1660–1750* (Cambridge: Cambridge University Press, 1992), pp. 213–54.

17. *ST* Ia, q. 4, a. 3.

it may be in the fifth of the *Disputationes Metaphysicae* of Suárez, in which he argues that the principle of individuation exists in the form and matter of an entity taken as a unity, that we find a telling moment in the break with medieval tradition.[18] More generally, however, it is in the work of Immanuel Kant that we find the most influential refutation of the traditional links between metaphysics and theology, which is to say the nature of the world and belief in its creator. In the *Critique of Pure Reason* Kant sets out a series of arguments against traditional forms of theistic belief, including the cosmological ('if anything exists, an absolutely necessary being must also exist'), the ontological ('the highest being necessarily exists') and what he calls the 'physico-theological' ('argument from design') proof.[19] Kant also delivers a powerful argument against traditional understandings of 'being' by arguing that being as such 'is not a predicate' and adds nothing to our knowledge of an object.[20] Very significantly, if it is the theory of the transcendentals which is most expressive of the pre-modern belief in the createdness of the world, as I have argued, then it is in Kant that we find a specific refutation of this. Again in the First Critique, Kant raises the issue of the principle of the transcendentals which 'has proved very meagre in consequences, and has indeed yielded only propositions that are tautological, and therefore in recent times has retained its place in metaphysics almost by courtesy only . . .'.[21] The error in the traditional application of this theory, in Kant's view, is to have mistaken unity, truth and perfection as properties possessed by objects rather than as necessary transcendental conditions in the perception of any object. In other words, Kant rejects these as holding for the real world and he refashions them as properties of knowing rather than as properties of the things known. He can thus dismiss them on the grounds that they are tautological and add nothing to our knowledge of the world.

Cosmological transformations

Over the course of several centuries the theophanic universe of the pre-modern period turned into the one that is more familiar to us today: a

18. Jorge J. E. Gracia presents his case for this view in his *Suárez on Individuation: Metaphysical Disputation v, Individual Unity and its Principle* (Milwaukee, Wis.: Marquette University Press, 1982).

19. I. Kant, *Critique of Pure Reason*, Part I, Second Division, Book II, Chapter 3, Sections 3–7.

20. Ibid., esp. Chapter 3, Section 4.

21. Ibid., First Division, Book I, Chapter 1, Section 3 (translation in Norman Kemp Smith, *Immanuel Kant's Critique of Pure Reason* (London: Macmillan Press, 1933), p. 118).

world conceived primarily in terms of physical quanta, as the interplay of measurable forces. This is a world-view dominated by what Amos Funkenstein has called 'ergetic' knowledge, which is to say knowledge of how things are constructed and accordingly a technological knowledge of how things may be reproduced.[22] However contextualised, this kind of functionalist knowing, which Francis Bacon embraced as the primary model and exemplum of knowledge, has taken on a pervasive influence in our culture, far beyond the limits of natural science or mechanics in any specific sense. Technology makes an industrial society possible and is integral to its success. Technology guarantees a society's wealth and defence; medicine improves and lengthens life; productive, innovative industry brings financial and social stability to a workforce. Such developments have brought very considerable advantages, but the culture of scientism and functionalism has led also to impoverishment in other areas of human life. For all its errors, the traditional pre-modern cosmos was as much an expression of the imagination of humankind as it was of our rational capacities, operating within the limits of the day. The predominance within our culture of a certain kind of thinking which is appropriate to particular types of scientific activity has left little place for the role of the imagination. But the imagination is an integral part of human cognition and identity. It is unsurprising therefore that in those cultures most influenced by technology and the scientific method we see many forms of resistance, some of which are responsible and complex expressions of the imaginative capacities of the human race, while others seem immoderate and undisciplined. Creationism, New Ageism, and diverse kinds of social, national and religious mythology are all pervasively present in modern society. Much of what we see on our television screens is escapist fiction. But the proper use of the imagination is intimately bound up with the principle of the 'cosmological', as defined in this book, in that the imagination allows us to map out ways in which we can comprehend the world *as a whole*. There is something in that kind of inquiry which intrinsically transcends the ordinary operations of reason and becomes more open-ended and intuitive. But where the imagination takes purchase, the human self who imagines begins to find him- or herself at home in the world. For the imagination is primarily about envisaging possibilities of new existence or new meaning which are constructed from and remain true to the realities

---

22. Amos Funkenstein, *Theology and the Scientific Imagination: from the Middle Ages to the Seventeenth Century* (Princeton: Princeton University Press, 1986), pp. 12 and 290–327.

that we already know. Our imaginations take us to new places and situations previously unconceived, but they do so by the disciplined reordering of the sensations, memories and perceptions of what is already familiar to us. Exercising a mode of responsibility before the world as we already conceive it, the imagination can be deeply creative and visionary, bearing comparison with the work of art. Or it may proceed in a way that has no real reference to what we already know, in which case it is vacuous and escapist, like the ephemera of day-dreams.

The imaginative reconstructions of cosmology with which we are concerned in this chapter belong roughly to the same historical period in which the new rationalism was taking root in European society. The works of the three individuals, Winckelmann, Jacobi and Hamann are therefore representative of alternatives to the trends which were to gain dominance, and they offer us an important insight into some of the most basic strategies of response to the fundamental changes which were afoot. In Winckelmann, for instance, we can see the appearance of art as a new focus for the spiritual and metaphysical values of a culture (in which he anticipates the Romantic cult of genius), whereas in Jacobi the issue is alternative readings of the scope and nature of reason (in which he anticipates Schleiermacher). In Hamann, in addition to his renowned critique of Immanuel Kant, we see the emergence of a language-centred and, indeed, scriptural account of the nature of the world. In each case moreover we find a concern with unity of the self and the world, not as an observed fact but as a project or goal to be attained. In fact, in many ways, we could say that if the new advances in natural science led – in their broader cultural expressions – to an alienation of the imaginative and spiritual self within the world, then these new 'cosmological' projects are all grounded in an attempt to open up new, disciplined ways in which human beings could experience themselves as being in fundamental unity with the world conceived as a whole. It is here then, in these cultural and intellectual formations of the mid to late eighteenth century, that we can discern the outline of a return of the cosmological principle conceived in diverse ways as the attainment of a new conceptual unity of self and world.

Winckelmann and art

Johann Joachim Winckelmann (1717–68), the author of *Thoughts on the Imitation of the Painting and Sculpture of the Greeks* (1755) and *History of the Art of Antiquity* (1764), was the inspired intellectual who inaugurated the engagement with classical Greek culture which was to mould European, and especially German, life and letters until at least the late nineteenth century and the work of Friedrich Nietzsche.[23] The Hellenist movement was one of spiritual and intellectual renewal which brought Christianity and 'paganism' (itself a fusion of ancient and modern impulses) into sustained and varied dialogue with each other. Through Winckelmann, for the first time, a new kind of cosmology entered modern Europe, which both had recognisable links with the traditional cosmology of the Christian past and yet strikingly differed from it in certain important respects.

Born in lowly circumstances in Prussia, Winckelmann rose to become one of the most influential literary and aesthetic thinkers of his day, before meeting an untimely and violent death at the hands of a thief in Trieste. From one perspective his work is dominated by immense learning, and by an exquisite scholarly attention to detail in the many statues, buildings and paintings concerning which he wrote. But with an eighteenth-century élan, Winckelmann combined his powers of scholarship with an inspired vision of the uplifting value of aestheticism and the moral and social ideals which it sustained. Winckelmann's main thesis, which is already articulated in his early *Thoughts on the Imitation*, was that ancient Greek civilisation – favoured by climate and situation – had had a particularly privileged access to the beauty and strengths of nature. He believed that the Greeks had become aware of the ennobling aspects of natural beauty in a way that was true of no other people. They had learned to celebrate and proclaim this knowledge through the power of the arts, above all through sculpture, which was the most mimetic of the arts. The skills of the artist served to heighten natural beauty by bringing together in a single work the very best features of a number of natural forms. The artists and the culture which supported and valued their work placed this representational art at the centre of Greek society and values, as the highest expression of an aesthetic ideal, which was intimately bound up with the cause of freedom in both the moral and political domain.

Winckelmann summarised his view of that Greek ideal in terms of 'edle Einfalt' ('noble simplicity') and 'stille Grösse' ('tranquil grandeur'). In an important passage from 'On Art among the Greeks', published in his *History of the Art of Antiquity*, Winckelmann distinguished between the *Bildung* or 'formation' of the work of art and its *Ausdruck* or 'expression'. The

---

23. Henry Hatfield surveys this tradition in his *Aesthetic Paganism in German Literature* (Cambridge. Mass.: Harvard University Press, 1964). Stefan George can also be included amongst these writers.

former was a kind of unity generated by the proportions of the art work: the harmony of its parts resolved as a formal unity which was the ground of its aesthetic appeal. The latter, on the other hand, marked the intersection of the work of art with the human world so that 'expression' is an extension of aesthetic contemplation into the domain of 'action and passion'.[24] In his celebrated analysis of the statue of Laocoön from *Thoughts on the Imitation*, Winckelmann had already pointed to the serenity of Laocoön's great spirit, who 'suffers, but suffers like Sophocles' Philoctetes: his pain enters our soul but we would wish to be able to endure pain as this man does'.[25] In 'On Art among the Greeks' he states that 'tranquillity [*Stille*] is the condition which is most particular to beauty, as it is to the ocean, and experience shows that the most beautiful individuals possess a tranquil and decorous nature'.[26] The quality of tranquillity, or 'serenity', as we can also translate *Stille*, looks back to the *apatheia* of Stoic ethics and shows that Winckelmann sees in art a programme of ethical formation as well as the refinement of taste. He makes the point in the following line from the same passage that 'the idea of sublime beauty can only be generated by the tranquil contemplation of a soul which is detached from all single forms'.[27] Effectively, then, the nobility of Greek art teaches us not only how to produce equivalent works of our own, but also instructs us in 'imitation' in a broader sense, as an ethical commitment to the values of purity, nobility and truth.

Winckelmann's synthesis of Greek themes with contemporary concerns inaugurated a new kind of aesthetic religion in Europe which in certain significant respects was distinctively pre-Christian. His identification of beauty with the divine lacks the accommodation with Christian culture and symbolics which we find in Dante, and seems a direct challenge to the Christian piety of eighteenth-century Europe. It is for instance rooted in a kind of transcendental humanism which finds expression in the divinisation of the human body: 'the highest beauty is in God, and the concept of human beauty is perfected the more closely it is identified with the highest being…'.[28] The artist is himself in the image of God who created all things.[29] The content of that religion can be grasped in Winckelmann's remarks about the transcendentalism of art: 'The spirit of rational

24. J. J. Winckelmann, *Werke* (Berlin: Aufbau-Verlag, 1982), p. 197.
25. Ibid., p. 18.
26. Ibid., p. 211.
27. Ibid.
28. 'Von der Kunst unter den Griechen', Winckelmann, *Werke*, p. 195.
29. Ibid., p. 201.

creatures has an innate tendency and desire to rise above the material world into the sphere of the mind, and its true contentment is the production of new and refined ideas.'[30] It is the function of the artists to 'overcome the hard object of matter and . . . to inspire it'. By their hands 'objects of sacred devotion were produced which, inspiring awe, must have seemed like images of a higher nature. The first founders of religion, that is, the poets, bestowed on these images noble ideas which lent wings to the imagination, raising their work above itself and above the world of the senses.'[31]

The complex relation between Christianity and Winckelmann's aesthetic religion, predicated upon idealised ways of reading Greek culture, can be seen from his application of the theory of the transcendentals, with its origins in both classical and Christian culture. Although there is no explicit discussion of the interrelation of the good, the true and the beautiful as such, his work is everywhere imbued with their values: the beauty of art simultaneously conveys the highest cognitive and instructional or ethical value. Art and the artist serve as the paradigm of the fully realised human being. The fact that Winckelmann privileges beauty above all else effectively removes the transcendentals from their Christian context (as the application of beauty primarily to art does from their Platonic one). Nevertheless they retain something of their cosmological character, or expressivity as cosmological indices, which was of such importance during the Middle Ages. In an essay written in 1805, towards the end of his own life, Goethe draws out the distinctive quality of Winckelmann's life and work in terms which derive both from antiquity and German Neoclassicism, reflecting upon the contemporary situation of humankind. Goethe begins by stating that Winckelmann was an outstanding individual who – untypically for his day – sought 'to grasp the external world with enthusiasm, to establish a relationship with it, to unite with it to form a single whole'.[32] Goethe laments the fragmentation of the human faculties, and argues that greatness in his own world is generally only achievable through 'the purposeful application of individual faculties' or 'by combining several of his capacities'. For the ancients, however, another way was possible, when all of an individual's 'resources are uniformly united within him'.[33] Almost uniquely therefore Winckelmann's ability to feel

30. Ibid.

31. Ibid.

32. 'Winkelmann und sein Jahrhundert', in *Goethe. Berliner Ausgabe*, vol. XIX (Berlin: Aufbau-Verlag, 1973), pp. 469–520 (here p. 480).

33. Ibid., pp. 481–2.

the unity of his innermost life with the world in its inexhaustible fullness marks him out as someone who lives according to an ancient pattern of life. Goethe expresses his achievement in distinctly cosmological terms:

> When the healthy nature of man functions as a totality, when he feels himself in the world as in a vast, beautiful, worthy, and valued whole, when a harmonious sense of well-being affords him pure and free delight – then the universe, if it were capable of sensation, would exult at having reached its goal, and marvel at the culmination of its own development and being. For what is the use of all the expenditure of suns and planets and moons, of stars and galaxies, of comets and nebulae, of completed and developing worlds, if at the end a happy man does not unconsciously rejoice in existence?[34]

Goethe unequivocally identifies this way of living, or what he calls 'an indestructible health', with 'pagan' religion which sets the human race within a different kind of cosmology from that which was available in the Christian Europe of his day. Goethe specifically celebrates the fact that Winckelmann's 'baptism as a Protestant had not succeeded in Christianising his thoroughly pagan nature'.[35] What Goethe in fact appears to be implicitly recognising is that the deepest problems of his age, and the fragmentation of the human faculties which is the distinguishing characteristic of the modern, are the product of a cosmological malaise, and that the healing of this disjunction between self and world and their ultimate unity requires the brilliant vision of a Winckelmann (or indeed of Goethe himself, which is the subtext of this paeon to Weimar classicism)[36] to make available the unity of a new kind of cosmological thinking and feeling which is inspired not by the remnants of a biblical cosmology, nor – for Goethe – by the Catholic neo-medievalism of the emergent Romantic movement.

It is the attainment of such a cosmology, set more as a task to be accomplished than a state of affairs to be discerned or recognised, which inspired many in the traditions which followed Winckelmann. The purification of sight to the extent that the work of art becomes the medium for the discovery of a new depth or immediacy of reality is extensively present in

---

34. Ibid., p. 482.
35. Ibid., p. 489.
36. It is useful to take this text alongside Schiller's estimation of Goethe in *Über naïve und sentimentale Dichtung* as an artist in whose poetic genius opposites are unified.

Goethe's account of his own Italian travels.[37] For Schiller, too, the artist is the one who transcends the alienation between self and world, ideas and the senses, by attaining a new freedom in the unity of the work of art. In his aesthetic philosophy, art effectively becomes the free, creative basis for a programme leading to the aesthetic, moral – and indeed political – renewal of society. Something of this same privileging of the work of art as representing the unification of what is ordinarily fragmented in human perceptions, and as conveying 'reality' with an unparalleled immediacy, is apparent in the Hellenic tradition of German letters from Herder to Hölderlin and, more remotely, in Nietzsche, but it is present too in the modern period in the *Erlebnisphilosophie* of a hermeneutic philosopher such as Wilhelm Dilthey and in the aesthetics of Hans-Georg Gadamer. In changed form, the final unity of the good, the true and the beautiful retains a certain force in what we might call the aesthetico-religious tradition, and becomes a place of resistance to the instrumentalisation of nature and the world.

Jacobi and reason

Like Hamann, Friedrich Heinrich Jacobi (1743–1819) gives us valuable insights into philosophical possibilities which are at odds with the Kantian rationalism and its aftermath that so formed later tradition. He too looked to a restoration, albeit in distinctively new terms, of the cosmological and with it a deep sense of the unity of the world and of the self within the world. Goethe's appeal for a unity of the faculties of the self grounded in the self's own relation with the world finds one of its chief modes of realisation in Jacobi's work. Jacobi is known in the history of ideas as one of the leading polemicists at a time when German thought and letters were a ferment of new ideas and perspectives. He played a major part in the 'Spinoza controversy', which led to an undermining of the influence of rationalism through the discovery – communicated in Jacobi's *Concerning the Doctrine of Spinoza in Letters to Herr Moses Mendelssohn* (1785) – that Ephraim Lessing, one of the leading spirits of the rationalist movement, was himself a Spinozist.[38] Spinoza was read by some as a pantheist who offered support to a pietistic world-view which stressed the immediacy of

---

37. Winckelmann's programme and Goethe's *Italienische Reise* are perceptively compared by Jeremy Morrison in his *Winckelmann and the Notion of Aesthetic Education* (Oxford: Clarendon Press, 1996), especially pp. 34–68 and 206–48.
38. A very thorough account of this episode in German letters is given by Frederick Beiser in his *The Fate of Reason* (Cambridge, Mass.: Harvard University Press, 1987), pp. 44–91.

God's presence in the world, and which was often linked with radical political movements of the day. For others, following Bayle's highly negative and fatefully influential assessment in his *Dictionnaire Historique et Critique*, Spinoza was a dangerous atheist. Jacobi himself, like Fichte, took Spinoza to be an apostle of reason and judged that his rationalism found its focus in an enquiry into the principle of sufficient reason, or the explanatory causes of the way things are. Spinoza was thus a philosophical representative of the new sciences of technology and mechanics. The deterministic kind of rationalism which Spinoza represented was one therefore which would inevitably lead to the extinguishing of faith in God and divine providence, free will and belief in the immortality of the soul, and to an abject fatalism. Jacobi's account of Lessing's confession that he was entirely in agreement with Spinoza raised the spectre that the rationalist philosophy of Moses Mendelssohn and others was self-contradictory and would inevitably lead to nihilism and the extinction of all human values.

The alternative to rationalism which Jacobi proposed was one which was grounded in a different understanding of the principle of reason. In the Preface to the treatise *David Hume on Faith* which Jacobi added in 1815 for the version published in his collected works, Jacobi set out the leading points in his critique of Kant's philosophy. He stressed that he saw in it an unnecessary and fatally contradictory disjunction between the role of understanding and reason. The failure to emphasise the place of reason, as a transcendental perceptive faculty equal to that of understanding, would lead inevitably to a form of absolute subjectivism. 'Representations' alone constitute a kind of 'negation of nothingness, a something that passes for mere "not-nothing" and would pass for plain "nothingness" if reason (which still retains the upper hand) did not forcibly prevent that'.[39] Jacobi defined reason as the faculty, uniquely characteristic of humankind, which had as its objects the true, the actual, the good and the beautiful.[40] These transcendental properties are possessed by reason as its objects of knowledge with an absolute certainty of 'faith', which Jacobi in turn describes as 'a knowing not-knowing'.[41] They are

---

39. F. H. Jacobi, *David Hume über den Glauben, oder Idealismus und Realismus*, ed. Hamilton Beck (New York and London: Garland, 1983), p. 102 [facsimile reproduction of 1787 edition and the *Vorrede* to the 1815 edition]. English translation in George di Giovanni, ed. and trans., *The Main Philosophical Writings and the Novel 'Allwill'* (Montreal and Kingston: McGill-Queen's University Press, 1994), p. 580.
40. Jacobi, ed. Beck, *David Hume über den Glauben*, p. 9 (ET *The Main Philosophical* Writings, p. 540).
41. Ibid., p. 20 (ET p. 545).

the secure foundation of the *actuality* of the world such that it resists absorption into the self, or into a transcendental self, in its irreducible alterity. They are communicated not through sensation (*Empfindung*), which easily becomes internalised and subjectified, but through true perception (*Wahrnehmung*).[42] Reason does not stand in opposition to understanding therefore but rather complements and contextualises it, for reason's knowledge of its objects, of the Kantian thing-in-itself, is not given *in* or *through* the appearances but *with* them in a way that is 'mystical' and 'incomprehensible both to the sense and to the understanding'.[43]

Jacobi is important for recognising that a rationalism predicated purely upon the principle of sufficient reason and causal explanation (mechanism), or a rationalism which saw no possibility of knowledge beyond that given by the senses (materialism), undermines the possibility of a world in which human beings might be free.[44] His response was one which derived in part from a critique of Kantianism and in part from his debt to pietistic currents of thought in eighteenth-century Germany, which stressed the place of faith and the immediate experience of God. These two trajectories came together in the theme of revelation, a term of which Jacobi makes frequent use.[45] We know the world to be real not on account of its demonstrability, which – in Jacobi's view – can yield only partial certainty, but because of the mysterious way in which it communicates itself to us:

> Just as the actuality that reveals itself to the outer sense needs no
> guarantor, since it is itself the most powerful representative of its
> truth, so too that actuality that reveals itself to that inward sense that
> we call reason needs no guarantor; in like manner it is of itself the most
> powerful testimony of its own truth.[46]

Jacobi evokes the notion of a unity of the faculties when he speaks of the 'sense-sensation' (*Sinnes-Empfindung*) or the 'spirit-feeling' (*Geistes-Gefühl*) that attends the reception of that truth, the lack of which makes understanding of his argument impossible.[47] On one occasion he speaks of it as a 'feeling of rapture' as the mind receives what is beyond the senses 'and yet

---

42. Ibid., pp. 39 and 34 (ET pp. 553 and 551).
43. Ibid., p. 23 (ET p. 546).
44. For a similar perspective, see Fichte, especially the discussion of determinism and freedom in *The First Introduction to the Wissenschaftslehre*.
45. See especially *David Hume über den Glauben*, ed. Beck, pp. 9–63 (ET pp. 540–64).
46. Ibid., p. 107 (ET p. 583).
47. Ibid., pp. 59–63, 76 (ET pp. 563–4, and 570).

given as something truly objective, and not merely imaginary'.[48] Jacobi's interest for us in this section therefore is that he is one of the first to acknowledge that the rise of comprehensive systems of explanatory thought can close out aspects of the self and of the world which are integral to human existence. He employs the cosmological motif of the transcendentals as a way of restoring the sense of a world that is something other than human construction. But he does so by emphasizing the importance of reason, which is the faculty by which we perceive the transcendentals, which in turn ground 'freedom, virtue, wisdom, art'.[49] Reason in this sense is the essence of the self and the sole guarantor of the fullness of human life. In this movement towards anthropology, which will be a distinctive characteristic of the following centuries, he anticipates the work of Schleiermacher. But Jacobi is of interest also in that he recognises that eighteenth-century rationalism is a form of evasion of the real, and therefore ultimately nihilistic. The alternative system of cognition which he proposes is one which draws explicitly upon the language of faith and of revelation, and it is here that his thinking takes on an explicitly scriptural shape:

> Just as the Creator's Word, calling worlds forth out of nothingness, is exalted above its echo eternally resonating in the endless appearance we call the universe, so too the productive power originally inhabiting man is exalted above the power in him of reproducing after experience.[50]

Hamann and language

Johann Georg Hamann (1730–88) was born at Königsberg, which was also the home of Immanuel Kant. He is a prophetic figure whose repeated criticisms of Kantian philosophy anticipated late approaches which were significantly at odds with Enlightenment values and assumptions (he was personally acquainted with Kant and was arguably the first to read the *Critique of Pure Reason*, having received a copy prior to its publication). Hamann also stands within the tradition of German aesthetic philosophy; his *Aesthetica in Nuce* became a classic text of the *Sturm und Drang* period and anticipates Romantic aesthetic philosophy in its insights. He follows Winckelmann in his belief that art imitates nature but attacks the notion that imitation entails reproducing Greek originals: 'As if our learning

---

48. Ibid., p. 60 (ET p. 563).
49. Ibid., p. 63 (ET p. 564).
50. Ibid., pp. 113–14 (ET p. 585).

were purely an act of recollection, our attention is constantly drawn to the monuments of the ancients, to give form to the spirit through memory. But why should we linger with the honey-comb fountains of the Greeks and neglect the living well-springs of antiquity?'[51] Hamann shares Winckelmann's belief that art gives access to an unparalleled immediacy of experience, but he does not structure this in terms of a revived classicism which becomes the skeleton of a new 'religion of art'. His engagement with art has to be seen rather in terms of an entirely new concept of world, and of our knowledge of the world, which Hamann develops in his early works on the grounds of a radical encounter with Scripture. This provides him with a powerful model for the nature of the world, as originating in the speech of God, which both anticipates in its own way the anti-Kantian turn to language-centred views of reality and stands in a tradition of creation-centred semiotics which looks back to Origen and Augustine.

In the early autobiographical piece *Thoughts on my Life's Course*, Hamann recounts his experience of conversion while reading Scripture, by which he was able to reimage the relation between self and world. Between April 1757 and the summer of 1758 Hamann resided in London, where he was a representative of the House of Berens, a merchant firm in Riga. His business affairs went badly in England and he underwent a personal and moral collapse. He began to read the Bible repeatedly and intensively and, on 31 March 1758, had an experience of reading which led to a deep reorientation of his life. The passage in which God says to Cain that the earth has opened its mouth to receive the blood of his brother Abel triggered in Hamann the sense that he was himself the murderer of Christ, his brother: 'I felt my beating heart, I heard a voice in its depths sighing and lamenting, as the voice of blood, the voice of a murdered brother . . .'.[52] Between March and May of that year, prior to his departure from London, Hamann wrote a number of brief works in which he began to outline a critical response to his experience of scriptural conversion; many of the themes indicated here would be taken up again and developed more exhaustively in later works. It is already evident in the early *Biblical Reflections*, however, that Hamann was linking nature with creation through divine speech, and embedding knowledge within the life of the senses: two themes which

51. *Aesthetica in Nuce* (Josef Nadler, ed., *Johann Georg Hamann. Sämtliche Werke* (Vienna: Herder, 1949–57), vol. II, pp. 195–217, (here p. 209).
52. *Londoner Schriften*, ed. Oswald Beyer and Bernd Weissenborn (Munich: Verlag C. H. Beck, 1993), p. 343 (Nadler, ed., *Werke*, vol. II, p. 41).

take on a particular importance for his distinctively scriptural cosmological thought on the one hand and for his contestation of Enlightenment reason on the other.[53]

Hamann's 'theology of the world' is predicated on an analogical system of thinking which aligns 'history', 'nature' and 'scripture' as distinct but related forms of divine revelation. In his *Socratic Memorabilia* Hamann argues that the pre-Christian history of the Greeks is integrated within the cycle of historical revelation. We can legitimately turn to the figure of Socrates therefore as someone who communicates much about the nature and content of divine revelation through his life and death, as well as through his teaching. History communicates the revelatory through instruction, so that '[j]ust as nature is given in order to open our eyes, so too history to open our ears'.[54] In his remarks on nature, repeated throughout his works, Hamann stresses that entities in the world originate in the divine speech and are to be understood as types of divine 'sign': 'Every phenomenon of nature was a word – the sign, symbol and pledge of a new, secret, inexpressible, and therefore all the more intense unity, communication and coalescence of divine energies and ideas. Everything which humankind first heard, saw with the eyes and touched with the hand was a living word; for God was the word.'[55] In his correspondence with Immanuel Kant concerning the joint project of a book on physics for children which Kant had proposed, Hamann described nature as essentially enigmatic and incomplete: 'Nature is the equation of an unknown grandeur; it is a Hebrew word which is written only in consonants, whose pointing the mind must provide.'[56] The physicist's knowledge of nature is only that of its 'alphabetical' character; its full meaning, or textuality, still remains beyond the capacities of the human mind to comprehend until aided by divine illumination. It is Scripture, however, that provides the hermeneutical key to the creation; history and nature are merely commentaries on the book of the Word of God, which is 'the sole key which opens to us the knowledge of both'.[57]

53. *Biblische Betrachtungen* (*Londoner Schriften*, pp. 65–271).

54. *Sokratische Denkwürdigkeiten*, (Nadler, ed., *Werke*, vol. II, pp. 57–82; here p. 64).

55. *Des Ritters von Rosencreuz letzte Willensmeinung über den göttlichen und menschlichen Ursprung der Sprache* (Nadler, ed., *Werke*, vol. III, pp. 25–33; here p. 32). The passage continues with an affirmation of the origins of human language in the divine 'Word': 'Mit diesem Worte im Mund und Herzen war der Ursprung der Sprache so natürlich, so nahe und leicht, wie ein Kinderspiel.'

56. Brief an Immanuel Kant (end of December, 1759) (*Johann Georg Hamann. Briefe*, ed. Arthur Henkel, Frankfurt am Main: Insel Verlag, 1988), p. 31.

57. *Brocken*, § 3 (*Londoner Schriften*, p. 411).

The alignment between history, nature and Scripture, all of which are grounded in the self-dispossessing act of divine revelation, lends Hamann's work a distinctively cosmological aspect. Harald Schnur has argued that Hamann's theological categories are fundamentally convertible into those of hermeneutics, and that Hamann therefore holds an important place in the history of interpretation prior to Schleiermacher.[58] Hamann's position is certainly one of a radical hermeneutics which takes human experience to be itself revelatory, or akin to the revelatory, and the human act of understanding to be integral to the emergence of world as meaning. This is to universalise the hermeneutical problem in a way that anticipates the work of Gadamer in the second half of the twentieth century. But Hamann's primary source is Scripture itself, which – according to a theology of creation – becomes the key to our understanding of the world. Hamann is thus first and foremost a scriptural pragmatist, the first modern Christian perhaps to discover in a distinctively Jewish reading of Scripture the outline of a divinely creative, language-centred, non-essentialist view of the world. Although he may point forward to modern hermeneutical philosophy, more fundamentally Hamann stands in close proximity to the pre-modern model of the cosmological-Christological sign, not now in the context of a hierarchically ordered universe of cosmic participation, but rather in terms which are given by Scripture itself. This comes into view above all in the extent that he looks to the divine agency as the model or ground of human interpretation of the world in its truth. God, as Author of the world, is 'the best interpreter of his own words'.[59] The Spirit interprets the Spirit: 'Whoever senses the Spirit of God in themselves, will certainly sense the Spirit in Scripture.'[60] But it is Christ who is most fundamentally 'the interpreter' of the Father, since 'none but the only-begotten Son, who is in the bosom of the Father, has given an exegesis of his fullness and grace of truth'.[61] If it is the case that 'the book of the creation contains exempla of general concepts, which God wished to reveal to creatures through creatures, while the books of the Covenant contain exempla of secret articles, which God wished to reveal to human beings through persons', then it is Christ who seems to be the 'Author's unity' which 'is reflected in the dialectic of his works; – in everything there

---

58. See the useful discussion in Harald Schnur, *Schleiermachers Hermeneutik und Ihre Vorgeschichte im 18. Jahrhundert* (Stuttgart and Weimar: Verlag J. B. Metzler, 1994), pp. 59–96.

59. *Aesthetica in Nuce* (Nadler, ed., *Werke*, vol. II, pp. 203–4).

60. *Biblische Betrachtungen* (*Londoner Schriften*, p. 189; Nadler, ed., *Werke*, vol. I, p. 128).

61. *Golgotha and Scheblimini* (Nadler, ed., *Werke*, vol. III, p. 315).

is a single note of immeasurable height and depth! A proof of the most glorious majesty and most comprehensive dispossession!'[62] It is Christ in whom God addresses us after he has 'exhausted himself through nature and Scripture, creatures and seers, grounds and figures, poets and prophets'.[63]

The emphasis that Hamann lays upon the materiality of the world order as the place of God's signifying self-communication with us leads to an unusually material understanding of human language as 'an act of translation – from a language of angels into a human language, which is to say, thoughts into words, – things into names, – images into signs, which can be poetic or kyriological, historical or symbolic or hieroglyphic'.[64] Words themselves have a double nature, part 'aesthetic' and part 'logical': 'as visible and audible objects they belong with their elements to the senses and to perception, but, according to the spirit of their application and signification, they belong to reason and concepts'.[65] In his anti-Kantian text *Metacritique of the Purism of Reason*, Hamann argues that reason itself is bound up with language and thus with the senses in a way that determines it as tradition-centred on the one hand and as dependent upon experience on the other. He passionately disputes the legitimacy of reason in abstraction from the senses and the world, and he embraces the sceptical philosophy of David Hume as showing the fragility of autonomous reason. Faith itself, Hamann claims, is not based upon the operations of detached reason but rather upon 'the testimony of the ears, eyes, and of feeling';[66] faith is thus 'not a work of reason and cannot yield to its attack'.[67]

Few works of the period are as stylistically demanding for the reader as those of Hamann. His dense and allusive texts, with multiple word plays and esoteric word formations, seem themselves to replicate his belief in the primacy of interpretation at the creative centre of the human experience of the real. But, despite the difficulty of his own preferred mode of expression, Hamann is an important figure for the modern world.

---

62. *Aesthetica in Nuce* (Nadler, ed., *Werke*, vol. II, p. 204).

63. Ibid. (Nadler, ed., *Werke*, vol. II, p. 213).

64. This typology derives from Johann Georg Wachter's *Naturae et Scripturae Concordia*, in which Wachter uses the term 'kyriological' – from Greek meaning 'direct' or 'literal' – to denote images of things (in contrast with images of what cannot otherwise be represented, which are 'symbolic' or 'hieroglyphic'). See Sven-Aage Jørgensen's commentary to the *Aesthetica in Nuce*, *Johann Georg Hamann. Sokratische Denkwürdigkeiten. Aesthetica in Nuce* (Stuttgart: Philipp Reklam jun., 1968), p. 88.

65. *Metakritik über den Purismum der Vernunft* (Nadler, ed., *Werke*, vol. III, pp. 281–9; here p. 288).

66. *Biblische Betrachtungen* (*Londoner Schriften*, p. 304; Nadler, ed., *Werke*, vol. I, p. 244).

67. *Sokratische Denkwürdigkeiten* (Nadler, ed., *Werke*, vol. II, p. 74).

A contemporary, even acquaintance, of Immanuel Kant, he sharply contested the rationalist's abstraction of reason from the work of the senses and from language itself. His scriptural cosmology, which was predicated upon an analogical field of resonance between history, nature and God's Word, focused upon language and thus interpretation in the act of knowing the world. If the Kantian system served to secularise reason by loosening its connection with the metaphysical and the religious, then Hamann's contribution was to embed reason again in the divinely created world order. Reason that fails to understand its own language-centredness miscomprehends itself.[68] And language itself, part human and part divine in its origins, part conceptual and part sensual in its structure, is the true medium of our knowing.

Conclusion

The fundamental evolution in understanding of both self and world that took place between the sixteenth and eighteenth centuries is a process of enormous and untraceable complexity. But it is possible to assert in general that by the end of this period the human imagination and the intellect were set on separate trajectories and that the self, no longer unified in itself by the sense of a *cosmos*, of itself as creature intimately ordered to and participant in a world of God's making, was in some profound way cut adrift or exiled from the world. Our increasing capacity to act directly upon the world through technologies of change only enhances the condition of our alienation and the uncomfortable awareness that we ourselves easily succumb to the very processes of manufacture and manipulation of which we are the agents. This is not to argue against technology and science, but is to recognise that the ways in which these can be appropriated in terms of social and cultural formation of human communities whose everyday lives are deeply affected by them can – and indeed generally does – lead to a fragmentation within the self. The force of the New Age in our society, of Gaia and deep ecology, of extra-terrestrialism perhaps, as well as interest in the pre-technological cosmologies of pagan Europe or Native Americans, must be understood, at least in part, against the background of just such a loss of cosmology and perceived need to restore it again in whatever ways become culturally available.

---

68. Cf. *Metakritik über den Purismum der Vernunft* (Nadler, ed., *Werke*, vol. III, pp. 284–6).

Whatever our general situation, for Christian communities the loss of cosmology signals a deep incoherence. How can we affirm that God is creator of the world unless at the same time we have some sense of what it means for the world to be God's creation? How can we be creatures of God unless the world itself exhibits and becomes expressive of the same power of divine creativity? The failure to see that – for the Christian – self and world must form a single unity, is in itself to risk building a Christian theology upon the implicit denial of what is perhaps the central tenet of the Christian faith: that God's creativity radically and continuously shapes history, selfhood and world. What we find in the work of Winckelmann, Jacobi, and Hamann, writing at the point where the fragmentation of the faculties was developing apace, is the drafting of alternative possibilities: new ways of retrieving and living the cosmological, not as a restatement of the medieval past, but precisely within the changed circumstance of the post-medieval world. Our inheritance from this period is immense. From them we have received the principles of 'religious experience' and of religious 'intuitions' as the inscription of the world order within the 'spiritual' faculties of the self. We have received from them the idea that art is or can be a form of transcendence. But there is also a further inheritance here, seen most clearly in the work of Hamann but present too in Jacobi, which is that Scripture itself can ground a revelatory understanding of the world and of the real and that the restoration of a scriptural cosmology – understood in the broadest and most flexible terms – can open new possibilities of *imagining* what it is to be alive in God's world and therefore what it is to think and feel as God's creature.

II

Scriptural cosmology

4

Speech revealed

בִּדְבַר יְהוָה שָׁמַיִם נַעֲשׂוּ וּבְרוּחַ פִּיו כָּל־צְבָאָם׃

By the word of the Lord the heavens were made,
and all their host by the breath of his mouth
Psalm 33

Scripture stands at the heart of the self-communication of God in history since biblical texts make present kinds of human speaking which
are interpenetrated by and formed within the creative rhythms of revelatory divine speech. Old and New Testament are canonical compilations
of hymns, historical narratives, dramatic interludes, stories, dialogues,
songs, texts of thanksgiving and celebration, prophecies and parables,
aetiologies and genealogies, proclamations and affirmations, ethical and
legal codes, which are inwardly shaped by divine speaking. This is the
distinctive characteristic of Scripture, that it is constituted as a form of
testimony, as a witness to God's unfolding presence in history, in and
through the creative power of the divine Word. But Scripture is also something other than the testimony of others, for it opens up to us new ways
of speaking. Through our reading of Scripture, we come to inhabit utterances that are already shaped by the divine communicative presence.
Our own voices enter the voices of others who have been reformed by
the power of divine speech, and we learn new modes of speaking and listening. Scriptural reading is the slow learning of these new practices of
speaking.

A further, defining particularity of scriptural reading is that we read
in Scripture of how Christ himself, who is the meaning of the text, is the
one through whom all things were made. This is to make a claim upon
the world itself, and thus upon the act of reading itself, practised at a

particular point in space and time. Therefore we can discover in reading Scripture that the Word precedes us and is already present in *this* particular act of reading. Furthermore, as the divine text pervades our mind, senses and feeling, we discover that the world we inhabit is already fashioned at its depths *in* the very same creative Word of God which manifests in the text. And so each and every act of reading, every attempt to make sense of and to find meaning in the world of which we are a part, is discovered to be a sharing in the creativity of the divine Word.

To read the scriptural text appropriately, which is to say, in its own terms, as it invites us to read it, is to read it in a way that is therefore different from any other text. No other text lays claim to the world, and thus to the space between ourselves and itself. Where we begin to understand that this is the character of its textuality, and respond to that invitation, then the possibility of a scriptural cosmology, as a way of making sense of the world from the perspective of the creative spirit-breath of God, begins to emerge.

Mosaic dialogues

What we may call the linguistic paradigm of the creation of the world begins with an important passage which extends from Genesis 1:1 to 2:4 (generally regarded as the work of the priestly source). While there is no apprehension in these verses of a *creatio ex nihilo*, for which we should look to a later period when a more overtly metaphysical way of thinking engaged with the creation narrative, we can discern here a sense of the presence of God as manifest in and through a sequence of divine speech acts.[1] The act of speaking itself manifests the divine creativity and does so in a way which communicates the presence of God with his creation. That presence-with is furthermore an intimate one, since the act of speaking implies the presence not only of the one who speaks but also of the one who is spoken to: orality commands proximity. The eight acts of creation which occur between Genesis 1:1 and 2:4 can reasonably be said to be an unfolding of

---

1. Djamel-Eddine Kouloughli, 'La thématique du langage dans la Bible', in Sylvain Auroux, ed., *Histoires des idées linguistiques*, vol. I: *La naissance des métalangages en Orient et en Occident* (Liège and Brussels: Pierre Mordaga, 1989), pp. 65–78 (here p. 66). On language in the Old Testament, see also Wolfgang Schenk, 'Altisraelitische Sprachauffassungen in der Hebräischen Bibel', in Peter Schmitter, ed., *Geschichte der Sprachtheorie*, vol. II: *Sprachtheorien der abendländischen Antike* (Tübingen: Gunter Narr Verlag, 1991), pp. 3–25, and Werner Weinberg, 'Language Consciousness in the Old Testament', *Zeitschrift für die alttestamentliche Wissenschaft* 92 (1980), 185–204.

a relationship which is already constituted in the initial act of speaking. Normally speech is a kind of relation which grows out of a spatio-temporal proximity (the speaker has to be heard by those who are spoken to or with); in the case of divine speaking, however, it bestows not just proximity but even the spatio-temporal parameters which enable proximity. Out of the will of God to exercise intimacy in speech, the structured world is born, and the human race as the creatures who receive the divine speech, and who participate in it, are conceived.

The process of linguistic generation which is embodied in the opening verses of the Genesis narrative, and which is continued in later texts, shows successive stages or degrees of realisation of the generative intimacy which is intrinsic to the originary speech act. The world itself is called into existence by the power of divine reference implicit in *yəhî* ('let there be . . .'), which is the jussive form of the verb *hâyâh* ('to be'). Just as divine speaking entails the creation of an intimate space in which speaker and listener share a physical reality (rather than deriving from it), so too divine reference entails the creation of world as that to which it refers. The sequence of jussives establishes a cosmology by instituting successively the existence of light, the dome to separate 'the waters from the waters', the gathered waters, the dry land, vegetation, lights in the dome 'for signs and for seasons' and 'to give light upon the earth', 'swarms of living creatures' in the waters and birds that 'fly above the earth', and finally 'human kind'.[2] On each occasion the Priestly source matches the *yəhî* ('let there be') with *wᵃyəhî* ('and there was'), with liturgical effect. This device serves to interweave the narrator's own voice with the divine speech, affirming the creative potency of God's words through an answering human response. The narrative of the unfolding creation is itself the performance of its own content, since the narrator's voice is moulded to the divine speaking with deep religious feeling.

Following the cosmological institution, God blesses firstly all the living creatures and then humankind, commanding them to be 'fruitful' and to 'multiply'.[3] The occurrence of blessing and of the imperative at this point sets up a new kind of relation between God and the created order, anticipating the parameters of the Covenant. Here the institutionary and cosmological function of the divine jussives gives way to modes of divine speech which establish a *relation* between living creatures and God within

---

2. Gen. 1:3–20.
3. Gen. 1:22 and 28.

that cosmology. In the case of non-human creatures, this is one of obedience and divine control which affirms their reproduction and flourishing. In the case of humans, however, this same blessing and command is linked with God's bestowal of 'dominion' over creatures, thus hinting that humankind, who are made in 'the image and likeness' of God, participate in the divine sovereignty: perhaps even, in a sense, they share in the divine creativity.[4] Following the blessing and the imperative at verse 28, God says to humanity: 'See, I have given you every plant yielding seed that is upon the face of the earth . . .' This marks the first use of shifters, or personal pronouns, which – as indexical features of language – are entirely empty of reference until filled out in a specific speech act. Their nature is to be interchangeable, and their use here in the divine speech at verse 29 represents an intensification of the communicative mutuality of humanity and God. We may note in particular that their function as signalling subjectivity, in this case subjectivity both divine and human, occurs within the perfect verbal form '*I give you*' (NRSV: 'I have given you').[5] This can itself be read as offering an internal thematisation of the process of creation-donation which takes place in these same words, heightening the reflexivity of the text.

The second stage in the deepening creativity of divine speech comes in the Exodus account of God's self-naming. The episodes at Exodus 3:1–15 and 33:12–23, in which God declares himself to Moses, express a heightened mutuality between God and humanity, but they are also set within the context of the granting of the commandments on Sinai and the freeing of the people of Israel from their captivity in Egypt. But these themes of Covenant, Law and Liberation do not constitute an entirely new departure in the history of God's relation with Israel. This is not the metamorphosis of the Creator God into the God of Covenant but rather the unfolding of the primary divine act of creation: salvation in history and the formation of an ethical community around the commandments of God are both modalities of divine creativity. The creationist subtext is apparent in the resonance of the name YHWH which contains an allusion to *hâyâh*, meaning

---

4. The idea of a human participation in divine powers is further strengthened by the account at Gen. 2:18–20 of Adam's naming of 'every living creature'. Note also the human power of giving blessing.

5. This verb is used first at Gen. 1:17. Norbert Samuelson takes it here in the sense of 'appointing' or putting something under the authority of another, which is to say, the different varieties of vegetation under the authority of humankind (Norbert M. Samuelson, *The First Seven Days. A Philosophical Commentary on the Creation of Genesis* (Atlanta, Ga.: Scholars Press, 1992), p. 132–3).

'to be', and is expanded at Exodus 3:14 as *ehyeh ašer ehyeh* and as *ehyeh*. Suggested meanings for *ehyeh ašer ehyeh* include 'I am that I am', 'I shall be who I shall be' and 'I am He who is'.[6] One possible reading of YHWH is as the causative form of *hâyâh*, although this is not attested in classical Hebrew.[7] But whatever its original derivation may be, YHWH as name of God richly resonates with the opening verses of Genesis. Its occurrence in these passages from Exodus, where the concern is with the liberation of Israel, suggests a continuity between God's act of creation, God's compassionate, liberating intervention in Israel's history, and the performance of divine speech which is the modality of divine presence with and for Israel.[8] Accordingly, God's self-naming to Moses at this point represents a new and fuller realisation of the mutuality of language that has been inaugurated in the Genesis narrative. It shapes Moses as one who 'speaks *with* God', and it is important to note that God's self-naming is also in a sense the naming of Moses, who discovers from God in this moment the names of his ancestors, Abraham, Isaac and Jacob, who form his lineage. From now on God speaks with Moses 'face to face' and knows him 'by name'.[9] The verbal phrase *dâbâr ʿim*, or 'speaking with', is infrequently attested in the Old Testament and is used almost exclusively to describe Moses' encounter with God at the granting of the commandments on Sinai (Exod. 19–20, 33–4).[10] It needs to be contrasted with *dâbâr ʾel* and *dâbâr lə* ('speaking to'),

---

6. In his authoritative discussion of the philological issues which underlie this text, see Roland de Vaux, 'The Revelation of the Divine Name YHWH', in John I. Durham and J. R. Porter, eds., *Proclamation and Presence* (London: SCM Press, 1970), pp. 48–75. His preferred option is 'I am He who is.' Stéphane Mosès reformulates the talmudic reading of Exod. 3:14 as signifying God's liberating *presence with* his people in the phrase: 'Dans la formule "Je serai qui je serai" le pronom relatif marque la distance qui à la fois sépare et relie les deux pôles du processus de Révélation l'un actif et l'autre passif, ou encore, l'un assumant une fonction d'émetteur et l'autre de récepteur' (Stéphane Mosès, ' "Je serai qui je serai." La révélation des Noms dans le récit biblique', in Marco M. Olivetti, ed., *Filosofia della Rivelazione* (Padua: Casa Editrice Dott. Antonio Milani, 1994), pp. 565–76; here p. 574).

7. It does occur in Aramaic, however. See de Vaux, 'Revelation', pp. 61–3.

8. See also notes 26 and 27 below.

9. Exod. 33:11–12.

10. For every usage of *dâbâr ʿim* in the Old Testament, see F. Brown, S. R. Driver and C. A. Briggs, eds., *A Hebrew and English Lexicon of the Old Testament*, s.v. 3, e. It is also used once to refer to God speaking with Balaam (Num. 22:19), but the use of 'speaking with' is generally reserved for Moses' relation with God. The occurrence at Josh. 24:27 (NRSV: 'all the words of the Lord that he spoke to us'; LXX: *pros hēmas*) is in the context of remembrance of the Covenant, as is Ezra's reference to 'speaking with' in his National Confession (Neh. 9:13). Gideon also uses 'speaking with' in his conversation with the angel, but his purpose is to establish whether he is conversing with God or not: 'If now I have found favour with you, then show me a sign that it is you who speak with (*dâbâr ʿim*) me' (Judg. 6:17). The occurrence in Hos. 12:4 comes in a passage that is notoriously unclear: 'He strove with the angel and prevailed, he wept and sought his favour; he met him at Bethel, and there he spoke with him.' The LXX correction of 'with him' to 'with us' shows the confusion over the subject of

which are more usually used of God's address. The encounter between God and Moses narrated in the Book of Exodus represents a new stage in the realisation of a divine intimacy with the created order, therefore, and its expression, the verbal phrase 'speaking with', is a linguistic inflection of intensified mutuality and deepening creation.

But the Old Testament shows another form of participative speech, which is the speech of prophets, and can be contrasted with that experienced by Moses. Moses himself is the supreme prophet, but still his status is like no other. The distinction between Moses and the prophets is itself the theme of a passage from Numbers (12:1–9), in which Aaron and Miriam challenge the primacy of Moses: '"Has the Lord spoken only through Moses? Has he not spoken through us also?"' (NRSV). The phrase rendered as 'speak through' here is *dâḇâr bə*, which has given commentators some food for thought. It can equally well mean 'to speak against', 'to speak in' or 'to speak through', the last two of which accord with the immediate contexts of this passage in which the indwelling of God in the speech of prophets is at issue. There is, however, a further possible meaning of the phrase as 'to speak to', although this is uncommon in the Old Testament (where, as noted above, the prepositions *lə* and especially *ʾel* are preferred).[11] God replies that whereas he speaks to the prophets 'in visions' and 'in dreams', he speaks to Moses 'face to face – clearly not in riddles' (v. 8). Here again, the phrase *dâḇâr bə* is used both of God's speaking to Miriam and Aaron, and to Moses, but the addition of 'face to face' (literally 'mouth to mouth') suggests that God's encounter with Moses is rather an intimate speaking *with* him than *to* him, in contrast with God's address to Miriam and Aaron.[12] If the medium of God's communication with the latter is that of non-verbal visions and dreams, then God communicates with Moses in words, speaking with him directly, and thus 'clearly', so that he bears a unique authority to interpret God's will. Martin Noth has suggested that the meaning here is that they speak 'as

the verbs in 4b. According to James L. Mays, the subject must be God (*Hosea* (London: SCM Press, 1969), p. 164), but see also Hans Walter Wolff, *Hosea*, trans. G. Stansell (Philadelphia: Fortress Press, 1974), pp. 212–13, and James M. Ward, *Hosea: a Theological Commentary* (New York: Harper and Row, 1966), p. 210.

11. George Buchanan Gray suggests that it expresses 'a closer and more intimate conversation than *lə* and *ʾel* (G. B. Gray, *A Critical and Exegetical Commentary on Numbers* (International Critical Commentary; Edinburgh: T. & T. Clark, 1903), pp. 122–3). It seems to have this sense at Zech. 1:13 and 14, and possibly at Hab. 2:1.

12. Cf. Exod. 33:11 ('face to face'), Deut. 34:10 ('face to face'). The form 'mouth to mouth' is found also at Jer. 32:4 and 34:3, where it refers to an uncomfortably intimate encounter of Zedekiah king of Judah with the king of Babylon.

men of equal rank speak with another'.[13] Such an intimacy of communication entails a privileged knowledge of God, as signalled by the final line of God's reply to Miriam and Aaron that Moses 'beholds the form of the Lord'.[14]

Prophetic activity is in general marked by the attendance of the Spirit of God (according to Moses), or by some other divine sign such as the 'hand of God' (Ezekiel) or the 'occurrence' of the Word of God to the prophet (Jeremiah).[15] In the case of Jeremiah, like Moses, his own natural speech fails him, and for Balaam, prophetic speech seems forcibly to replace his own natural words.[16] The role of the prophet is to act as vehicle for divine interventions in the formation of Israel as the holy people of God. Deborah gives inspired military advice to Barak in his struggle with King Jabin of Canaan, while Samuel is at hand to anoint both Saul and David.[17] But Samuel will also berate Saul for his disobedience to the divine command, as Elijah rebukes King Ahab for his idolatry.[18] Prophets such as Isaiah, Amos and Joel give voice to criticism of clerical practices, where these seem purely ritualistic and are unaccompanied by a genuine personal devotion.[19] As commissioned guardians of the Covenant, they call attention to the discrepancy between the divine caritative imperatives and the actual practices of social and political life in Israel. Samuel calls upon Israel to serve the Lord faithfully, while Isaiah instructs Israel to 'seek justice, rescue the oppressed, defend the orphan, plead for the widow'.[20] This tradition is summed up by the eighth-century prophet Micah, who declares to Israel: '[W]hat does the Lord require of you but to do justice, to love kindness, and to walk humbly with your God?'[21]

The prophetic theme entails a call to righteousness and the exercise of an active compassion. Ezekiel, Jeremiah and Hosea give witness to the intimacy, self-sacrifice and struggles of faith in their own lives and Ezekiel – like Moses – intercedes for Israel before God.[22] As a participation in the divine speech, prophecy shows that the divine presence which is given

---

13. Martin Noth, *Numbers. A Commentary* (The Old Testament Library; London: SCM Press, 1968), p. 96.
14. Cf. Exod. 33:18–23. See also the statement that God knows Moses 'by name' (Exod. 33: 12, 17).
15. Num. 11:16–30; 1 Sam. 10:6; Ezek. 33:22; Isa. 8:11; Jer. 1:4; Hag. 1:1.
16. Exod. 4:10; Num. 23:1–12.
17. Judg. 4:4–24; 1 Sam. 10:1, 16:12–13.
18. 1 Sam. 15:10–35; 1 Kings 18:17–19.
19. Isa. 1:10–14; Amos 5:23–4; Joel 2:13.
20. 1 Sam. 12:24–5; Isa. 1:16–17.
21. Mic. 6:8.
22. Ezek. 11:13.

with language, and which is an intrinsic part of the divine creativity, is itself structured as compassion. Not only does God's self-naming in Exodus take place within the context of God's compassionate and liberating action on behalf of his people, but the human life which is lived out within the Covenant is one which is orientated to the suffering other, to the 'widow, orphan and stranger'. The righteous, who shall be blessed, are 'gracious and compassionate', just as the God of Exodus has revealed himself to be 'gracious and compassionate', while those who fail to show such compassion to the weak and vulnerable in society must face God's anger.[23] Furthermore, the prophetic voice contains a certain knowledge about the operation of divine justice where the call to righteousness and compassion is not heeded. The true prophet is known by his or her ability to tell the future.[24] And it is the prophets who warn Israel of the impending 'day of the Lord', when all shall be called to account for their actions.[25]

The link between divine creativity, compassion, speech and presence is repeatedly brought out in early rabbinic sources, in both Targum and Midrash. In the former it is expressed through the use of the divine *Memra*, which is the hypostasised 'speech' or 'word' of God which is present during the creation narrative from Genesis.[26] In the latter, the connection is made through the identification of YHWH as the appropriate name of God to be used where God's compassion is to be highlighted.[27] But there is also a clear theological rationale at work in what we might call this fourfold

23. For the 'graciousness' and 'compassion' of God, see in particular Exod. 3:1–17, 33:19 and 34:6.

24. Deut. 18:15–22.

25. E.g. Zeph. 1:7.

26. See Peter Ochs, 'Three Post-Critical Encounters with the Burning Bush', in Stephen E. Fowl, ed., *The Theological Interpretation of Scripture. Classic and Contemporary Readings* (Oxford: Blackwell, 1997), pp. 129–42.

27. Two marginal glosses on Exod. 3:14 from the Targum Codex Neophiti exemplify the connection between divine speech, presence-with, creativity and compassion:

First Gloss: 'The Memra of the Lord said to Moses: He who said to the world: "Be", and it came into being, and who again will say to it: "Be", and it will be. And he said: Thus shall you say to the children of Israel: "WHO I AM (*'HYH*) has sent me."'

Second Gloss: 'I have existed before the world was created and have existed after the world has been created. I am he who has been at your aid in the Egyptian exile, and I am he who will again be at your aid in every generation. And he said: Thus shall you say to the children of Israel: "I AM (*'HYH*) sent me to you."'

(*Targum Neofiti 1: Exodus*, translated, with Introduction and Apparatus by Martin McNamara, MSC (The Aramaic Bible 2; Edinburgh: T. & T. Clark, 1994), p. 19; translation slightly adapted).

We find the identification of the name YHWH with God's quality of compassion in the passage from the Rabbah on Exodus (3:14):

Rabbi Abba bar Mammel said: God said to Moses: I am called according to my acts. At times I am called El Shaddai, Seba'ot, Elohim and Yahweh. When I judge creatures, I am called

unity. The linguistic structure of the cosmological institutionary narrative in Genesis entails a deepening mutuality between God and the created order, leading to blessing and command. This linguistic-creative process of the Old Testament culminates in the conversation, or 'speaking with', that takes place on Mount Sinai between God and Moses, who is to be God's agent in his intervention for the sake of his people. Divine presence here is not exercised from outside language, by some sovereign and independent agent, but is rather enfolded within language which acquires revelatory functions. Such an active penetration by God into the heart of human history implies a particular structure of revelation, grounded in the mutuality which inheres in language as such. By creating the world through speech, God himself becomes part of that world, as a figure, or voice, within it as well as a divine author who stands outside it. This interpenetration of the world by God comes into view as a shared subjectivity at the point where God first speaks with humanity in a way which entails the use of 'shifters'. Thus human beings come into existence as creatures to whom it is given to possess the subjectivity presupposed by the personal pronouns ('I', 'we', 'you', etc.), but this is also the point at which God allows Godself to inhabit the same realm of personal speaking.[28] In making of us an 'I', God too must become an 'I', and then also a 'me' (as receiver of action). As a God whose speaking is originary and creative of the world, God too must enter the realm of human speaking, acting and knowing. This kenotic, revelatory movement is necessarily a saving moment, for the divine presence of itself redeems and liberates as it enters and shapes the human condition in a deepening creativity.[29] God's own statement that he is 'gracious' and 'compassionate' in the Exodus narratives, especially at Exodus 3:1–17, 33:19 and 34:6, where there is a link with the divine name,

Elohim; when I forgive sins, I am called El Shaddai; when I wage war against the wicked, I am called Seba'ot, and when I show compassion for my world, I am called Yahweh.

(S. M. Lehrman, *Midrash Rabbah* III (London: The Soncino Press, 1961), p. 64).

28. In his *Divine Discourse* (Cambridge: Cambridge University Press, 1995), Nicholas Wolterstorff offers a discerning account of 'the claim that God speaks'. But the sharp distinction which Wolterstorff makes between 'revelation' and 'speaking' (Chapter two: 'Speaking is not Revealing') in terms of the human world tends to exclude the significance of the Genesis narrative as establishing the institutory or originary nature of *divine* speaking as ground of the world in which God also 'speaks'.

29. Paul Ricoeur captures this well in his comment 'we can affirm that the theology of Creation constitutes neither an appendix to the theology of Redemption nor a separate theme. The always-already-there of Creation does not make sense independently of the perpetual futurity of Redemption. Between the two is intercalated the eternal now of the "you, love me!"' ('Thinking Creation', in André LaCocque and Paul Ricoeur, *Thinking Biblically. Exegetical and Hermeneutical Studies* (Chicago and London: University of Chicago Press, 1998), p. 67).

points to the deep logic of this divine self-communication and summarises its content.

Trinitarian speech

The third stage in the unfolding of the linguistic institution of creation comes with the Incarnation. At this point God, who already uses the 'I', enters fully into the linguistic world by himself becoming an embodied speech agent among other speech agents. The hypostatic union entails the full realisation of God in the world as an 'I' and thus also as a 'me', whereby God becomes himself fully the object of others' actions. In the person of Christ, God speaks with us, as we do with him. This pivotal revelatory movement bears the marks of the Genesis–Exodus account of the creation in that Jesus Christ is recognised as 'the compassion of God'. The person and activity of Jesus of Nazareth is repeatedly linked in the Gospels with the Greek words *splanchna* and *splanchnizomai* which translate the Old Testament *raḥəmîm* (compassion) and *raḥam* (to show compassion) respectively. Jesus is 'the compassion of the mercy of our God' (Lk. 1:78), and he shows active compassion when he teaches, feeds the hungry, heals and raises the dead.[30] As the Word of God uttered to humanity, Jesus is also the realisation of the divine compassion.

Viewed against the background of the Mosaic dialogue in which God speaks with Moses 'mouth to mouth', the structure of the hypostatic union is that of the closing of the communicative distance between God and Moses, however intimate, so that now, in Jesus Christ, God and humanity speak with a single voice. So fashioned is the human nature of Christ by the divine nature, so internalised within the divine speech dynamic, that now God inhabits the voice of the man, Jesus, and Jesus inhabits the voice of God, in a radically new coexistence of person and speech. The 'envoicing' of Jesus by God is manifested in the many passages from the Gospel of John in which the authority of Jesus is at issue: 'Do you not believe that I am in the Father and the Father is in me? The words that I say to you I do not speak on my own; but the Father who dwells in me does his works.'[31]

---

30. Matt. 9:36; 14:14; 15:32; 20:34; Mk 1:41; 6:34; 8:2; 9:22; Lk. 7:13. These terms are used only of Jesus himself or of figures in three separate parables who represent divine forgiveness and mercy (Matt. 18:23–35; Lk. 10:25–37; 15:11–32).
31. Jn 14:10.

The unity of the human and divine voice conveys a communication by God to humanity which is so perfect that the recipient of the revelation of God – which is to say, the human nature of Jesus – is permeated by and made one with the divine life.[32] Tradition expresses this in terms of *homoousios* and the Chalcedonian unity of the two natures in the person Jesus. The Incarnation is not just revelation by virtue of its content but is itself the supreme form of revelation as such, where revelation is understood to be something revealed by one to another. It has moreover two consequences. On the one hand, it leads to the unity of Jesus and God expressed in the single voice, while on the other it leads to the emergence of a plurality of divine voices, as the Trinity unfolds in history. Through the new oneness of God and humanity, the Threeness of God comes into view. And the speaking *with* returns not as a mode of dialogue between God and humanity (Moses) but as a mode of conversation between God and God, which becomes the content of God's speaking *in* Jesus. In other words, what is revealed in the Incarnation of the Word is itself a mode of speaking: a polyphonic, inner-Trinitarian discourse of total transparency, communication and surrender.

Just as the Old Testament is substantially structured around the divine disclosures through the prophets concerning Israel's histories and futures, the New Testament narrative is built around a dialogue or conversation between Father and Son, in which the Spirit too plays a vital role. The speaking of Father and Son with each other occurs at critical points in the Gospel narrative, in so far as their unfolding relation is itself integral to the Gospel drama and divine speech is itself central to that relation. Thus we can in a sense say that while divine speaking through the prophets shaped the history of Israel as God's people, in the New Testament history itself is taken up *into* the redemptive drama of divine speech, in and through Father, Son and Spirit.

Father and Son

Speech between the Father and Son in the Synoptic tradition is divided into two groups of texts: the affirmations of baptism and transfiguration on the one hand and the tortured speech of the Passion narrative, at Gethsemane and on the Cross, on the other.[33] In the former the emphasis

32. See below, pp. 122–8, for a discussion of the redemptive and sacrificial characteristics of this unity.
33. The exception to this is the development of divine speech in the Johannine tradition, where the communication of the Father and the Son takes on a more fully conversational

is upon the Father who speaks with the Son (although Jesus' life is one of prayer to the Father), while in the latter it is the Son's speaking with the Father that comes to the fore. The baptism of Jesus plays a particularly important role in signalling the new dispensation. It marks the beginning of Jesus' ministry, and in all three Synoptic Gospels immediately precedes the account of the temptations of Jesus which are associated with his messianic mission.[34] John recognises in Jesus his successor who is to baptise not with water but in the Holy Spirit.[35] The first sign of that new dispensation is the descent of the Spirit upon Jesus, as he rose out of the waters after his baptism by John, followed by the sounding of a voice 'from heaven'. The symmetry of Jesus' upward movement and the downward movement of the Spirit which we find in Mark and Matthew is replaced in the Lucan account by a reference to Jesus' act of prayer, following his baptism. Although we are not told anything about the content of that prayer, we may assume that it was addressed to the Father and that Jesus therefore was implicitly 'raising his voice to heaven'. In neither version, however, is there anything of the sense of a radical intrusion such as we tend to find in the commissioning narratives of the prophets. Rather, the emphasis is upon a pre-existing mutuality, of which the baptism of Jesus is an expression. The pericope differs from commissioning narratives also in that the descent of the Spirit and the sounding of the divine voice are closely linked within the narrative structure of all three accounts. Both are symmetrically aligned with Jesus' rising from the water, or with his prayer, and both come 'from heaven'. The visibility of the Spirit, intensified in Luke by the phrase 'in bodily form like a dove', and the sounding of the divine voice, together suggest a coinherence of the Third Person with the Father's act of communication with the Son.

In the Father's words 'You are my Son, the Beloved; with you I am well pleased' (Matthew: 'This is my Son, the Beloved, with whom I am well pleased'),[36] which conclude the baptism narrative, the Old Testament

---

form (see the Lazarus episode in which the speech of the Father is silent, and the pericope narrated at Jn 12:27–36, in which Jesus says to the Father 'Father, glorify your name').

34. Matt. 3:13–7; Mk 1:9–11; Lk. 3:21–2.

35. In the account of the descent of the Spirit given in the Gospel of John (1:32–4), the motif of the baptism has disappeared, as has the sounding of the voice of God.

36. Lk. 3:22; Mk 1:11; Matt. 3:17. In Luke and Mark the syntax allows the alternative reading: 'You are my beloved Son . . .', which may be preferable (I. Howard Marshall, *The Gospel of Luke* (NIGTC; Exeter: Paternoster Press, 1978), p. 156 and John Nolland, *Luke 1–9:20* (Word Biblical Commentary 35A; Dallas, Texas: Word Books), 1989, p. 164). The text also supports the sense 'You are my only Son . . .', a common construction in the Septuagint.

theme of adoption into a filial relationship with God (cf. Ps. 2:7) is evoked together with the 'servant of God' motif as developed in Isaiah 42:1–9.[37] The latter conveys the intense and intimate affirmation in a moment of divine election, expressed in the bestowing of the Spirit upon God's servant.[38] In the Septuagint, the phrase *eudokēsa en* often has the sense of 'to take pleasure or delight in', translating the Hebrew verb *râṣâh*.[39] The Greek verb also has a volitional and social force, however, and can mean 'to consent to' as well as conveying the sense of 'election'.[40] At this point, the Father's *spoken* affirmation of his Son, enacting his relational and affective 'delighting in', sets out a historical and social reality between Father and Son based upon election and consensus.[41]

In the account of the transfiguration of Jesus in the Synoptic Gospels, the Father reiterates his affirmation of the Son, but in this case the context is more explicitly one of continuity with Old Testament tradition.[42] In Exodus we are told that the glory of the Lord rested on Sinai for six days, and that the voice spoke to Moses on the seventh day.[43] This typology may underlie the opening of the transfiguration accounts in Mark and Matthew, which state that it occurred after six days (although Luke prefers eight days). Similarly, Moses' three companions on Mount Sinai – Aaron, Nadab and Abihu – are perhaps a type of Jesus' three companions on Mount Tabor: Peter, James and John. Matthew tells us that Jesus' 'face shone like the sun', recalling Moses' shining face when he descended to

---

37. Ps. 2:7: 'I will tell of the decree of the Lord: He said to me, "You are my son; today I have begotten you." '

38. Isa. 42:1 differs from the baptism of Jesus however in that the word *pais* ('servant') is used and not *huios* ('son'), and we do not find *eudokēsa* for 'delights in' (as in the three Synoptic accounts) but the weaker *prosedexato* ('welcome' or 'accept'). The quotation of this same passage from Isaiah in Matt. 12:18 substitutes *eudokēsa* for *prosedexato*, by assimilation perhaps to Matt. 3:17.

39. Gottlob Schrenk, *Theological Dictionary of the New Testament*, vol. II, p. 738.

40. Ibid., II pp. 739–40.

41. The use of the aorist here may be 'equivalent to a Hebrew stative perfect, expressing God's continuing delight in his Son' (see Matthew Black, *An Aramaic Approach to the Gospels and Acts* (3rd edn, Oxford: Oxford University Press, 1967), pp. 128–9.). But see also Joel Marcus, who sees here a prior election of Jesus by the Father which is 'ratified at the baptism' (Joel Marcus, *Mark 1–8* (The Anchor Bible; New York: Doubleday, 1999), p. 163). For a more general discussion of the background to the baptism of Jesus, see A. Feuillet, 'Le baptême de Jésus', *Revue Biblique* 71 (1964), 321–51.

42. Matt. 17:1–13; Mk 9:2–8; Lk. 9:28–36. The transfiguration itself does not find a place in the Gospel of John, perhaps because of a potential clash with the Johannine development of the theme of glorification.

43. Exod. 24:16.

the people from Sinai.[44] In the Lucan account Moses himself speaks with Jesus about his forthcoming 'departure' (*exodus*) from Jerusalem, together with Elijah, suggesting that Jesus fulfils both the Law and the prophets.[45] The voice that sounds from the cloud again recalls Sinai. The Father's final affirmation of the Son in the words 'This is my Son, the Beloved', followed in Matthew by 'with him I am well pleased' (Luke has only 'This is my Son, my Chosen'),[46] closely links this pericope with the baptism of Jesus, matching the Mosaic background with the messianic motifs of filial adoption and the 'servant of God' theme.

The baptism–transfiguration nexus sets out the principle that the Father speaks in affirmation of the Son, whose very existence as Son and as beloved of the Father is made manifest by the Father's acts of speaking with Jesus. As we turn to the Passion narrative, however, it is the voice of the Son that we hear, struggling with fear at what is to come. In the account of Jesus' prayer in the garden of Gethsemane from all three of the Synoptic Gospels, Jesus prays fervently, in a highly agitated state, and calls out (in Matthew's version) 'My Father, if it is possible, let this cup pass from me; yet not what I want but what you want.'[47] The theme of Jesus' isolation is stressed as the disciples fail to be with him in his need, and the passage is resonant with apocalyptic tones concerning the coming 'hour'. Jesus' isolation is intensified by the absence of an answer from God in contrast with the earlier affirmations, and by the imagery of the 'cup', which is the Old Testament 'cup of staggering' or 'cup of wrath' that God in his anger gives his errant people to drink.[48] Here Jesus is taking upon himself more than the threat of physical death, for it is to be a death which expresses humanity's alienation from God.

The sense of Jesus' isolation becomes yet more intense in the crucifixion passages which follow. In this case it is the silence of the Father which represents the dramatic culmination of the Son's sense of loss and abandonment. Jesus' cry 'My God, my God, why have you forsaken me?' is a quotation from Psalm 22:1, which is shaped around the Father's silence

---

44. Exod. 34:29–35.
45. On the senses of the word *exodus* as 'departure' and 'death', as well as its resonances with the historical Exodus, see Marshall, *The Gospel of Luke*, pp. 384–5.
46. Luke's preferred word *eklelegmenos* (chosen, elected) recalls the use of *eklektos* in the Septuagint to describe Moses, David and the suffering servant. Cf. Ps. 106:23; 89:19–20; Isa. 42:1.
47. Matt. 26:39.
48. Ps. 60:3, Isa. 51:17, 22. See *potērion* in the *Theological Dictionary of the New Testament*. See also R. Le Déaut, 'Gouter le calice de la mort', *Biblica* 43 (1962), 82–6 and H. A. Brongers, "Der Zornsbecher", *Oudtestamentische Studiën* 15 (1969), 177–92.

and which brings that silence before us.[49] Within the semiotics of the Old Testament, the silence of the Father is a deeply resonant motif.[50] The Psalmist pleads with God not to 'remain silent' and far away, for if God is silent, then he may die.[51] Death itself is imaged as silence.[52] And in Isaiah, God's silence is identified with his wrath towards Israel: 'Why do you keep silent and punish us so severely?'[53] The silence of the Father in the context of the Cross suggests therefore that the Son's experience of abandonment is an extension of the 'cup of wrath' metaphor of Gethsemane.

But we find a further semiotics of divine silence in the distinction between God 'falling silent', as an expression of his anger and removal of his favour within a specific situation, and the possibility that God will withdraw his speech altogether, thus annulling his original creative act. Such a silence, as Job knows, would mean cosmic annihilation: 'If he should take back his spirit to himself, and gather to himself his breath, all flesh would perish together, and all mortals return to dust.'[54] The threat that God's silence as passing wrath might become cosmic silence, and thus the wholesale destruction of all that is, is intrinsic to the eschatological terror of the later prophets, who form such an important element in the apocalyptic background to the story of Jesus.[55] In the context of Jesus' speaking relation with God, we must say, then, that the Son experiences in his abandonment both the divine silence which signals personal death and the silence which speaks the end of creation.[56]

Spirit

Father and Son both play the role of speech agent in the New Testament texts surveyed above. The same cannot be said of the Spirit, however, who is not after all personified as a figure who speaks (in contrast with a father

49. Matt. 27:46; Mk 15:34. Luke has "Father, into your hands I commend my spirit' (Lk. 23:46), which is a quotation from Ps. 31:5.

50. For a discussion of the specific terminology of silence in the Old Testament (ḥārēš, ḥāšâh, dâmam), see my 'Soundings: towards a Theological Poetics of Silence', in Oliver Davies and Denys Turner, eds., *Silence and the Word* (Cambridge: Cambridge University Press, 2002), pp. 201–22 (here pp. 204–8).

51. Ps. 35:22; 28:1.

52. Ps. 115:17: 'The dead do not praise the Lord, nor do any that go down into silence.' See also Job 13:19: 'For who is there that will contend with me? For then I would be silent and die.'

53. Isa. 64:12. In Ps. 83:1 it is seen as a divine refusal to destroy the enemies of Israel.

54. Job 34:14–15. Speech is linked with life and the Holy Spirit in Job at 27:3–4 and 33:3–4 (cf. Gen. 2:7).

55. See also Zeph. 1:7: 'Be silent before the Lord God! For the day of the Lord is at hand.'

56. Matthew may be drawing out this apocalyptic motif in his account of the earthquakes and rending of the Temple veil (27:51). See the following chapter for a further discussion of this theme.

and a son). This raises the significant theoretical issue that the speech relation outlined above is fundamentally a dialogical one, whereas the argument I have proposed concerning the new dispensation is that the unity of human and divine voice in Jesus releases the threefold structure of divinity which can therefore be designated as 'triadic' or 'Trinitarian speech'. But the Spirit is nevertheless fundamental to the communication between Father and Son. The Spirit plays a central role in facilitating the Incarnation by 'overshadowing' Mary, and thus establishes the foundational context for the conversation between Father and Son (no speech act can take place outside a particular spatio-temporal context which allows it to happen). In a passage from the Gospel of John, the Spirit-Pneuma becomes the breath of Jesus and as such is the medium of his communication with the Father (speech requires breath and air to carry sound).[57] Further, the conversation between Father and Son is open and public, and is itself revelation. Here the Spirit is the principle of communicability, whereby the words of Father and Son, and of the Father in the Son, are made available to the world (conversation is inherently open, or 'voyaging', within the speech community at large, and is frequently shared out through social relations becoming part of the broader cultural formations).[58] Indeed, one of the chief functions of the Spirit is to intercept and break open the conversation of Father and Son in a movement which Rowan Williams has referred to as 'deflected love', universalising their relation of dialogical intimacy.[59]

It is primarily with the third category, the Spirit as facilitator of human participation in the divine conversations, that we shall be concerned here. At the heart of the Passion is the divine silence between Father and Son which – in the context of the creativity of divine speech – has cosmic significance. But the new pneumatic speech of Pentecost springs from this silence and signals a renewed intervention of the creativity of God as redemption. The presence of the Spirit in the room as a 'sound like the rush of a violent wind' and 'divided tongues, as of fire' marks the possibility of a new kind of human speech which is responsive to and integrated within

---

57. Jn 20:22.

58. Cf. Jn 16:13–15: 'for he will not speak on his own, but will speak whatever he hears, and he will declare to you the things that are to come. He will glorify me, because he will take what is mine and declare it to you. All that the Father has is mine. For this reason I said that he will take what is mine and declare it to you.'

59. Dialogical relations contain an implicit tendency towards narcissism and mutual gratification; see Rowan Williams, 'The Deflections of Desire: Negative Theology in Trinitarian Disclosure', in Davies and Turner, eds., *Silence and the Word*, pp. 115–35.

the triadic, life-giving speech of God.[60] Immediately following the descent of the Spirit, Peter preaches to the crowd, reminding them of God's promise to pour out his Spirit 'upon all flesh'.[61] Preaching itself is part of this new kind of Christian speaking in which – through the Spirit – the voice of the one who preaches is itself informed and shaped by the one who is preached about. The Letter to the Romans depicts a new kind of life in the Spirit since the Church lives 'in the Spirit', who gives 'life and peace', and not in the flesh.[62] The Spirit puts to death 'the deeds of the body', and manifests also as a distinctive kind of Christian prayer 'bearing witness' when we cry 'Abba! Father!'[63] According to Galatians 4:4–7, we have become the children of God: 'God has sent the Spirit of his Son into our hearts, crying, "Abba! Father!" So you are no longer a slave but a child, and if a child then also an heir, through God.' It is the Spirit that supports us in our weakness, when we do not 'know how to pray as we ought', since it intercedes for us 'with sighs too deep for words'.[64]

The Letter to the Ephesians depicts the transformed speech of the Spirit in terms of praise, celebration and the social construction of the community. The Holy Spirit is linked with the praise of God's glory that follows upon the new life of redemption; the unifying Spirit gives both Jew and gentile access to the Father; the Spirit reveals the mystery of Christ to the holy apostles and prophets; the Spirit grounds the love and peace which is the unity of the Church.[65] Furthermore, the Spirit is grieved by dissension and evil talk and Christians are urged to say only 'what is useful for building up', 'obscene, silly and vulgar talk' must be replaced with 'thanksgiving', the 'empty words' of those who wish to deceive are to be eschewed, and the saints of Ephesus are to 'pray in the Spirit at all times in every prayer and supplication'.[66] They are especially to pray for the author himself so that a message may be given to him 'to make known with boldness the mystery of the gospel'.[67] The theme of the new kind of pneumatic speech which extends throughout these verses reaches a climax in

---

60. Acts 2:1–3. For the image of the wind, cf. Ezek. 37:9–14 and Jn 3:8. For the image of fire, cf. Exod. 3:2–12. Matthew and Luke both report the prophecy of John the Baptist that one will come who baptises 'in the Holy Spirit and in fire' (Matt. 3:11; Lk. 3:16).
61. Joel 2:28. This parallels the way in which, according to Luke, Jesus preaches in the synagogue soon after the Spirit descended upon him at his baptism (Lk. 4:16–30).
62. Rom. 8:9; 8:6.
63. Rom. 8:13; 8:15.
64. Rom. 8:26.
65. Eph. 1:12–4; 2:18; 3:5; 4:2–4.
66. Eph. 4:29–30; 5:4; 5:6; 6:18.
67. Eph. 6:19.

the motif of being 'filled with the Spirit' as the Christians of Ephesus 'sing psalms and hymns and spiritual songs' amongst themselves, 'singing and making melody to the lord' in their hearts, 'giving thanks to God the Father at all times and for everything in the name of our Lord Jesus Christ'.[68]

Conclusion

The semiotic system outlined in these sections is one which stands in stark contrast with what we might call the Greek tendency, which is also well represented in the modern age, and which likes to abstract presence from language. This is to make the speech agent prior and to consider language as an expressive instrument for the communication of ideas that reside within the mind of the speaker. In Augustine's *On the Trinity*, for instance, we find just such an analysis of language as that which connects the world and the mind. There Augustine argued that the capacity of words accurately to describe the world is itself grounded ultimately in the unity of the Trinity. Words depict the world truly where they correctly order the relationship between the ideas in the mind of the one who speaks and the essences of those things which are spoken about, as unity in diversity.[69] This later became enshrined in the formula *nomen-ratio-res* of the scholastics. This model in various forms has predominated in the Western tradition, with its characteristic emphasis upon the control of language by a reasoning subject, and it is only in the modern period with the work, for instance, of Ludwig Wittgenstein, Maurice Merleau-Ponty and the speech-act theorists, that alternative linguistic paradigms have come to the fore.[70]

The Old and New Testament texts which I have surveyed support a different kind of semiotics, which is one of linguistic self-presencing, whereby subjectivity and sound are fused as voice and divine voice goes before, forming the ground that constitutes the givenness of the world. This is to place an enormous emphasis upon the originary character of language. To adapt a phrase from Merleau-Ponty, language precedes us as an 'element' in which we come to our own linguistic self-realisation. In terms of this reading of our biblical texts, the prior nature of human speaking

68. Eph. 5:18–20.
69. *De trinitate*, IX, 12–15 and XIV, 19–20.
70. Wittgenstein begins his *Philosophical Investigations* with a critique of Augustine's theory of language as given in the *Confessiones*, I, 8.

embedded in those texts is itself preceded by an originary divine speaking which sets up conditions for the former that determine its true realisations. The most primary character of that speaking, which is the creativity of God, orders human speech, and with it all the semiotic manifestations of human life in terms of culture, praxis and belief, as well as divine interventions, such as theophany ('speaking with' – leading to law-giving and Covenant), prophecy and proclamation ('God speaks in or through us'), and Incarnation ('speaking in or as') or Spirit-filled speech ('we speak in God').

The refusal of a subjectivity outside language does not, however, entail the eradication of agency as such; rather it envisages it as shaped by the plural structures of language itself. For God to speak, is for God to 'come into existence' as a subjectivity within language who is set in relation – by God's own granting – with those who are spoken to, or with, or about, and whose own 'voice' and subjectivity is interactively grounded in and informed by the divine speaking. This is an 'open' speech in the most radical sense of the term: it is speech of 'opening'. And the presence of God as enfolded within that speech-relation is itself an opening out to presences of the others who are themselves, according to the Genesis–Exodus paradigm, co-constituted by the originary creative speech of God. In other words, the model of revelation in operation here is that of language itself. The very phenomenon of language entails such an openness, as a condition which precedes any specific utterance or action towards others. But where the one who speaks is God, whose utterance is the very institution of both language and world, we must also observe a certain act of descent, a kenotic self-emptying, which allows the co-positing of creator and created within the same field or domain of language. This is already implied in the linguistic model of revelation, where language is understood to be intrinsically plural, and the repeated preference for the terminology of compassion as a primary, or perhaps the primary, name of God – as God of Exodus and in the Person of Christ – is the dramatic and cosmic unfolding of what is already richly present in the institutive narrative of the opening verses of Genesis.

It is precisely this enfolding of subjectivity within language as a modality of self-presence which underlies the coincidence of speech and compassion which we find repeatedly in scriptural texts. God's speech is God's compassion, since speech is always a 'speaking with' and for 'speaking with' to be perfect as divine 'speaking with' must be, then the one who receives the divine speech must themselves be perfected as an interlocutor: as a conversation partner in a sense equal with God. It is this structure which is apparent in the process of linguistic creation which I have traced in Genesis and which culminates in the granting of the commandments and the establishing – through God's speaking with Moses – of the Israelites as a people covenanted with God and fundamentally shaped by his 'graciousness' and 'compassion'. In our texts this 'speaking with' attains its fullest realisation in the triadic speech which is opened up to us in the Person of Christ, and in the dynamic process of 'envoicing' which I have preferred here to the conventional Christological terminology of the two 'natures'. As one who speaks with the Father in the Spirit and in whom the Father speaks also with us, in the Spirit, and who speaks with us and with the Father, in the same Spirit, and in whom we speak both with the Father and with each other, again in the Spirit, the single, wholly distinctive and personal voice of Jesus Christ – as the speaking compassion of God – is the dynamic and redemptive intersection of the divine and human order.

5

Spirit and Letter

Primum principium fecit mundum istum sensibilem ad declarandum
se ipsum, videlicet ad hoc quod per illum tanquam per speculum et
vestigium reduceretur homo in Deum artificem amandum et
laudandum. Et secundum hoc duplex est liber, unus scilicet scriptus
intus, qui est aeterna Dei ars et sapientia; et alius scriptus foris,
mundus scilicet sensibilis.

The first Principle created this perceptible world as a means of
self-revelation so that, like a mirror of God or a divine footprint, it
might lead human kind to love and praise the Creator. And so there are
two books, one written within, which is God's eternal Art and Wisdom,
while the other is written without, and that is the perceptible world.
St Bonaventure, *Breviloquium*

The presence of God *within* the creation, as the one whose speaking is the
origin of the creation, sets the parameters for a distinctively Christian understanding of language, world and sign. This is a model which proposes a
double operation of divine language. In the first place divine speech is that
which institutes the world. The world, of which we are a part, must therefore be constituted as a domain of signs whereby things created point to
the divine creativity as the source of their existence. This is not the scholastic principle of the likeness between cause and effect, with its origins in
Aristotelian science, which formed the theoretical basis of medieval analogy, but is governed – as I shall argue – by a relation which is analogous
to that which obtains between voice and text. That which was spoken by
God speaks the Creator, as a text bodies forth its author's voice. In linguistic terms therefore the things that constitute the world can be said
to *refer*, in both a primary and a secondary sense. The secondary referents

are those other things that belong with them and that together form the world. The primary referent, to which the world as a whole can be said to refer, is the creativity of God, which is the site of the world's own origination. But our scriptural texts also communicate a second operation of language which intersects with reference. This is the mode of address, which is implicit in all language but which becomes explicit in the commands and blessings of Genesis 1.[1] It is the 'speaking with' of Moses' encounter with God on Mount Sinai which is the fullest expression of this structure in the Old Testament. The Incarnation itself can be seen to continue and to intensify this theme with the complete closure of the hermeneutical distance between the divine and human voice so that both voices become one: Jesus Christ speaks both as a human being and as God. In him there is a complex simultaneity of speech since in him God speaks with God, God speaks with humanity, and humanity with God. So intense is the mode of divine address here that God speaks with his creation, and with humanity, from the centre of the created order: from within the domain of signs. It is this that forms the first principle of Christian semiotics: in the light of creation *through* Christ, the sign which refers can become, must become, also address. Christian semiotics has to take account of the intimate connection between the world as product of divine speech, signifying its source, and the divine speech itself as it breaks through the created order and speaks *with us* directly. This is a unity finally predicated on the role of Christ in the creation, a theme which enjoys ample scriptural warrant, and which must stand at the heart of the Christian understanding of the sign.[2]

If the first principle of Christian semiotics is the joint axis of reference and address, then the second is that the voice which speaks is itself a plurality, or triad of voices, in a simultaneity of speech identity and speech distinction. This emphasis upon the Word as conversation critiques traditional applications of the verbal metaphor of Incarnation which characteristically stress the expressive qualities of language, from the perspective of a pragmatic linguistics which highlights its dynamic, interactive

---

1. All linguistic signs combine a referential with an addressive function, whereas natural signs (which is to say, objects in the world) are rarely said to address us in any way. Within Judaeo-Christian tradition, however, natural signs can also be addressive since they are understood to be constituted by the divine speech (cf. the Hebrew homonym *dabar-dabar*, meaning both 'thing' and 'word'). For a fuller discussion of reference and address, see my article 'The Sign Redeemed: towards a Christian Fundamental Semiotics', *Modern Theology* 19.2 (April 2003), 219–241 (especially 227–30).
2. E.g. Jn 1:3; 2 Cor. 5:17; Col. 1:6.

and social nature. What is revealed to us then in Father, Son and Spirit, is the outline of a triadic, Trinitarian conversation, but it is revealed in such a way that we can ourselves participate in it. It is opened out or disclosed to us, not only as a divine speaking-to but also a divine speaking-with. In other words, the Son's speaking with the other Trinitarian Persons is communicated as an address to us but in such a way that the content of the address is that same speaking-with.

And at this point a third principle of Christian semiotics appears, a theme which was alluded to briefly in the preceding chapter. It is apparent that divine speech in the New Testament is structured around fragments of a conversation between Father and Son. The Spirit stands apart from these in so far as the Spirit is not itself figured as a speech agent and does not itself address; rather we have seen that the Spirit is the underlying ground of the communicability which inheres in conversation and which makes it possible. The linguistic model has at its centre a disjunction, therefore, between the Christian affirmation of the full equality of the three Persons and the fact that Father and Son appear to have a certain priority as speech-agents. Dialogism is not Trinitarianism. This serves to remind us, however, that God is realised within the creation in the modality of God-for-us rather than God-in-Godself. The imperfection of that image, expressed in a certain inequality of the Persons, results from the nature of the created order. If we are to reflect upon the Trinity in its uncreated immanence, then the linguistic model must be thought to an extreme such that the domain of world itself becomes personified as the Third Person: speech, conversation, address and reference are all subsumed into a single triadic act of divine communication which contains all that is. From that – divine – perspective the 'outer' domain is itself a moment within the 'inner' domain and, as such, is nothing other than the Trinity itself. The consequences of this disjunction between triadic equality of the Persons and the dialogism inherent in a Father–Son relation, are both necessary and profound. The model itself reminds us that it is a model and is a representation of something which is beyond our capacity to understand. But if we do not attempt to hold this reality before our minds, then – as Karl Rahner warned – the economic Trinity becomes a type of myth, detached from its ground in the uncreated life of the Godhead.[3] If we forget the dialectic of divine transcendence and immanence which plays even through God's self-representations, then God will

---

3. Karl Rahner, *The Trinity* (Tunbridge Wells: Burns and Oates, 1970), pp. 31–3.

be for us no more than a character in God's own text. And indeed, it is the Holy Spirit, with its characteristic subversion of boundaries, between the human and divine realm, between human and divine speech, which testifies to the ultimate and eschatological unity of world and Creator.

The model of the text

Pre-modern conceptions of creation tended to turn either on Platonic forms of participatory exemplarism or upon the Aristotelian principle that the likeness of the cause is visible in the effect. The principle of efficient reason, which is one of the critical elements in the emergence of the modern world-view, postulates no such symmetry: causality for us is a generally random collision of forces rather than the interaction of substances within a divinely ordained natural world. It does not make sense for us today to ask in what way the effects of gravity themselves reflect the nature of gravity, since gravity does not of itself have a nature. The attempt to construct a modern understanding of how the created order relates to its creator in fact requires an act of radical translation. Above all, a new mechanism of relation between the created world and the Creator needs to be established which does not fall victim to pre-modern systems of thought, such as the likeness of cause and effect or a causality predicated on participation.[4]

Such a move also needs to be made in the clear awareness that we are not describing the generation of the physical universe. That is better left to scientists. What we are doing is unfolding from Scripture, in dialogue with certain kinds of modern thinking, an account of what it is to live in a world which is fundamentally ordered to God as Creator and in which therefore the divine creativity is manifest. The emphasis here is upon seeking to draw out the rich *coherence* of the Christian revelation in terms of theological dimensions which have suffered serious neglect in the modern period on account either of a Christian reluctance to engage with the issue at all or of a desire among theologians to reconcile the data of Christian revelation with the findings and perspectives of natural science. But as we

4. It is not enough to act *as if* we live in a participated or allegorical world, for that is only to substitute a modern relativism for what was in its own time a thoroughly realistic manner of belief. Although the object or data of belief may be the same, the manner of its believing will not be. The harnessing of a modern linguistic relativism for the purposes of a return to the medieval world-view will produce a hybrid model which is neither authentically medieval nor authentically modern.

saw in the Introduction, such a reconciliation, while offering valuable insights, can only be partial and tentative, and will tend to fall short of providing the kind of conceptual life-world which is presupposed in Scripture and which was so richly developed in their own terms by the major pre-modern systematic theologians.[5]

The identification of a religious account of the origin of the world with a scientific one, which was particularly characteristic of Augustine's use of Genesis for instance, cannot be part of such a theological development of the creation in the contemporary world. But this need not be a matter of undue concern. The core of scriptural belief about the world is that God speaks with us through it. It is not extraneous or additional to him; rather God is implicated in the world order at the most fundamental level. As we look upon the world, and use its fruits, we find that we are already set in relation with God, who is inchoately present in the ground of our relating with the world and with those with whom we share the world. Questions to do with God's ownership of the world – implied in much of the current literature concerning God and physical cosmology – or indeed to do with the compatibility of Christian belief with the rationalism of scientific discourse are not, for all their intrinsic interest and value, particularly germane to the deeper theological issue of how we are to understand the nature of the God–world relation on the basis of the eschatological decision to live our lives out in the encounter with Christ and within the co-ordinates of a scriptural faith.

The model of God–world relation presented here draws therefore upon the resources of scriptural Christian faith rather than those of science and does not do so in a way which looks to a reconciliation between the two. But it is not in any sense a contesting of science in terms either of outcomes or method. What it does contest, however, is the general attitude of 'scientism' or materialism which is frequently the concomitant of scientific advances as these are received by the population at large. While the scientist may be charged with a sense of wonder at the complexity of the universe and of the world under the microscope, and may also be all too aware of the fragility of scientific knowledge in the face of that complexity, as new data and ideas constantly emerge, the popular culture of the day may be permeated by a deeply complacent view of the power of human scientific

5. Amongst those who work on the relation between science and religion, it is perhaps John Polkinghorne who most addresses the question of how the world might manifest God through its very nature as world, and whose work thus most approximates to what I am seeking to do here through extended scriptural exegesis. See Introduction, note 2.

intellect and a credulity regarding what has been achieved.[6] This reductionism can easily lead to attitudes of materialism and instrumentalism which have nothing to do with the true spirit of scientific inquiry and its accomplishments. One of the effects of this scientism for the religious believer is a deep-seated secularisation of the understanding of the self in its relation to the world, and particularly with respect to the faculties of the self which govern its knowledge of the world: principally the intellect and the senses. And, as we saw in chapter 3, this leads to a disjunction between the way in which we know the empirical (created) world and the way we know God (the Creator), so that our familiarity with God becomes the domain of a specific 'religious experience' or is designated by spiritualised faculties of abstract intellection.

It is as an attempt to heal this divergence between cosmos and creator as it plays out in the faith and life of the Christian community that I am proposing a new model of God–world relation which derives from a fresh reading of scriptural texts. The belief that the world is of God's making is intrinsic to faith in Christ, and the full realisation of the latter – if Galations, Hebrews and the Fourth Gospel are to be followed – entails also the acceptance that Christ is the one through whom that creation was accomplished. As he dwells in us and we in him; so too the world is his and he is the world. Indeed, there is a deep incoherence in accepting Jesus Christ through faith but rejecting the scriptural role of Christ in the creation. That role is the deepest expression of the divine modality of address which is already strongly signalled in the Old Testament and which – by the argument presented here – is integral to the linguistic model of creation that is foundational to the Judaeo-Christian tradition.

What is a text?

The paradigm developed in these pages seeks to articulate the long-neglected creationist aspect of Christology by drawing upon scriptural readings and contemporary theory of the text alike. There are in fact many different ways of understanding textuality, or the nature of the text, which are current today but the definition of a text proposed by J. J. E. Gracia offers a valuable starting-point for reflection as it takes account of the intentionality of the one who creates the text and the recipients for whom it is composed: 'A text is a group of entities, used as signs, which are

---

6. For a discussion of the problems of scientism with respect to our understanding of ourselves and the world, see Mary Midgley, *Science and Poetry* (London: Routledge, 2001).

selected, arranged and intended by an author in a certain context to convey some specific meaning to an audience.'[7] Texts are not simply any semiotic system, therefore, or 'anything that needs to be interpreted', as is sometimes argued in types of deconstructive philosophy.[8] All texts, according to Gracia's definition, reflect the activity of an ordering mind and communicative intent. But they may be of very many kinds, ranging from patterns of stones left on a beach to works of literary art or instruction manuals for washing machines. They are composed of 'entities constituting texts' (or ECTs, as Gracia calls them), which are material. And in the case of written texts, the constituent signs are words, characters or script which are material lines or shapes upon the blank page or whatever medium supports their visibility. There is, therefore, something fundamentally dual about the nature of the text for, in so far as it is constituted by its meanings, the text itself is immaterial. This combination of material signs and immaterial meanings is what allows us to speak of 'texts' both as material objects ('this is a long text') and as immaterial concepts ('this text is not coherent').[9]

The dual nature of the text is fundamental to its composition, but the material basis of the sign, and thus of the text itself as a combination of signs, is often not immediately apparent.[10] We conceive of texts in the main in terms of their abstract significations rather than their material properties. In the case of a written text, the visible element that is manifest to us in the shapes of a script (such as the print on this page, which is uniform and monochrome) is suppressed in the interests of an immediate apprehension of the meaning of the text. But occasionally texts may be reproduced in a way that employs their visibility in order to convey meaning. The use of italics is one convention which allows the communication of *emphasis*, for instance. The use of red characters in medieval liturgical books to pick out the important feast days gives us the phrase 'red letter day'. Poems may be printed in a way that subverts the principles of

---

7. Jorge J. E. Gracia, *A Theory of Textuality. The Logic and Epistemology* (New York, Albany: SUNY Press, 1995), p. 4.

8. See for instance Jacques Derrida, *Of Grammatology* (Baltimore and London: The Johns Hopkins University Press, 1974), especially pp. 6–26. While extending the notion of text to include any contextual 'arrangement' of signs, such as we find in natural phenomena, or in social structures, may be a reasonable strategy on certain grounds, it is one which effectively eradicates 'text' as a category of human communication, in which the subject's act of interpretation is matched by the desire on the part of an author to convey meanings to a recipient or audience.

9. Gracia, *Textuality*, pp. 6–7.

10. See Hamann's remarks on this above, p. 70.

efficient use of paper in order to underline the 'high value' of poetic discourse. But most generally we fail to see the visible signs which constitute writing unless they are in some way deficient and require repair, or when, perhaps, we are seeking to identify someone from the characteristics of their handwriting.

Writing and voice

The deconstructionist tendency to prioritise texts as a cultural artefact over and above the manifestations of voice and communicative presence reflects a failure to observe that the texts are realised for us at a subtle level as voice in the act of reading. As our eye passes over a text (in a language and script that we understand), we see signs that relate to other signs, both within the given text and extraneous to it, from which we construct its possible meanings through an act of interpretation. But as we recognise words, the materiality of the sign is transformed *from the visible to the oral*. The presentation of the written text is itself visible (we cannot read the text until we have first seen it), but in its cognitive reception within the mind of the reader it is constituted as sounds. In other words, the act of reading unlocks the sounds from the visible signs; or alternatively understands the visible signs to represents the sounds that constitute words.[11] Perhaps one reason why we may not be so aware of this shift resides in the fact that both written and spoken words are material entities (the former predicated on the visual and the latter on the audible) in which the material element is so transfigured by meaning as to be virtually no longer recognisable as materiality.[12] The transference from one material medium whose materiality is saturated and overtaken by communicative conceptuality to another

11. There are exceptions to this general rule of reading, of course, where signs are complex visible elements for which the reader lacks the appropriate scheme of pronunciation (even though the tendency here is for the reader to substitute some kind of sound analogue; as in the case of the Russian poet Pushkin who 'read English as though it were Latin').

12. It is important to remember that sounds, as uttered by the human voice, are themselves signs to such an extent that the pure sound properties of utterance may well escape our hearing as much as the visibility of script escapes our seeing. In other terms, whether they are organised as visible or audible signs, the signifying properties of words are so powerful as to virtually extinguish the purely sensory media within which they are encoded. The very term 'voice' implies the uttering of sounds that are so saturated with meaning as to be only recognisable as words. If someone sitting unseen in the corner of the room grunts or makes some other inarticulate noise, we are unlikely to say that we have heard their 'voice'. But we do hear the 'voices' of those who speak in languages we do not understand. This is because we recognise that they are speaking words: the sounds seem to signify, even if we do not have access to their meanings. The exception to this principle occurs when the sound properties of the voice itself are of interest, as in the case of professional singing. In this instance the aesthetic qualities of the voice take on a value in themselves, in parallel with the art of calligraphy in the case of the written word. And yet, even here, it is not pure sounds that we hear but still voice, which is to say, sounds so governed by meanings and so embedded within

such medium is easily made. The consequence of this transference from the point of view of the reader is that the written textual signs are integrated into his or her own 'vocal' life. The multiple voices of the text which are refracted through and in the visual medium combine with the remembered, imagined and real voices of the reader's own communicative world. Texts 'speak to' the reader, however diffusively and indeterminately this may be at times. Only very specific practices of reading eliminate our subjectivity (generally academic ones) or so reduce it as to make it barely a factor in reading. Otherwise texts are referred back to our own social and communicative world through the act of reading.[13] They link with and feed into the world of our actuality, in which human presences speak, and voices draw our attention.

Voice and writing

From the perspective of the reader, meaning moves easily between written and oral signs, but from the point of view of the one who speaks, the difference between voice and text – the visual and auditory medium – can be much greater. Conversation, speaking together, is the primal site of language. Of course, conversations, like any other mode of discourse, can be entirely formal and ritualistic, but where each speaker recognises the other as centre of their respective world, there is an attentiveness to the speech of the other which can prove generative and creative from the perspective of what each discovers that they wish to say. In other words, true conversation is deeply interactive, and therefore unpredictable. Precisely because conversation is interactive, and social, it is also ethical. We can choose not to hear what the other has to say. We can contradict or abuse, or simply refuse to converse. In extreme cases we can shout the other down, using our own voice as a weapon against their speaking. But we can also listen sympathetically, drawing the other person into self-expression. We can encourage or console them, inform them or bring them to new understandings. We can rejoice with them. Or we can simply speak with the other as an equal, and receive their gift to us of speaking as an equal. If culture is the domain of shared meanings, as Clifford Geertz for instance defines it, then conversation is a place in which the shared symbolic structures which form our cultural community can be creatively shaped.

an embodied and personal expressivity as to be virtually indistinguishable from the presence of the one who speaks.

13. Hans-Georg Gadamer calls this element in reading 'prejudice' or 'pre-judgement'. See his *Truth and Method* (London: Sheed and Ward, 1975), pp. 235–74.

When we write a text then, we pass from this dynamic and creative moment of embodied, dialogical speech. Our expressivity now moves from an oral, interactive and context-specific discourse to one which is supported by a different kind of materiality. *Visibility allows the detachment of what we have to say from the immediate spatio-temporal context of orality and the original utterance*. It embodies and incarnates our utterance by giving it enduring form in a way that the sound of the voice alone cannot do. And so by analogy with our own body, the text becomes a kind of deferred body: an extension of ourselves which carries our voice into the world to be reconstructed at every stage by the minds of others. From now on our voice, which has moulded and informed the text, will be alienated from ourselves and subject to a more radical process of interpretation and construal.[14] Others will not 'hear' in the way we have 'spoken'. They will substitute for the unique and personal sound of our own voice, the voices of others. They will bring to our text a range of interpretative 'pre-judgements', as Gadamer calls them, which are not part of our own world. They will 'misread' our text; they will read it in ways that are new.

The divine text

The creation of the world has something about it which is like the generation of a text. The scriptural record presupposes the priority of the voice, and of divine speaking, which calls all things into existence. It is the voice of God, or the triadic speaking of the divine Trinity, communicated through the multiple speech-agency of Jesus Christ, which generates and redeems. Moreover, the scriptural text itself, of both Old and New Testaments, exhibits signs of the human voice answering to the divine voice, as hymnic, celebratory and testamentary passages dissolve the historical text into an orality of confession and praise.[15] The triadic speech of the Trinity itself remains an ideal, however, of which we glimpse only an outline in the representations of Trinitarian life as they unfold in the missions of Father, Son and Spirit. But we can conclude that the Persons in some sense speak with one another in perfect equality of loving communion and self-communicating love, and that it is this rhythm which underlies the great speech narratives of Genesis,

---

14. Cf. 'Hermeneutics begins where dialogue ends' (Paul Ricoeur, *Interpretation Theory* (Fort Worth: Texas Christian University Press, 1976), p. 32).
15. For the theme of testimony, see Walter Brueggemann, *Theology of the Old Testament: Testimony, Dispute, Advocacy* (Minneapolis: Augsburg Fortress, 1997).

Exodus and the New Testament. According to Genesis 1, the creation is sequenced as stages in a process of generation and objectification through the unfolding structure of divine speaking; and according to the dispensation of the New Testament, that divine speaking is itself a triadic discourse. The process of objectification from multiple speech powerfully evokes the notion of text as the distillation of a divine and subjective economy of speech, which is the fluid process of oral communication between Trinitarian Persons, into another, objective economy which is that of the written sign, gathered up and opened out for the interpretation of others. And as we have seen, a text is of itself the displacement and in part alienation of the oral communication by its transposition into another, visual medium, which – as a form of embodiment – both communicates and conceals the vocality and vital content of the original discourse.

According to this paradigm, therefore, the world in all its diversity and variety, in its material and abstract dimensionality, is most essentially a divine text: a 'text' which is the deposit of the divine speaking and which bodies forth the essence of the communication between the divine Persons in a cosmic objectification willed by the Persons that is itself the foundation of the world. It is not the case, of course, that the move from the inner-Trinitarian speaking of the divine Persons to objectification through reference, blessing and command exactly parallels the transposition from an oral to a written medium in human communication, since the speaking of God within God is 'silent' and uncreated, while the speaking of God to and with us is both generative of world and intrinsically part of it. The transposition of words from speech to written text on the part of the human creature is not exactly like the emergence of the world-generating speech of God from the divine and uncreated silence. And yet there are useful parallels. God 'precedes' his creation, even if the manner of that 'preceding' is not strictly chronological (since time is created with the world) but rather the consequence of the divine transcendence: whereby God remains 'above', 'beyond', or finally unconsumed by his creation. There must also be some sense in which the creative speaking of God marks the coming into view of some dynamic which is already present in or characteristic of the inner-Trinitarian life prior to the act of speaking. If language is the primary model of revelation, then speaking must bear some kind of likeness to the God who shows himself, and who does so, in Origen's terms, as the interpreting Word. In the same way, the fullness of the world generated by the divine breath must reflect something of the abundance of the inner divine life which we glimpse in its scriptural representations.

And it is here that the textual parallel gains strength, for it is exactly this sense of presence within an alienating medium which is characteristic of the textual dynamic. Authors 'speak' in and through their texts, though always in ways that require interpretative construction on the part of the one who receives the text. The voice is both heard and not heard, received and not received; and it is not only the authorial voice that comes into play. We hear also the voices of others who are in no way associated with the production of the text but who have left an impression upon ourselves which has become formative of who we are, and thus of the way in which we read texts. As we construct the authorial presence, mediated through the deixis and indexicality embedded in the text, we do so in a way that reflects the presuppositions and impacted experiences of other people, other conversations, which shape our histories. Not everyone will relate to the character of Anna Karenina in the same way: do I admire strong women, or am I nervous of them (am I myself a strong woman, have I suffered at the hands of strong women)? Do I perceive the character to be forthright and bold, or rather to be the victim of her own unassimilated and ultimately self-destructive motivations? Although it is perhaps literary texts which most clearly illustrate this point, some degree of construction, and therefore of subjectivity, is intrinsic to the reading of any text, where the authorial voice is diffused through the accumulation of signs which require a deliberate act of interpretation.

The following taxonomy will serve as well as any other. There are texts which are literary, descriptive (history, biographies or travelogues), enigmatic (puzzle texts), discursive (which present an argument, or are educational in some way), which present a record (where comments or conversations are recorded by another), which are instructional (telling us how to operate the new washing machine), confessional (autobiographies) and epistolary.[16] The model of world as text resonates in a particularly positive way with the first and the last of these categories. In the terminology of Paul Ricoeur, the artistic text functions as a 'second world', or new horizon of imaginative experience, whereby its world-generating properties are reflected in the capacity of the literary text to draw us in to what we experience as another existence, overlapping with our ordinary, extra-textual

---

16. Religious texts do not belong in this taxonomy since any of these can become religious texts by virtue of their status within the contexts of specific groups of readers.

life in the world. But although our access to such texts mimics our apprehension of the world in many ways, and is the secret of their power, the role of the author is not symmetrical with that of God as divine Author. Where the author's own voice is inserted in a literary text, for instance, as occurs in some picaresque novels or certain kinds of postmodern writing, then the reader understands that voice to function as a narrative element within the fabric of the fiction itself. In other words, we apprehend this as a fictional device, a further strategy of the text, and not as direct authorial comment from outside the parameters of the work. Where such authorial comment is to hand, we may well be suspicious of it. Authors are not necessarily the best commentators on their own texts. The nature of human creativity in fact grants a thoroughgoing autonomy to the text itself. In the case of the Judaeo-Christian creation, however, God's authorship remains the governing structural principle throughout the evolution of the creation-text's history. When God speaks, it is with the total authority of the Creator who stands both at the heart of the creation, through divine immanence, and at a point that is transcendentally beyond it, as the one who brought it about. God's speaking is profoundly transformative of the nature of the world and generative of the realisation of its intrinsic dynamics. But it is also rooted, as noted above, in an inaudible divine and uncreated speaking: a 'speaking' which is simultaneously 'silence' and which entirely escapes the horizons of the world.

It is the category of the epistolary text which reflects most closely the relation between voice and text in the present model of divine creation. Letters may be written by those who are absent to those with whom they wish to remain in close relationship. Such letters constitute the attempt to bridge spatial distance and to restate an intimacy of relation through the medium of a text. Letters may often be the carrying on of a conversation by other means, and the texts that pass between friends, or lovers, may after a period of time be reordered within a living relationship of proximity and speech. In other words, unlike most kinds of writing, in the epistolary text the falling of a vocal presence into the visual presence/absence of the text can be marked by a sense of longing for the beloved and grief at his or her absence which necessitates recourse to the sign. Written signs, unlike softly spoken words, risk falling into the hands of those for whom they were not intended: private speech, in written texts, can be denuded and become the object of voyeurism, derision or entertainment. If the literary text is the most vigorous and productive example of the fertility of the sign, then the epistolary text is the greatest witness to the primacy of intimate, subjective address as it struggles against its will with the public and objective commonality of the sign.

Sign and address

Following the above constructive metaphor, the 'text' which is at the same time the alienation and communication of the triadic speech of God, remains within God, as 'Author', and exists outside God, as a domain of divine self-communication *sub contrario*. It precisely reflects the extension of God beyond himself, the divine self-donation, which is at the same time a mode of divine revelation and concealment. Just as someone who writes a letter to a loved one is genuinely present in the words that communicate a depth of relation, while being also spatially and temporally absent, God communicates himself in the creation while also being absent from it. This structure of indwelling forms the theological rationale of Old and New Testament alike, for at every twist and turn of history the 'text' of the world is attended by the authorial voice, breaking through the surface of the text, and reintegrating the objectified divine self-communication into the dynamic orality of God. Each divine utterance is an extension of the divine presence within history and a deepening of the creativity of God which gives life to the world.

The intensity of God's concern with his world, as author of the text, is evident in the Exodus narrative, where God gives Moses knowledge of his name as the one who shall lead Israel out of Egypt. It is evident also in the granting of the Law by which the existence of the people of God is structured according to the divine creativity, as compassion and holiness of life. It is the meaning of the speech of the prophets, through whom God acts by utterance to protect and restore the purity of his people. We can see it too where God intervenes on behalf of Israel by protecting its material existence against the weapons of its enemies. The Old Testament is pervaded with the sense of God's 'jealousy' regarding his text-world and his abiding commitment to the creation. The divine interventions here are in a real sense 'authorship', for God possesses sovereign power within the world and can shape it from within, but nevertheless it is the authorship of an author who has himself become a figure in his own text. The 'authorial voice' is not God in himself, but rather God as he has freely chosen to make himself known to us within the world of his own making, as a speaker who is implicated in the originary act of speech. The text of the world 'bears' or 'houses' God's voice therefore by extension, in analogy with textual replications, or reflexes, of the human body, which propagate speech beyond the immediate spatio-temporal contexts of the original speaker. God in himself remains unseen, known only by faith as a reality that makes the figural speaking truly revelatory as a speech that points beyond the world and not to (human) processes within it.

Spirit

It is the particular role of the Spirit to thematise precisely this divine authorial commitment to or attendance on the creation. It is in this context that we must see the rich ambiguity of the word *rûaḥ*, which has a range of meanings including 'spirit', 'breath', 'wind' and 'life'. The occurrence of *rûaḥ əlohîm* in the cosmic institutive narrative of Genesis 1:1–2 already signals the expressive power of this ambiguity. As 'the wind of God', or 'a mighty wind', it parallels a topos in ancient Eastern creation myths, according to which the wind dries land from the sea.[17] As the Spirit of God, it points to the extension of divine creative power which shapes the world. Although its original meaning is likely to have been the movement of air, *rûaḥ* derives from an earlier root *rwḥ*, which also underlies the verbal form *râwaḥ* meaning 'to be wide' or 'spacious'. It thus has a secondary historical association with spatiality. From this perspective, therefore, *rûaḥ* suggests the formation of the very structure of the cosmos as 'atmosphere' and 'space', that is, as extension which is 'breathed out' by divine words, which appears also to be the reading found at Psalm 33:6, where we read 'By the word of the Lord the heavens were made, and all their host by the breath of his mouth.'[18]

The theme of *rûaḥ* as wind, in service of the divine will, can be found also in later texts. It was a 'strong east wind' that divided the waters for the escaping Israelites, and it was 'a very strong west wind' that 'lifted' the locusts of the eighth plague and 'drove them into the Red Sea'.[19] The wind represents God's judgement, eradicating Israel's enemies with a 'fierce blast' or scattering Israel 'like chaff'.[20] As Hosea says of Israel: 'Although he [Ephraim] may flourish among rushes, the east wind shall come, a blast from the Lord, rising from the wilderness.'[21] The wind can also be associated with theophany, as in Isaiah's proclamation that 'the Lord will

---

17. H.-J. Fabry, *Theologisches Wörterbuch zum Alten Testament*, vol. VII (Stuttgart: Kohlhammer Verlag, 1993), cols. 386–425.
18. See D. Lys, 'Rûach. Le souffle dans l'Ancien Testament', *Etudes d'Histoire et de Philosophie Religieuses* 56 (Paris, 1962), 19.
19. Exod. 14:21; 10:19.
20. Isa. 27:8; Jer. 13:24.
21. Hos. 13:15.

come in fire, and his chariots like the whirlwind', or indeed be the site of God's speaking, as in the mysterious *dəmâmâh*, which can be translated as 'breeze' or 'breath of wind', in which Eliphaz and Elijah encountered God.[22]

Spirit is also closely associated with the principle of life, particularly with the divine life which inhabits human beings as God's creatures.[23] In contrast with terms such as *ḥayîm* ('life'), *nepeš* ('soul'), *lêḇ* ('heart'), it is only said to *indwell* the self and does not represent the human person as such. It also returns to God after death.[24] In the valley of dry bones passage narrated at Ezekiel 37:1–14, *rûaḥ* is linked with the 'word' of God, which God instructs the prophet to utter to the dry bones, with breath to animate the bodies 'from the four winds', and with spirit as divinely ordained life.

The *rûaḥ* as Spirit of God also marks the points of divine intervention in the world. In the Book of Judges, the 'spirit of the Lord' descended upon Samson, giving him exceptional strength, as it came also upon Gideon, Jephthah and Othniel.[25] In 1 Samuel this tradition of the descent of the Spirit upon individuals continues, albeit in a royal context, with the anointing of Saul and David.[26] Ezra tells that God instructed his people through his 'good spirit' and he proclaims to God: 'Many years you were patient with them, and warned them by your spirit through your prophets; yet they would not listen.'[27] It is the prophets, chiefly, who become divine agents through the advent of the divine spirit-breath, calling the powerful to account for their abuse of power and failure to care for the weakest and most marginalised in society and warning Israel of divine judgement to come.

This complexity of meaning that we find in the term *rûaḥ* shows its central function as signalling the implication of the divine, expressed as wind-breath-spirit, within the world. Space, or extension, the movement of wind, the animating power of breath and life, are all cross-referenced in an interplay of meanings which generate a sense of the connectedness of God with the world. If *rûaḥ* in its anthropological applications expresses the intrinsic relation that exists between God and his human creatures, in what Aubrey Johnson referred to as 'theo-anthropology', then in its

---

22. Isa. 66:15; Job 4:16; 1 Kings 19:11–12.
23. Gen. 6:17 and 7:15 make clear that *rûaḥ* can refer also to the life of animals.
24. Eccl. (Koh) 12:7.
25. Judg. 13:25; 14:6; 6:34; 11:29; 3:10.
26. 1 Sam. 10:6; 16:13.
27. Neh. 9:20, 30.

cosmological applications it is suggestive of the pervasive presence of God within the physical fabric of the world as creative energy, power, breath and wind.[28] From the perspective of the model of the world as text, these significations express the extent to which the world-text is sustained by the dynamic of the authorial voice. The words or body of the text are shaped by the Author's breath, which remains in a sense internal to them within the otherness of their inscription. The Spirit, then, is the world's remembrance of its origins within the divine originary speech. But it is also the dynamic resonance of those origins: the co-ordination of the divine voice as it breaks through the surface of the text, in a manifestation of the divine logic which is the deep history of the world. Again in terms which derive from our governing model, the Spirit is the original creativity of God at work, whose generative words shape the world in an interconnectedness of text and voice.[29]

Word

It is fitting therefore that the Spirit, who is the Spirit of the creativity of God, should play a vital role with respect to the Incarnation of the Word which, for Christians, marks the point at which what we are calling the 'authorial voice' is fully realised within the creation, in the form of a speech-agent. The advent of the Messiah, who will inaugurate a new age of universal peace and righteousness, is signalled by the inspired speech of the prophets. But the Messiah himself will be marked by the Spirit, for, according to Isaiah, 'the spirit of the Lord shall rest upon him' and he shall possess 'the spirit of wisdom and understanding, the spirit of counsel and might, the spirit of knowledge and the fear of the Lord'.[30] According to Deutero-Isaiah, the messianic figure, conceived of as the suffering servant,

---

28. Aubrey R. Johnson, *The Vitality of the Individual in the Thought of Ancient Israel* (2nd edn, Cardiff: University of Wales Press, 1964), pp. 23–37.

29. This is to affirm Schleiermacher's hermeneutics in so far as the spirit of the author permeates the text, which needs to be resolved against the background of authorial intention. But the fact that the author in this case is God means that the Spirit-Presence of the divine author fulfils the text and overwhelms the recipient in a way that is more reminiscent of postmodern conceptions of the text as a field of irreducible indeterminacy. This combination of Schleiermacher's model with a theological account of the creation of the world produces a form of pragmatic hermeneutics to the extent that God's meaning can truly be known by the interpreter of the text, who is filled by it, but the meaning remains unconsumed by any particular act of interpretation. God's meaning within the text both saturates the mind of the interpreter and escapes any totalising or hegemonic appropriation of it. This is a hermeneutics both of indeterminacy and of authorial intention, therefore, in which the indeterminacy is the result of an *excess* of presence.

30. Isa. 11:2.

will also put into question in an ultimate way the abuse of power which is the corruption of divinely granted freedom. The servant, upon whom God 'puts his spirit', 'will not grow faint or be crushed until he has established justice in the earth'.[31] The same link between the Spirit and messiahship is sustained in the Lucan birth narrative, where at the Annunciation Gabriel tells Mary that the Holy Spirit will come upon her.[32] The Spirit is present when Elizabeth, bearing John, greeted Mary who was with child.[33] The role of the Spirit at the baptism of Jesus, and in his own ministry as one who baptises not with water but with the Spirit, shows the continuity between the Spirit of the Old Testament and that of the New with regard to the ultimate, eschatological fulfilment of the divine presence on earth.[34]

Jesus teaches and heals, encourages the good and opposes evil. His words are 'a light to the world' and Christians see in his life and death the structure of an irreversible and consummate intervention of God which has foundational cosmic and historical significance. The Incarnation is the supreme manifestation of what Walter Brueggemann calls the divine 'power for life'.[35] For all its continuity with the life of the Spirit, therefore, the intervention of God in the Incarnation is a modality of God's presence in the world which differs in significant respects from that of the Spirit. In terms of the textual metaphor for the world as divine creation, the Spirit is the text's own memory of its origins in the divine voice. It is the knowledge encoded in the text that that voice remains in attendance on the creation in such a way that the breath can be withdrawn and the text be dissolved in cosmic destruction. Alternatively, the text can be 'repristinated': transfigured by the realisation or sounding of the voice in attendance – taken back, while remaining text, into the divine breath. The former knowledge is expressed in prophetic voices that warn of divine destruction and the 'day of the Lord', while the latter is heard in the messianic prophecies which envisage history in terms of a dramatic fulfilment. Both of these forms of utterance show an internal relation with the function of the sign as reference; they are grounded in the awareness of God as Creator. The incarnate Word, on the other hand, provides a narrative of origination, much like the Spirit, but it is also and paramountly a modality of *address*.

31. Isa. 42:1–4.
32. Lk. 1:35.
33. Lk. 1:41–2.
34. Matt. 3:11–12.
35. Brueggemann, *Theology of the Old Testament*, pp. 528–51.

The question of the nature of God's definitive intervention in Jesus Christ is closely bound up with the scriptural account of human nature, and the role of the Spirit in its formation. In Genesis 2 we read that when God had formed man from the dust of the ground, he 'breathed into his nostrils the breath of life'. This already signals that there is an intimacy of relation between humankind and the divine breath. Speech is intrinsic to the status of humanity as being 'in the image' of God. Adam, too, possesses the power of naming, as he does that of blessing and cursing, in a way that suggests that he shares something of the originary power of God's speaking, however partially and remotely.[36] But contained within the human capacity to *speak*, as given by our affinity with the divine nature, there is also the human capacity to understand (or 'to listen', as it is most frequently expressed in biblical language). The scriptural self is one who is summoned into a reciprocal relation with the God who speaks, in terms of our attentiveness, our openness to what is said, or ability to comprehend, to follow and to obey. The *interpretation* of God's word is therefore at the centre of the human condition, as we struggle to make sense of what has been given to us to understand by the divine initiative. Our hermeneutical tasks are part of our spiritual character as reflective linguistic beings. The interpretation of the divine will, as expressed in the world, in dreams and in Scripture, is a human activity which is especially associated with the Holy Spirit. Interpretation of this kind entails an element of divine illumination, or intervention, therefore, which draws the individual interpreter more fully into the realm of divine power. The prophets who testify to the failure of Israel to follow the divine will are inspired by the Spirit, and their lives are touched by the power of God. Additionally, Joseph interprets Pharaoh's dream and has 'the spirit of God', just as Daniel, who interprets Nebuchadnezzar's dream, is 'endowed with a spirit of the holy gods'.[37] Jesus' own acts of interpretation are likewise spirit-filled. As a boy he disputes with the teachers in the Temple so that '[a]ll who heard him were amazed at his understanding' (a phrase which recalls the messianic passage at Isa. 11:12, referring to 'the spirit of wisdom and understanding').[38] And subsequently the Gospel of Luke records that when Jesus returned to Nazareth, he read a messianic passage from Isaiah: 'The Spirit of the Lord is upon me, because he anointed me to bring good news to

---

36. Gen. 2:18–20. Note also the power of human speech, as blessing or cursing, as in the Letter of James 3:1–12.

37. Gen. 41:38; Dan. 4:8 (also 5:11 and 14).

38. Lk. 2:47.

the poor. He has sent me to proclaim release to the captives and recovery of sight to the blind, to let the oppressed go free, to proclaim the year of the Lord's favour.'[39] Jesus' interpretation of the Scripture to those present with him, that it had been fulfilled in their hearing that day, seems reflexive to the extent that he is not only the one who is empowered by the Spirit to bring the good news and to release captives, but it is by the same Spirit that he is *able to read the Scripture to them in this way*. Jesus' own interpretation of Isaiah on that day is itself an aspect of his life in and through Scripture and of his particular ability to discern its meaning.

But Jesus' reading of Scripture differs from any possible reading of our own in a way that is determinative of Christian salvific history. Jesus read Scripture as the one of whom Scripture speaks. His reading of it, which is to say, his entry into its foundational meanings, was at the same time the point at which the Creator's voice re-entered, or reanimated the text of the world. The unfathomable act of generosity which was the creation of the world represented also the fundamental alienation of the divine voice, as a divine orality of pure presence was exchanged for a textuality at the heart of which was the act of – human – interpretation. The divine meanings presupposed a human interpreter, subject to all the vagaries of reading and reconstruction. The world was poised at its centre on the contingencies of the human mind. Human beings made in the image of God might correctly understand the divine purpose, under the guiding influence of the Holy Spirit, or they might misunderstand and reject such a purpose, preferring their own partial and distorted constructions. In either case, the originary divine voice was now under alienation.

Texts are like bodies, and bodies like texts. For both are voice-bearing. The body frames the voice, while the text carries the voice, like a semantic echo, away from the living immediacy of the body's reality. In order for the text of the world to be united once again with the divine voice, something other was needed than the sounding of God's speech within the creation. The divine had itself to become body, and that body had itself to become world.

Conclusion

The model of author and text represents a postcritical attempt to recreate the structures of a pre-modern paradigm of the universe as participating

---

39. Lk. 4:16–30. The reading is taken from the LXX version of Isa. 61:1–2 to which has been added a phrase ('to let the oppressed go free') from Isa. 58:6.

in the life of God. In the patristic and medieval periods, sophisticated forms of metaphysics predicated upon specific notions of a causal relation between the divine being and contingent, created being provided a structure for a theological logic and semantics. Speech about God was meaningful since the world from which language derives bore a certain likeness – by virtue of its state as *caused* – to the divine nature itself. Running through these paradigms was the idea that a cause replicates itself in some degree in its effect, and thus the caused bears a likeness to its cause. This sat uneasily with Thomas' insight that divine causality was not like any other kind of causality (since it was 'creatio ex nihilo'), but nevertheless the notion that causes and the caused are linked by *likeness* was so fundamental to the pre-modern understanding of the world that it necessarily had a great influence upon the way that theologians conceived the relation between the world as created and the nature of God as Creator.

The cosmological idea advanced in this book, which is that the relation between God and the world is akin to the relation that obtains between an author and his or her text (or more specifically the authorial *voice* and the text), seeks to replace the traditional metaphysical view with a non-metaphysical dynamic of voice and sign. This is to replace likeness with implication (the divine voice is implicated in or given with the world) and causality with embodied extension. There is a sense in which this language of voice and embodiment seems closer to the scriptural world than are extrinsic notions of causality and existence, and thus more *theologically* coherent. But there is a further advantage in the voice-text model which is to do with the emphasis it places upon interpretation as a human activity. Peter Ochs has drawn our attention to the extent to which modern pragmatism resonates positively with ancient rabbinic forms of exegesis. Pragmatism seems in a way to be the practice of an implicit theology of creation. If we hold that the interpreter is an intrinsic part of the textuality of the world (which we must do if we hold to a 'world-text'), then the act of interpretation, indeed of experiencing, understanding and perceiving, must itself be viewed as being integral to the textuality of the world. It is not that we are observers, standing outside the world and looking within. What we might call 'right' or 'deep' interpretation on our part will be interpretation which grasps the nature of the world's textuality, therefore, and which – under the guidance of the Spirit – receives it as divine relation and covenantal gift which is transparent to the divine author who gives. This sequence is already adumbrated in the movement between Genesis and Exodus, between the creation of the world and the giving of the Law. Law is interpretation governing principles of action which is ordered to the world as divine breath or word. Judaic Law issues from the belief that right understanding is tied in with practices of living which are grounded in the order of creation, and which cannot be exercised outside that relation. Judaic Law also places great emphasis upon the bodies of those who interpret the world 'textually', in implied recognition of the analogy that flows between the world as divine 'body' and the body of the one who interprets or receives that body rightly or in depth, as the self-communication of God.[40] What we can term the 'embodied interpretation' of Jewish Law, which is to say interpretation that takes place in and through the body, its vestments and practices, is an important signal of what in the Christian dispensation is understood to be the uniquely radicalised interpretative practices of Jesus as the embodiment of divine life.

40. I shall return to this theme in chapter 8 below, pp. 156–69.

6

Voice and sacrifice

Scriptura est sicut panis, qui nisi frangatur et distribuatur, non satiat.

Scripture is like bread which until it is broken up and given out does
not satisfy our hunger.

Nicholas of Cusa, *Sermones*

The extended exegesis of the preceding two chapters posits that the world
precipitates from the living and plural speech of God as a text crystallises
from the dynamic speech-processes of human culture. But the 'text' that
deposits through the divine creative act is more properly to be thought
of as a 'Primal Text', that is to say, it cannot itself be known as text, for
it eludes all our constructions, but is that by which textuality is possible. This Primal Text is the very bedrock of spatio-temporal existence and
from this our world emerges. It is a kind of primal matter, though not
in the sense that the scholastics used this term, for even a Primal Text
must combine the material and the notional in a way that primal matter did not. It is not a foundational passivity, which is what the scholastics understood by primal matter, but something far more dynamic, for
it already stands in the most intimate relation with divinity, from whose
speech it has precipitated, as the human voice, personal and immediate,
is encoded and made strange in the visible and material signs of the text.
This Primal Text participates in and communicates the divine speaking,
but it does so through something other. Like a text, it contains the author's
voice in encoded form, but does so in a way that requires interpretation:
only through a sequence of interpretative acts by others can that voice be
released and 'heard'.

The Primal Text that I am proposing represents the point at which God willed the divine speaking to turn outwards, through originary reference, thus calling the material world as that which is other than God into being. The status of the Primal Text as that which offers itself to understanding suggests that semiosis is intrinsic to the Trinitarian life itself. The Word must in some sense give itself utterly to be interpreted or exegeted by the Father with the Spirit, and by the Spirit with the Father, and must itself exegete the Father with the Spirit, and the Spirit with the Father, in a continuous and infinite perichoresis of knowing and understanding through love and self-giving. It is from that inexhaustible fount of meaning that the world-text itself must flow. The Primal Text must itself be a kind of overflow from the infinitely fecund semiosis that is the inner life of the Trinity. And even if it is unknowable in itself, since it is too intimately bound in to the inner life of God, the Primal Text, as first reflex of the Trinitarian life, must underlie every aspect of the created order. For the world itself is known to us in and through interpretation. It yields itself to us as a multitude of textualities, each in interaction with the other. Text, as a combination of material signs and notional meanings, is the very structure of existence and is the readability of the world. We see textuality in the recent understandings of the way that brain and consciousness interact, or in the genome which maps the genetic inheritance of the human race. Some fields of meaning are dominantly of the senses and to do with the physical construction of the world as a unity of objects. Other semantic fields are more notional, or cultural, in kind and mediate the universe of interpretations and social meanings embedded in language and social actions. Others again are literary or more properly textual in form. These include the products of art, high culture and education. If textuality itself can be defined as the ordering of material entities in such a way as to engender more complex meanings, as the combination of the material and the ideational, then some manifestations of this primal textuality show a primacy of the material and others of the ideational or notional. Perception itself is the recognition of a concept within the material order, as we discern distinct objects about us. High-level social or cultural meanings, on the other hand, seem to have no base in the material order despite the inherent materiality of the sign, since in them the signifying function of the sign has attained an almost absolute power. This deep textuality is manifest, then, in the participation of all the semantic fields which constitute our experience in the same unity of the material and ideational, and in their consequent capacity to interact with each other in the formation of an infinitely complex structure which we call world. It is only the capacity of the material and the ideational to interact, together with the astonishingly diverse dimensions of existence which they embody, that forms world, and it is this principial intertextuality, never to be discerned directly in itself, which creates the possibility of the analogical, world-generating interrelation of all things.

Textualities can be material, cultural, social, artistic, ideational, literary or any combination of these, but among those textualities which are textual artefacts and which we most commonly denote as conventional texts, we must give a special place to Scripture. Scripture, in the definition given above, is the aggregation of texts which body forth the human voice, shaped and transformed by the divine speaking in history, which it records and to which it testifies. Without the biblical text, we could not know of God's action in history, or the formation of the world. But the proximity of Scripture to createdness of the world is greater than this. We find in the Bible, in fragmented but analogical form, the pure reality of the divine speaking within history, captured by human voices whose own celebratory expressivity was constituted in a vital response to the originary speech of God. Thus we hear a kind of echo of the creative speaking of God, the divine voice, which is the ultimate historical referent of the text. We can think of Scripture, then, as a textual and therefore accessible performance of the unknowable Primal Text. It stands as an icon of the divine creativity and offers those communities who enter into it through repeated acts of deep reading the possibility of access into the vital structure of the world as divine text. As a reflex of the divine creativity, Scripture offers a celebratory conformity to the life-giving compassion of God that is the ground of the world.

Inhabiting the Text

I argued in the previous chapter that human interpretation of the world is itself part of the world. In other words, if the world at its root is Primal Text, then our capacity to interpret the world must itself be part of our own participation in the Primal Text. It is one of the chief fallacies of human consciousness that the mind observes the world without itself being part of the world. But there is a significant distinction to be made between the human mind and the world it cognises since – from a scriptural perspective – the world is itself composed of signs. A sign, whether conceived of as a word or an object in a divinely instituted world, only truly comes into view to an observer, or interpreter, who stands outside it. Signalling is an exterior act in which the sign's own resting in itself is given out, and is exhausted, by its signifying function. If we ourselves are part of a textual world, and are in essence signs, then we cannot ever apprehend our own nature, as signs, but can be realised only in the ecclesial gaze of others.

This appears to be the predicament of human nature. We are constituted as those for whom the world signifies; our inner nature is that of an interpreter. And thus, if we are part of the divinely ordered world of signs, we are destined always to remain alienated with respect to our own self-knowledge. Our true, signifying nature, can only ever be known by others, and never by ourselves. But in fact this view rests upon a misunderstanding of human existence. The fact that we cannot *see* ourselves as sign does not mean that we do not carry out the inner functions of the sign in our daily living. According to a scriptural view of the world, the signifying properties of the world are grounded ultimately in the inner life of the Trinity. Trinitarian speech, made accessible to us in and through the person of Christ, is a kenotic discourse and the exteriorisation of that speech, which I traced in chapters 4 and 5, entails the compassionate engagement of God with his creation. In so far as we embrace our own compassionate nature, therefore, exercised before the other, we actually realise our own signing nature. Compassion is an act of self-renunciation which, paradoxically, leads to an enhanced or enriched state of existence. We gain life through self-risk undertaken for the sake of the other, on account of the dialectical character of our own being in the world.[1] But in so far as we realise our own compassionate nature, which is a condition of our existence in the world, we actually enter into our own nature as divinely constituted sign, and thus give realisation to our own participation in the Primal Text which is the root of the world.

The final question in this section, then, concerns the relation between our own participation in the Primal Text and self-realisation as compassionate sign and the reading of Scripture. I have already argued that Scripture, as the congregation of texts written by those whose own voices have been shaped in celebration by the divine speaking, authentically mediates to us the structure and dynamic of God's originary, revelatory speaking. As a textualisation of that compassionate, creative dynamic, Scripture awakens us to the possibilities of our participation in the Primal Text and

---

1. I attempted to give a phenomenological account of this structure and dynamic in my earlier *Theology of Compassion* (London: SCM Press, 2001; Grand Rapids: Eerdmans, 2003), especially pp. 24–46.

gives us access to it, as the deep structure of the createdness of the world. But the question remains as to why it should speak to us, those who hear or read the words of Scripture, in the way that it does. The answer traditionally has been that we attend to the Bible in and through the power of the Spirit, which signals the supernatural quality of authentic scriptural reading. But this needs to be given a somewhat fuller theological content if it is to be useful as providing an insight into a Christian biblical hermeneutic. The Spirit, in the analytic given in chapters 4 and 5, is not address as such but the dynamic which makes address as communication possible. From the perspective of a theology of creation, it is the world-text's memory of its origination in the divine speaking: as *rûah* meaning 'wind', 'breath' and 'spirit', it is the divine imprint within the world and is its capacity to be integrated again – as text, as materiality – into the divine breath.

The Spirit in us, then, is the mark of our own elemental belonging to the created order and is to be found as a propensity, a tendency, or even an inchoate memory of our origins, deep within us. It is the Spirit that allows us, if we allow the Spirit, to enter the biblical world. It allows us to 'hear' the divine voice that speaks within the biblical word and to become integrated into the perichoretic speaking, and kenotic way of life, which circulates within the Gospels and their Hebrew foundation. As Trinitarian, the Spirit is a participation in the economic life of God. Its movement within us, in the domain of biblical reading and interpretation, is at the same time the discovery that the power of God has preceded us: the Word of which we read is already present to us, as Word and Spirit of the Word, in the act of reading.[2] But further, the role of the Spirit is the guarantee that the authentic appropriation of Scripture can never be purely individualistic but is always in essence an ecclesial act. We put on 'the mind of Christ' when we read Scripture in and through the Spirit; we become one with his body the Church in a conforming of the self with the divine logic of Scripture which shapes in us a new celebratory and compassionate form of life.

---

2. I hope to address the theme of scriptural reading more fully in a future work. What I am advocating here is neither fundamentalist (since interpretation is at its centre) nor relativist (since agency lies with the text). It is perhaps most easily understood by analogy with the pragmatist school of philosophy. In his study *Pierce, Pragmatism and the Logic of Scripture* (Cambridge: Cambridge University Press, 1998), Peter Ochs has set out a contemporary rabbinic scriptural hermeneutic. There are likely to be some subtle distinctions to be made in the formation of a Christian analogue to Ochs' programme, but the Christian scriptural hermeneutic I have begun to outline in this volume is greatly indebted to Ochs' insights and work, as it is to those others, whether Jews, Christians or Muslims, who reflectively practise it.

Christology

The Bible speaks to us of Christ who is himself the ground of the world and, as divine–human presence with us, as a divine–human speech-agent, is the realisation in the created order of the originary Trinitarian speech of creation. The question now arises as to the alignment between the way in which we read Scripture, and the way in which Jesus himself read Scripture. If reading Scripture authentically in the Spirit is for us to become increasingly conformed to the structure of the divine creativity manifest through an ecclesial speech, presence-with and compassion, then what of Jesus himself? What insights can we gain from the Gospels about how Jesus may have read Scripture and how this may have found expression in his life and values?

The relation between the world of the New Testament and that of the Old as reflected in the practice of intertextuality has come in recent years to establish itself as a primary area of thematic concern for New Testament scholars.[3] The New Testament abounds in direct and indirect references to the Old, in both Hebrew and Greek versions, and the practice of reading is itself at the heart of the Gospel message. This is the case not only in terms of the use made of Scripture by the Gospel writers and the early Church in order to present Jesus as the fulfilment of the Hebrew prophetic and legal traditions but also in Jesus' own application of Scripture within his ministry. The reconstruction of the place of scriptural quotation in Jesus' own teaching shows that he had an extensive knowledge of the books of the Hebrew Bible.[4] He is generally supportive of Old Testament perspectives but is also capable of bringing striking new interpretations to bear. Following the Beatitudes, Jesus expands the moral precepts of 'ancient times' in terms of a radical ethic of interior righteousness, purity of intention, and the thoroughgoing practice of non-violence.[5] Jesus applies

---

3. See Steve Moyise, 'Intertextuality and the Study of the Old Testament in the New Testament', in *idem, The Old Testament in the New Testament. Essays in Honour of J. L. North* (Sheffield: Sheffield University Press, 2000), pp. 14–41, for a useful overview of the theoretical parameters of intertextuality, as dialogical, or two-way, or postmodern, which is to say indeterminate, and its history in biblical scholarship. Joel Marcus' discussion of intertextuality in Mark (*The Way of the Lord. Christological Exegesis of the Old Testament in the Gospel of Mark*, Louisville, Ky.: Westminster/John Knox Press, 1992) is an exemplary study of the way in which a Synoptic author engages in a coherent and extended act of reading, in the sense of interpreting, Old Testament sources within the narrative framework of his Gospel.
4. Henry M. Shires states that the sources of Jesus' citations include thirty of the thirty-nine books of the Old Testament (*Finding the Old Testament in the New* (Philadelphia: Westminster Press, 1974), p. 88).
5. Matt. 5:21–48.

texts directly to his own situation, as when he quotes the account of how David and his men ate the bread of the Presence (1 Sam. 21:1–6) in order to underline his own authority, in the Gospel narrative, as 'lord of the sabbath'.[6] Repeatedly the Gospels present occasions on which Jesus makes implicit or explicit claims regarding his own status as the one who comes to fulfil the Old Testament promise.[7] At Luke 4:16–30, Jesus is shown reading a text based on Isaiah 61:1 in the synagogue at Nazareth and interpreting it in terms that are to be significant for his own ministry.[8] Whatever historical-critical arguments are brought to bear, which may persuade us of the historicity or otherwise of any individual pericope, the engaged reader of the New Testament cannot but feel that Jesus himself was steeped in the language and precepts of the Old Testament and that his own life was patterned upon it, in a fusion of prophetic 'Exodus' traditions which stemmed from Galilee and royal, priestly traditions which were associated with Jerusalem and the Temple milieu.

'I am He'

One of the ways in which Jesus most explicitly inhabits the scriptural text is the 'I am' sayings. In the Deuteronomic phrase 'I am he', or *'ani hû'*, God expresses his own unique sovereignty. God's claim against the 'foreign gods' is one that is grounded in his manifest power of control over Israel's history, and specifically his support and deliverance of his people, as it is in his status as creator of the world. This kind of language of divine subjectivity reaches its climax in a passage from Deuteronomy 32:39 where the intensive form *'ani 'ani hû'* is used as God declares: 'See now that I, even I, am he; there is no god besides me. I kill and I make alive; I wound and I heal; and no one can deliver from my hand.'[9] This declarative form which articulates God's subjectivity as supreme ruler of the world reoccurs in the New Testament in the Gospels of John and Mark. The most interesting passage in Mark is the point at which Jesus identifies himself to the disciples when walking on the sea. At one level the words

---

6. Matt. 12:1–8.

7. For an analytical summary of the use of the Old Testament motifs of exodus, conquest, temple and kingship, see William M. Swartley, *Israel's Scripture Traditions and the Synoptic Gospels* (Peabody, Mass.: Hendrickson Publishers, 1994).

8. Lk. 4:16–21; cf. Lk. 24:27 and 44. Swartley, *Israel's Scripture Traditions*, pp. 74–7. See also C. K. Barrett, 'Luke/Acts', in D. A. Carson and H. G. M. Williamson, eds., *It Is Written. Scripture Citing Scripture* (Cambridge: Cambridge University Press, 1988), pp. 231–44 (here 235–6).

9. For a detailed and nuanced discussion of the deuteronomic *'ani hû'*, see Catrin H. Williams, *I am He. The Interpretation of 'Ani Hû 'in Jewish and Early Christian Literature* (Tübingen: Mohr Siebeck, 2000), pp. 42–50.

'Take heart, it is I' serve to alleviate the disciples' shock at what they are seeing, but at another they are a declaration of the divine subjectivity in Jesus who – with echoes of Genesis 1 – stands above the waters and controls the wind.[10] It is primarily in the Gospel of John, however, that the Old Testament resonances of the Greek 'I am' (*egō eimi*) are most extensively present. Early in his ministry Jesus uses the phrase to identify himself as the Messiah to the Samaritan woman: 'I am he, the one who speaks to you.'[11] In later passages *egō eimi* is used in order to assert the identity of Jesus against his detractors, again in an overtly messianic sense: 'Very truly, I tell you, before Abraham was, I am.'[12] Following Jesus' washing of his disciples' feet, Jesus alludes to his own forthcoming death and states: 'I tell you this now, before it occurs, so that when it does occur, you may believe that I am he.' In the verse that follows this line, the messianic content of the phrase is again made explicit: 'Very truly, I tell you whoever receives one whom I send receives me; and whoever receives me receives him who sent me.'[13]

It is impossible to know whether and to what extent the 'I am' usage, found equally though differently in Mark and John, is grounded in the early kerygma of the Church or reflects something of Jesus' own self-understanding. But it is the case that the Gospel narrative records Jesus' inhabiting of the Old Testament text in this particular way. What we can discern here is the outline of what we might call 'a Christology of textual awareness' as a criterion of the subjectivity of Christ which is not, however, 'consciousness Christology' or 'degree Christology' but rather an attempt to articulate in a variant form what Karl Rahner has termed 'ontological Christology'.[14] This represents an attempt to maintain a continuity between Jesus' experience of God with our own experience of God without, however, reducing the former to the latter. It seeks to locate Jesus Christ within human history without, however, compromising the freedom of God with respect to that history. A Christology of this kind attempts to give expression to the dialectical nature of the revelation itself, by affirming that the divinisation of Jesus Christ is at the same time recognisably our own divinisation and the entry into the world of the divine presence in a new and unparalleled way.

10. Mk 6:45–52.
11. Jn 4:26.
12. Jn 8:58; cf. 8:24 and 28.
13. Jn 13:19–20.
14. Karl Rahner, *Foundations of Christian Faith; an Introduction to the Idea of Christianity* (London: Darton Longman and Todd, 1978), pp. 302–3.

I argued in the previous chapter that human nature is intrinsically hermeneutical, and that the human nature of Christ, therefore, is hermeneutical in the inclusive sense in which I have used the term. The distinction between Jesus' interpretation of Scripture and of the world, and our own interpretation of Scripture and the world, is that he exegetes these as the one who is their ultimate meaning. Jesus therefore understands himself to be the centre of both Scripture and world in a dialectic of identity and difference which is grounded in the Word's own contemplative exegesis of the Father. And if the Word 'exegetes' or 'interprets' the Father as the Father's image (cf. Jn 1:18, in which the word *exēgēsato* occurs), as scriptural cosmologists such as Origen and Hamann have maintained, then we can further say that humanity is formed 'in the image of the image', to adopt another patristic insight. Our capacity to interpret, indeed our intrinsic nature as interpreters in a world that gives itself for interpretation, is the divine image in us and is the mark of our own integration into the world-text as part of that text, and not as extraneous to it.

A second point of continuity and distinction with respect to the incarnate Son and ourselves rests in the principle of compassion which, by the argument given above, is an intrinsic part of the way in which we exegete the world as God's creation. In so far as we enter the Primal Text, which is to say, the Trinitarian ground of creation, we are ourselves conformed to it in a life of celebratory holiness and commitment to the other. This involves a transformation of body and spirit, along the principle of the perichoretic kenosis and compassion which is the structure of the creation itself. The act of interpreting the world as God's creation, under the guidance of the Spirit, leads to a sanctification of life. In the case of Jesus himself, that transformation is a total one and entails the complete emptying of himself into and for the world.

Further, each single act of human compassion signals the compassion of God and communicates a deepening of the divine creativity in the world. In the case of Jesus, however, that human compassion is identical with the divine compassion, the creativity of which extends to the regeneration of the world. Since Jesus himself, as the Word, is the centre and meaning of Scripture and the world, his own act of *reading* Scripture and world, which is the evolving understanding and – with it – acceptance of his divine mission, brings about the re-creation of the world. In terms of the present textual metaphor, this marks the point at which a single created individual becomes the total presence of the principial and originary voice of God, speaking now from *within* the text of the world. This is a divine movement which necessarily entails the redemptive healing of the world-text. The textual alienation of the divine voice leads inevitably to misinterpretation and misappropriation of the created order. The manifestation or realisation of the voice of the Creator, speaking from within the creation, brings with it the healing and repairal of what has been lost or damaged or misunderstood through a divine act of compassion which is the assimilation of the otherness of the text, the otherness of creation itself, back into the divine order.

'This is my body'

The institution of the Lord's Supper is recorded in all the Synoptic Gospels as well as in St Paul's First Letter to the Corinthians.[15] It takes place immediately prior to his betrayal and arrest, and marks a point in Jesus' mission which both looks back to his struggle in Gethsemane and looks forward to the Passion. It thus communicates to us something of Jesus' self-awareness as he undergoes and accepts the unfolding logic of his scriptural life. The occasion of this pericope is the Passover meal, when the Jewish people recalled their liberation from the Egyptian exile by God's power and the consecration of the firstborn in remembrance and thanksgiving for it. Jesus attended that meal in Jerusalem with his disciples and, according to the New Testament record, blessed the bread and the wine in the traditional Jewish way, adding words which expressed his understanding of his own imminent fate as being one of sacrifice for others, covenant with God and the advent of God's kingdom.[16] The words of institution represent in the first place Jesus' own self-possession as one who inhabits Scripture, the realisation of which is an utter emptying of the self for the sake of the other, for the sake indeed of the whole of the creation, expressed in terms of the coming of the kingdom and the reign of heaven on earth. For Jesus to know who he was, was for him to know that he was utterly given out, sacrificed, for the sake of the world. Jesus inhabits Scripture then as the one of whom Scripture speaks, as the fulfilment of time and sign of the kingdom.

But in the second place there is in the words of institution a perfect coincidence of creativity of speech, presence-with and compassion. We can note for instance a linguistic trace which sets up a subtle resonance with the baptism–transfiguration nexus which was explored in chapter 4. The

---

15. Matt. 26:26–30, Mk 14:22–5, Lk. 22:14–23, 1 Cor. 11:23–6.
16. For the argument that the Last Supper was a Passover meal and that the words of institution contain signals that they represent the *ipsissima vox* of Jesus, see Joachim Jeremias, *The Eucharistic Words of Jesus* (London: SCM Press, 1966), pp. 15–88 and 201–3.

Lucan structure of the declarative '[t]his is [my body; my blood] which is given for you' with a command 'Do this in memory of me' is already given in the transfiguration pericope where we have: 'This is . . . [my Son] . . . Listen to him.' The parallel 'This is my Son . . .' 'This is my body . . .' can be read as a chiasmus since a son is in a sense an extension of the body of the father.[17] There is no reference to the Holy Spirit at this point in the text, but the epiclesis of the Spirit which occurred in many early liturgies could be said to pick up the descent of the Holy Spirit recorded in the account of the baptism.[18] This is a divine speaking which is therefore at once declarative and institutionary. When Jesus blessed the bread and wine, and when he declared them to be his body and blood, he spoke not with a human voice but with the voice of the Father: he instituted the very thing which he declared to be the case. This was not originary speaking in the sense of the *fiat*, for it did not bring something from nothing. But it marked his point of entry into the biblical metaphor. The 'cup of wrath' of Psalm 60:3 and Isaiah 51:17, 22, which Jesus feared and with which he struggled in the Gethsemane pericope, is now internalised and assumed into his own identity as blood poured out for others. In a parallel way, Jesus himself now becomes the 'bread from heaven' and 'the bread of life', in Johannine phraseology, recalling the act by which Yahweh fed his people in the wilderness.[19] In the words of Eucharistic institution, therefore, symbols both of God's justice and his nourishing, life-giving love constitute Jesus' point of entry into Scripture in an act of personal appropriation of its meaning and *telos* as the one of whom Scripture speaks.

The institution of the Lord's Supper is a critical moment in the nexus of Passion, resurrection and ascension. Its position immediately before the Passion narrative signals Jesus' own acceptance of what is to come, as an expansion of the line 'yet, not my will but yours be done' (Lk. 22:42), and it offers an insight into his state of textual awareness at this significant point in his mission. His speaking at this point is both glorified and sacrificial, for the voice with which he speaks is simultaneously his own human voice and the voice of his Father. Voice is actually a radically corporeal notion, and the fusion of two voices, the one human and the other divine, in the person of Jesus has profound implications for the condition of his

---

17. This is more evidently the case according to pre-modern understandings of procreation, which tended to view the child as the product of the man's seed.
18. The epiclesis can also be found in the second, third and fourth Eucharistic Prayer of the modern Roman Rite.
19. Jn 6:22–59.

embodiment. This now becomes dual in a real sense: as the bearer of the divine speaking, the body of Jesus is also the body of God. This is a highly contradictory notion, since the body of God is infinite while the human body of Jesus is finite. It is this unendurable paradox which is resolved, or perhaps better to say *realised*, in the sacrificial pouring out of the body and blood of Jesus *into* the material elements of the world which is first signalled in the institution of the Lord's Supper and is accomplished in the Passion, resurrection and ascension. Jesus' body resurrected and ascended is the unity of the world as text with the authorial voice of God. His sacrifice in and through this 'dual' embodiment is the regeneration and repristination of the world. In the vocal terms that are being developed here, it is the point at which the words of the text are filled again with the authorial voice, and the text, while remaining text, becomes the divine body.[20]

Eucharist

The celebration of the Christian Eucharist is a primary way in which those who follow Christ come to inhabit Scripture, and it is one which is accomplished through a ritual participation in the way in which Jesus himself inhabited Scripture. Located at the centre of Christian life, the Eucharist is the most radical way of reading Scripture. The participation in Jesus' own entry into the Word of God as the Word of God shows a twofold structure. In the first place there is the characteristic of a pluralistic dialogism, a Trinitarian rhythm of speech which centres on the presence of the Word with and for the people. Secondly, there is the more metaphysical structure of what has been known in Catholic tradition as the Real Presence, which articulates an appropriation through faith and in the Spirit of the transformation of the bread and wine into Jesus' own body and blood effected by the original words of institution. These are recapitulated, performed or actively remembered by the community who gather in his name to celebrate and give thanks for his creative love.

Multivocal speech
At the centre of the Eucharistic celebration, in the modern Catholic model, is the priest who speaks from within the heart of the community, with

---

20. In 'Silences of the Cross' (unpublished paper given to the Society for the Study of Theology, April 2003), I sought to describe the particular role played by silence in the context of the divine sacrifice.

the voice of Jesus, for the sake of the community. Eucharistic speech it-self is multiple and celebratory, grounded in praise and thanksgiving. Dialogical rhythms (responses, absolution, kyrie), recontextualised with triadic, Trinitarian disruptions (doxologies, petitions), play throughout the Eucharistic service and are apparent already in the priest's greeting in the name of Father, Son and Spirit, following the Entrance Song, to which the people give the reply Amen. The Liturgy of the Word sets this speech rhythm firstly in the context of the divine speaking-with, but it also evokes the person of Christ intertextually, against the Old Testament background. An Old Testament reading is placed side by side with a Psalm and a passage from the New Testament, setting up a structured series of internal resonances. The responses at the end of the readings reinforce the dialogism here, as do the repeated responses within the Psalm.

According to the rubric of the Order of the Mass, '[t]hrough the read-ings, God speaks to his people of redemption and salvation, and nour-ishes their spirit with his word; Christ is present among the faithful in his word'.[21] Effectively the ground of Eucharistic speaking as thanksgiv-ing and celebration now comes into view: Christ is present in his word and speaks through Scripture with the people of God who are assembled around him. The role of the homily is to help to integrate that divine speaking into the lives of the faithful, so that they may increasingly be formed in the breath or Spirit of God and so live lives that are opened out with thanksgiving into the compassionate creativity of God. The affirma-tion of the three Persons in the Creed which follows the readings is the peo-ple's response to that revelation, and it too must be allocated to the work of the Spirit in a particular way. The Spirit is also invoked in the Memorial Prayer of the second and third of the Eucharistic Prayers as it is in the In-tercessions for the Church of the fourth Eucharistic Prayer. In each case the emphasis is upon the loving unity of the Church, formed around the recep-tion of the Eucharist, which finds expression also in the exchange of the sign of peace prior to the act of communication during the rite of commu-nion. Further, the Prayer of the Faithful, which concludes the Liturgy of the Word, points to the fact that the dialogism of Eucharistic speech is fun-damentally triadic and perichoretic in form. In the intercessions for the world, the voices of those who are oppressed, who suffer or are sick, who struggle or are needful in some way break into the Eucharistic speaking: through the compassionate concern of those celebrating the Eucharist,

---

21. *The Sunday Missal* (London: Collins, 1975), p. 25.

their voices enter into the flow of celebratory-compassionate speech, enriching it and extending the speech inclusively into the world.

If in the Liturgy of the Word the Church hears Scripture, read out as text and reflected upon in the homily, then in the Liturgy of the Communion the priest performs with and on behalf of the people Jesus' own speaking. As the words of institution are repeated at the consecration of the elements, the priest is indwelt by the voice of Jesus who speaks from the midst of the text, transforming and sanctifying. In the most intimate sense, this is a ritualistic form of reading in which the Church corporately partakes. But here the distantiation of the text is left behind, the voice of Jesus is no longer alienated under the aspect of a visible sign: through the priest's own voice, the voice of Jesus becomes present *under the aspect of speech and not as written text*. This movement recapitulates and makes present Jesus' own inhabiting of the scriptural text when he declared the bread and wine to be his own body and blood that was to be given for all.

Real presence

The formal expression of union with Christ in the Eucharist in Catholic tradition is the belief that in the act of consecration, the bread and wine truly become the body and the blood of Jesus Christ. If the rite of consecration represents our own entry into the way that Jesus entered into the biblical text, then we can say in Pauline language that it marks the point at which we put on the 'mind of Christ', or in patristic language, the point at which we participate in Christ's own nature as Wisdom. One of the fundamental expressions, if not the most fundamental, of that new condition of mind is an entirely new way of seeing the world: not as a sphere of reference but rather as divine address.

The transformation from sign to address which takes place in the Eucharistic act of consecration is an intensification, or culmination, of a tendency which is foundational to sacramental theology. The term sacrament, as we find it in Augustine, for instance, expresses the belief that the things of creation have some kind of signifying relation to the Creator; only gradually did the term come to be restricted to the seven sacraments we know today. With that development in the twelfth century, however, a new intensity of signification was achieved whereby the 'pointing to' occurred only within a specific rite and overtly Christological context (in contrast with the implicit and diffuse Christology of the earlier usage). Under Aristotelian influence, the sacraments were now *efficient signs*, which caused or brought about that which they signified. The grace of God was not only suggested by the application of the material elements within the rite but was actually made manifest in the world, and specifically in the lives of those who participated in the sacrament. The technical term for this kind of sacramental sign was *signum et res*: the material sign and the divine reality it signifies in combination.

The theology of the Eucharistic presence constituted a further and ultimate degree of intensification, for it was now asserted – in the classical expression that we find in Thomas Aquinas – not only that the signs signify invisible grace in a way that makes it effective but also that they now signify it so comprehensively that it becomes 'substantially' present. In other words, the materiality of the Eucharistic signs becomes so transfigured by signification that the object of their signifying, that is, the body and blood, take on presence. But the manner of that presence is not that of ordinary objects in the world. It is not a form of replacement, whereby some item A takes the place of item B, which is no longer there. Nor is it a transformation such that B changes into A, and again ceases to be there: the sight, touch, smell and taste of the elements are evident to all. The change is of a more subtle kind and cannot be conceived outside the frame of reference established by the sacramental tradition. Eucharistic presence marks the intensification of signification to an extreme of plenitude. Integral to this dynamic is the preservation of the sign, which must remain intact if the act of signifying is to be accomplished. But the manner of its persistence is peculiar. For to the eyes of faith, the elements become the body and blood of Christ. But the body and blood is not present in any normal sense, otherwise we would not see the remaining elements. In other words, the elements are both present and absent, just as the body and blood are both present and absent: the one cannot be conceived without the other. This kind of presence then, which is the extreme of signification, is not an ordinary presence but a presence which is simultaneously an absence. Neither the bread and wine nor the body and blood are present on the altar in any ordinary sense, but both are present and absent in a reciprocal sense, thus instituting a new and quite unique modality of presence.

The fact that the Eucharistic presence grows from the process of sacramental signifying is fundamental for our understanding that the presence of the body and blood is not imposed upon the elements from without, but received from within. The transformation of the elements marks the unity of two sets of intersecting trajectories. The first is that of a theology of creation which affirms that the world is created through Christ, together with the creative speaking of Christ at the institution of the Lord's Supper,

whereby Christ continues the movement of divine revelation by perform-
ing within the company that is to be his church his own unity with the
created order, with the world. This is the semiotics not of referring signs
but of address, as sublimation of the sign. But at the same time what we
see in the Eucharistic celebration is the intersection of Christ's own inhabiting of Scripture, and embrace of its kenotic meaning, as the Word of God
indwelling the Word of God, with the Church's depth reading of the Scriptural text. In the Eucharist, we read as Jesus read, but only by virtue of his
creative power, by his own infinite act of reading which was the fulfilment
and end of Scripture's meaning.

Union with Christ in the Eucharist is therefore a union that is accomplished across the gap of the ages through the retrieval of a written text
into its oral medium: a liturgical moment which is itself founded on the
Passion and resurrection of Christ, whereby the material text of the world
became again the divine breath. The Eucharistic moment is not a moment
of presence but one which so fills presence as to be no longer graspable under that aspect: it is the pleroma of time itself. Paul Ricoeur has argued
that the temporality of Genesis is one in which the 'always-already-there'
of Creation does not make sense independently of the perpetual futurity of
Redemption' and that 'between the two is intercalated the eternal now of
the "you, love me!"'.[22] The Eucharist proleptically grasps the end and the
beginning of things in a complete transparency of the world to its creator.
The effects of our own participation in this transformed reality are also not
easily grasped but come into view only gradually in the slow mediation
of the everyday. They concern the substrate of our senses, our fleshliness,
and the contours of our thinking, in the slow diffusion of wisdom through
senses and mind. Integral to the reception of the world as a New Creation,
is the discovery that perception itself is redeemed.

Conclusion

In the previous chapter I identified three primary stages in the dynamic
movement of revelation of the Judaeo-Christian tradition, each of which
was simultaneously a moment of deepening creation. The first is the cosmic institutionary narrative of Genesis 1, with the consequent entry of God
into language as himself a speaking subject; the second is the encounter

---

22. André LaCocque and Paul Ricoeur, *Thinking Biblically. Exegetical and Hermeneutical Studies*
(Chicago and London: University of Chicago Press, 1998), p. 67.

between God and Moses in which God revealed his name and established a relation of conversation – or 'speaking with' – Moses 'face to face'. This was concomitant with the granting of the Decalogue and establishing of the Covenant. The third such stage is the Incarnation with the fusing of the divine and human voice in Jesus, revealing the triadic nature of the divine speaking. This unity of voice, divine and human, undermined the onto-logical stability of the voice-bearing body of Jesus, leading to his sacrificial self-identification with the material world which is itself the text, or ex-tended body, of God. Only through his death, resurrection and ascension did the voice of God enter once again into the text of the world, effecting redemption.

At each point the deepening movement of revelation through divine speech grounded a new kind of humanity. In the first case, it was the es-tablishing of human subjectivity, summoned into existence through the divine subjectivity (Gen. 1:29: 'I give you'). In the second case, it was the es-tablishing of the self as an ethical subject, with the reception of the divine commandments and the obligations which flow from a 'speaking with' re-lation with God through Moses. This manifested in some cases as a self-risking prophecy and in others as speaking for the marginalised and vul-nerable in society: for the 'stranger, widow and orphan'. In the case of the self-emptying of the Son in the Incarnation, human nature was called into existence in its perfection, as wholly transparent to God. That new ex-istence was subsequently shaped as the Spirit-filled speech of Pentecost, leading to praise, prophecy, celebration and thanksgiving.

With the creativity of the universalisation of the Son, who was 'given' and 'poured out' for all, in his post-Resurrection body, there was a further opening out in the creation of the Eucharistic community. This is the com-munity of those who are moved by God's address in and through the per-son of Christ, and who are empowered with a new way of seeing the world: as divine body. The recognition of the world as divine text-body is itself constitutive of a new kind of human embodiedness, one which is celebra-tory, Eucharistic and compassionate, and which discovers itself to be joy-fully at one with the world-text's ceaseless play.

Eucharistic Wisdom

The abundant real

וְהִנֵּה יְהוָה עֹבֵר וְ רוּחַ
גְּדוֹלָה וְחָזָק מְפָרֵק הָרִים וּמְשַׁבֵּר סְלָעִים לִפְנֵי יְהוָה לֹא
בָרוּחַ יְהוָה וְאַחַר הָרוּחַ רַעַשׁ לֹא בָרַעַשׁ יְהוָה׃
וְאַחַר הָרַעַשׁ אֵשׁ לֹא בָאֵשׁ יְהוָה וְאַחַר הָאֵשׁ קוֹל דְּמָמָה דַקָּה׃

And behold, the Lord passed by, and a great and strong wind rent the
mountains, and broke in pieces the rocks before the Lord, but the Lord
was not in the wind; and after the wind an earthquake, but the Lord
was not in the earthquake; and after the earthquake a fire, but the
Lord was not in the fire; and after the fire the voice of a gentle breeze.
                                                    1 Kings 19:11–12

In the first section I surveyed some pre-modern perspectives on the cosmological which seemed – albeit at the cost of a liaison with archaic science –
to give powerful theological expression to the principle that creation is
through the Word. In the second section I proposed a scriptural cosmology, predicated upon an oscillation between sign and address. According
to this view, the world and its objects are of God's making, and have a dual
signifying function. They can be said both *to refer* and *to address*. Their referential function can be further classified into two types. We have world-
constituting reference, which is to say, the way in which linguistic signs
refer to entities which are at the same time natural signs that point to yet
further entities in a complex weave which grounds our experience of and
participation in the world. Things refer to other things, words to other
words, and language combines with things in the formation of world. We
can term this type of world-constituting reference the secondary referential function of the sign. But we can discern also a primary or fundamental mode of referencing, as things refer back to their maker, as an effect to

its cause. It is this primary referencing which is the foundation of natural theology. The second function of the sign as *addressivity* can also be divided into two types. There is a weak addressivity in which all utterance participates. The use of language implicitly or explicitly presupposes one who listens to or otherwise receives the communication. But a strong addressivity occurs where one speaker directly addresses another.[1] At this point the dialogism which is implicit in language as such is explicitly realised within the context of a relation between speech-agents. In the framework of the present argument, this entails a semiotic, predicated on a movement between reference and a strong mode of address, which is the ground of a new cosmological principle.

That semiotic needs to be distinguished from natural theology on the one hand just as it does from a direct, unmediated experience of God on the other. To be a sign which refers is a form of self-emptying as the existent is evacuated into the presence of another entity. This can be described as a form of veiling as one entity is overshadowed by another whose own visibility is commensurate with the vanishing of the signifying entry. In pointing beyond itself to the divine Creator, which is the referential function of a natural theology of the sign, the world does in a sense recede from us and become instructional: the world is veiled as it points back to and casts light on a divine causality. Natural theology tends to organise the world as a diaspora, then, constituted by its memory of a prior and truer homeland. The functional modality of the sign as address, however, structures the world in an entirely different way. Here we can say that addressivity overwhelms the referential function. It does not eradicate it – the world-constituting reference of the sign retains its force – but the sign receives a new intensification of meaning through the sense of a divine presence which communicates with us *from within the world*. Thus we can say that a reading of the cosmological passages of the New Testament proclaims the possibility that the referential function of the sign can be *overwhelmed* by a divine addressivity, which operates within it at a new level of communicative intensity.

Such a semiotics of divine address leads to a cosmological structure of fullness and of voice. God speaks with us from within his creation. As the spatio-temporal realm in which the voice of God is heard, we can say that

---

1. All speech is in a sense address; for example, if I say to you, 'John has fallen asleep', then I am speaking to you about John. But if I say, 'I love you' or 'Please don't do that', then my address to you is a form of transaction with you and is an attempt to directly influence our relationship.

the world becomes in a sense *the voice-bearing body of God*. It is this dynamic which first comes into view in Jesus' words of institution of the Lord's Supper, as the human and divine voice merge, or speak together, and their unity – manifest at the level of body – precipitates the universalisation of the body of Christ, which is at once the body of an individual speech-agent and the body of the world.

In this third section of the book I shall investigate the nature of the reality of the world at work within that semiotic of Eucharistic disclosure. I shall contrast a Christian realism with secular accounts of the nature of reality and begin to reflect upon the kinds of claims the real makes upon us and the varying possibilities that inhere in the different ways in which we can learn to receive the world in its abundance. Within such a Christian cosmological framework, the role of the body of Christ, and of the world reconfigured within the body of Christ, will be a primary element in the embodied Christian experience, understanding and practice of the real.

Realism and Eucharistic semiotics

The reality of the sign is itself a contestation of the real. We cannot think away signs, any more than we can shed the relativism which is deeply ingrained in a contemporary world-view which understands differences between languages and perspectives to be innate to the order of things and to embody as much a claim to the real as any sense of 'immediacy' which inheres, in Humean terms, to belief as distinct from fictions of the imagination. Since the discovery of the centrality of the sign to human cognition, the realisation of the reality of the sign will determine how we conceptualise the world. If we take it as something which is governed by a reality which is 'external' to it, then our philosophy will take on the colour of a correspondence theory whereby the sign articulates and is in the service of the world, as an extra-semantic sphere. If we understand it also to govern the world of objects, then we shall find we have much in common with the critical realist school, for whom the constructions of language make known an 'external' world, but only heuristically and partially. According to this perspective the cultural traditions we inhabit are as important an element within our cognitions as the objects or reality which are external to them. Further, we may take the view that signs are essentially all that we have; they are free-standing and independent elements which are themselves constitutive of what we know as the real. We need not look beyond them for anything corresponding to reality, but should learn to discern within them the shape and formation of our world. According to this – deconstructionist – reading, the reality of the sign is its reference not to any extra-semiotic realm but merely to other signs, whose reality-reference in turn is realised only within language as the ultimate notional aggregation of possible meanings which attain the density of a world. Meaning is generated by self-evacuating signs which simultaneously constitute the world, or the real, while emptying it of anything which might cohere with traditional notions of presence.

A Christian semiotics based on a Eucharistic metaphysics is somewhat at variance with all three of these – lightly sketched – paradigms. First and foremost it insists that all questions to do with the sign, whether that of the Eucharistic elements or not, must be located within a broader semantic field which is that of the *world-text*. It is important that we do not replicate the move of secular semiotics at this stage, which is to proceed from the sign as a *given*, without taking cognizance of the fact that – from a Christian perspective – the givenness of the sign resides in the giving of God: as creator of the world, its origins and destiny. In chapter 5 we saw that the analogy of literary or epistolary texts helps us to envisage this world-text as being itself informed or animated by the authorial breath (Spirit) or voice (Word) of God, which – together with the Father – are missions of the inner life of the Trinity. *This means to say that the nature of the sign as referring is held ultimately in the act of Trinitarian address: signs only refer because they are part of a world which is itself constituted as the issue or outflow of an act of communication between God and God.* God as Trinity is therefore implicated in the very ground of the world. As one who speaks, who enables speech, and is himself spoken of, God moves at a central point in human history and in the created order as such. The Eucharist is the making present in the everyday of that redemptive inhabiting of the text of the world by the divine voice, as Author of that world; and is the assimilation of reference back into its originary ground as address. In the Eucharistic presence as received by the worshipping community, reference does not cease but is overwhelmed by the divine presence which is its ground, as sign is overtaken by voice.

The Eucharist does not in itself constitute a unique instantiation of Christian semiotics, but is rather a particularly intensive representation of the principles of Christian cosmological semiotics as such. It can therefore be used to illustrate the relation between sign and origin, which is to say, the createdness of the world, with particular clarity. Such a Eucharistic account of realism stresses the place of divine initiative on the one hand and the incompleteness, or 'journeying', of the world on the other. It also gives a fundamental role to the human community, which is shaped by the divine speaking and which in turn can shape and sanctify the world through action, culture and expression, conceived in the fecundity of a new kind of perception and responsivity to the creativity of the divine revelation. Such an account will seek an ultimate unity between all three of the elements of semiosis: the world itself, as sign of God's authorship, God as both origin and referent of the sign, and humanity as the one who interprets the sign and draws out its meaning, the ground of which is Christ's own reading of the world. This unity becomes the site of the emergence of a new vision of the real, as the hospitable and habitable space, both human and divine, in which the world will be released into its ultimate destiny as New Creation.

The sign fulfilled

In the natural state, signs are 'under-way' or transitional entities whose claim to reality is balanced by their condition of self-evacuation, or self-emptying, in the act of pointing beyond themselves to something other. For a sign to exist is for it to be poised on the brink of vanishing for the sake of the reality which it designates: whether conceived as objects in an extra-semantic world or the infinite deferral of other signs. In the natural state, similarly, human beings who live in a world of signifying signs, and for whom signs 'mean', occupy a shifting space as interpreters whose own existence is conditioned by the fugitive character of the signs which exist for them. We cannot see beyond the contingent surfaces of the world's flux, the cosmic semiosis, a richly effervescent but also irreducibly mobile and potently anarchic assemblage of meanings that self-evacuate for other meanings in a spiralling turbulence of deferred resolutions. And we can ourselves seem in that display to be what Hegel described as 'an appearance' or 'surface-show' of 'being that is directly and itself a non-being'.[2] Or, as Fichte stated, we become a 'dream of a dream': a nomadic, de-spirited point of self-awareness adrift in a chain of disconnected narratives.[3] Indeed, what holds us and gives us balance are those points of address, the voices of others who speak with us and for us, who are

---

2. *Phänomenologie des Geistes*, in G. W. F. Hegel, *Werke*, vol. III (Frankfurt am Main: Suhrkamp, 1970), p. 116; *Hegel's Phenomenology of Spirit*, trans. A. V. Miller (Oxford: Oxford University Press, 1977), p. 87.

3. J. G. Fichte, *The Vocation of Man*, ed. and trans. Peter Preuss (*Johann Fichte. The Vocation of Man* (Indianapolis and Cambridge: Hackett, 1987), p. 65).

epiphanies of reality, and in whom the sign with all its magical multitude of meanings achieves the stability of presence.[4]

A Christian fundamental semiosis offers a radical alternative to the conventional semiotic systems outlined above. The question of whether signs point primarily to objects, through ostensive reference, or whether they point primarily or purely to other signs, is not essential to the deeper insight that their mode of reference, or constitution as sign, is itself grounded in the divine address as God speaks with God. As we have repeatedly noted, Christian thinking on the createdness of the world, and hence on the nature of the sign which is foundational to the structure of the world, must start from the scriptural passages which identify the Word as the originary cosmological principle: the one through whom all things were made. The claim of a Eucharistic semiotics is that Jesus' own complete entry into Scripture, which was marked by his utter self-giving for the sake of others – as broken bread and wine poured out – in an anticipation of the coming of the kingdom, was also the point at which the Word through whom all things were made became again the speaking ground of all that is. The Eucharistic claim is further that the human communities who gather in his name at particular times and places can – by the power of Jesus' words – enter into his very act of reading through the liturgy of their common life and can thereby receive a new way of seeing the world. That renewed perception belongs to the New Creation and is grounded in the sense or awareness that the world itself is in some profound and incommunicable sense the breath of God and the body of Christ, through and in whom God speaks creatively with us. It is here that the Spirit plays a particular role, since the Spirit is at the same time the breath that forms speaking and the breath that animates bodily life. Just as, in Ezekiel, it is the advent of the Spirit of God that raises the dry bones and sinews into living bodies, so too it is the coming of the Spirit in a new way through the Word's unity with the world that makes of the world a divine body, shaped in and through the Son. The descent of the Spirit at Pentecost and in the Eucharistic epiclesis draws the themes of new speech, renewed creation and cosmic, resurrected life richly together.

Understood as an exemplum of the real, then, Eucharistic metaphysics offers a model of reality which takes the world to be in a sense the body of God. This is not a device to explain the relation between the world and its Author, as is commonly the case, but reflects an understanding of body as

---

4. See Fichte, *The Vocation of Man*, Part III.

relation: space configured as love. Traditional Christian discourse on the body has tended to be influenced by notions of the materiality of the body as a mode of individuation, or self-realisation within the world.[5] Here, in contrast, I am arguing for a view of the bodiliness of the world which understands it in terms more of a divine erotics than definitional logic: as divine embrace. The deep reality of the world, therefore, is not to be found in the sign, whose necessary emptiness is a form of pregnant expectation, nor is it to be found in the ostensive reference of the realists. Rather, the deep reality of the world, in which the sign is fulfilled, is the presence of God speaking with us, in our specific temporal and spatial locations, through the textuality of the world: as an overwhelming which is the fulfilling of the created sign by the self-communication of the triune God with us as voice which is simultaneously body, as body which is at the same time world.

A Christian philosophy of the real

There have been numerous attempts during the history of philosophy to capture what can be designated as 'the given', which then becomes the ground of the 'ultimately real'. Indeed, the traditions of Western philosophy can be viewed as successive projects based upon a prioritisation of some element within experience, or our knowledge of the world, which is deemed to be more foundational than others and which takes on the role of a governing principle within a conceptual system which, in what Strawson calls the 'prescriptive' or 'metaphysical' tradition, attempts to give a unified account of what it is to be in the world.[6] In this chapter, my concern lies with the question of how a distinctively Christian philosophy of the real is to be formed (while in the final chapter I shall reflect upon distinctively Christian ways of *reasoning* which are predicated upon it). The principal problematic is that the real, which becomes manifest in the address, or voice, which overwhelms the signifiers, emerges at a point which is prior to the constructions of our language, reasoning and feeling. It is an event which constitutes the core of our experience and hence eludes thematisation *as* experience. A Christian philosophy of the real cannot begin as philosophy, therefore, for this would be to evade reality through networks of thought; it would be the fabrication of what

---

5. Paul S. Fiddes, 'Incarnation and the Embodiment of Christ' (unpublished paper).
6. P. F. Strawson, *Individuals* (London: Methuen, 1959), pp. 9–11.

can be packaged and offered as the real, and which quickly becomes as remote from the real as any other cultural scripting. A Christian philosophy
which began in a process of reasoning would be in some sense a contradiction in terms since – as philosophy – it would be an act of evasion, and the
adjective Christian would simply describe the colour of its inauthenticity.
Christian philosophy must begin in another, more primordial place, with
another state of mind, neither rational nor non-rational, neither reflective
nor naïve. It must begin in a mood, or intuition or condition of the self
which mediates the sense of an encounter with the other that is beyond or
beneath language, and yet which is still a condition of experience: recognisable, even familiar.

Christian philosophy must begin with the exercise of a certain passivity, which is a long hesitation, a waiting in patience, before the intractable
otherness which is at the core of experience.[7] It is this that registers the
presence of the real, prior to its deflection into avenues of evasion. Passivity is the mark of the authenticity of our perception before the irreducible actuality of reality. But where is this passivity to be found, for it
cannot be self-induced? Where is it to be learned? The attempt to make
ourselves passive would be a striving of the will and thus a form of activity. The more we struggled to achieve it, the more it would elude us. It cannot be self-induced because passivity as such is always the gift of another.
But the learning of a deep passivity is also a difficult concept: for who shall
teach us? Who could mediate to us such a primal posture of the self before reality? And yet in a certain sense passivity of this kind can be learned,
but only if the learning is a form of discovery of what is already there and
available to us.[8] In other words, we can learn to see what is already a possibility. So the questions which mark the beginning of a Christian philosophy of the real are these: where shall we learn this deepest passivity and
be awakened to its possibilities? How shall we make its discovery?

7. I am using the term 'passivity' here in an entirely neutral sense, to denote a condition
which is ordered to a pure divine activity or dynamic presence that is pre-conceptual. This
condition might also be described as 'submission' or 'resignation' but in both of these cases
the object, or that to which they are ordered, can be taken to be something akin to
'command' or perhaps 'power', both of which already function at the conceptual level. The
medieval theologian Meister Eckhart made extensive use of the terminology of *wirken* (divine
acting) and *leiden* (human suffering or passivity) to designate the foundational relation
between humanity and God as one conditioned at its heart by the divine reality. It is this that
my use of the term 'passivity', which means something like 'stillness' or 'responsivity', seeks
to emulate.
8. This condition of passivity is not drawn out from within us, therefore, but is a state that is
given from outside ourselves, by the Teacher, to borrow a phrase from Kierkegaard's
Philosophical Fragments.

For the Christian there is a place where passivity is exercised before all others, with a primordiality which is a listening or attentiveness to the ground of existence itself. This is the passivity exercised before Christ, as redeemer and saviour. For Catholic Christians that passivity finds its focus in the Eucharistic celebration, where it comes into view as a responsivity of thanksgiving. Here there is a new possibility of the apprehension of the real, for the Eucharistic mind is a mind trained in attentiveness, an unparalleled state of being given over to the other beyond all limits. In the moment of 'transubstantiation', when the signifying elements are overtaken by the spoken Word, and by an alterity which transfigures their material form, breaking sign into presence: in that moment the mind learns a new form of dynamic stillness. This is not a stillness of the heart or intellect alone, but of the whole self, summoned into dialogue with God through the Word of the Trinity: called out of our own meanings not through interpretation but by the embrace of the speaking other whose voice, as the Spirit's voice, inhabits our own speaking as celebration and intercession.

In the Eucharist, the dynamic that we might call Eucharistic perception becomes the ideal ground of all human perceiving. And it does so because it forms us in the possibility of a new way of receiving the real, through sight, hearing, touch, smell and taste. We discover in worship a primordial attentiveness before the one who is the ultimate other-in-relation, which becomes a training in the apprehension of the real, perceived not as a domain to be conquered through a controlling interpretation but as a fecundity and an abundance that excessively fills our minds and our senses, making possible the infinite variety of human ways of knowing, sensing and feeling. It is this, the fecundity of the divine creativity made visible in the person of Christ, but intrinsic no less to the web of the world, that forms the ground of the pragmatic theory, or theology, of the world's createdness which this book articulates.

A Christian philosophy of the real reflects an immediacy which is prior even to the notion of experience but which does not represent, nevertheless, a kind of aporetics; it is not itself known as the alien and strange which becomes resident among us through the operations of the sacrament (although that is indeed one of its possible constructions). The real, as I have defined it, is the state which is not knowledge itself but is the pre-conceptual ground of knowing, in which self and other are not separable and in which sentience and perception, subject and object, still form a unity. The unfolding from that first moment of the constructions and operations of subject and object, sense and knowledge, is an inevitable process, though one which can be delayed by an attitude of attentiveness which is akin to prayer: the posture of a self which is given over utterly to the apprehension of what eludes our categories, which is prior to our thought and yet which lays claim to us totally as the primordial place from which subject and object first emerge within the unfolding horizon of a world.

The pre-conceptual, then, cannot itself be received by us as the object of knowledge; it is known rather in the claims it makes upon us. For a self, tutored in the experience of Eucharistic presence, the claim of the real manifests as the formation of a certain kind of embodiment. This type of embodiment is as foundational, and as pre-conceptual, as the real itself. We can only ever know it, therefore, in the transformations which it effects in our lives. Amongst these we must point in particular to the increased sense of compassion, and of celebration, which develops in the Eucharistic self who is set in relation with the transformed elements as the body and blood of Christ. The ecclesial body which is formed in this encounter is one which is foundationally committed to the other, and is foundationally worshipful or celebratory (I shall discuss these themes in the following chapter). But what we can know about the real in itself, from our experience in the Eucharist, is that it is itself a form of relation: the real is itself a kind of *bodiliness*. The Eucharist teaches us furthermore that this bodiliness or relation, which is the point of meeting between self and other prior to their differentiation, is also a form of hospitality: a pleroma of generous fecundity, in which the subject, as it emerges, knows itself to have been welcomed and received. What we encounter in the thematised body of Christ given in the Eucharist, then, is the shape of the real itself, as divine hospitality, divine embrace, in which we are received even as we receive. And the Eucharistic attentiveness teaches us that it is Christ himself who holds us, at the core of our experience: calling, communicating, and receiving us from *within* the world as the ground of existence.

Intensities of the real

In line with the above argument that the semiotic which comes into view in the Catholic understanding of the Eucharist is a semiotic of the world itself and not just of one part of the world, it is important to see also the ways in which the real, as the self-communication or embrace of God, manifests in other areas of our living. In this section we look at some of the other ways in which we can come into an embodied awareness of our relation to the real, itself manifest as the pure relatedness of the divine body. It is naturally the case that every individual's experience of this will be their own, and there are no prescriptive norms that can be set down. But there is perhaps a certain structure which such 'passages' or 'events' in life will have in common. We may see in them the structure of belonging and over-whelming which parallels the inner form of the Eucharistic celebration, as an intensive mode of Christian cosmic semiotics. These occasions will be grounded in the sense of the self being given over into the otherness of the real in such a way that the self remains a principle of identity, even if the parameters of that identity can undergo dramatic transformations. But above all, it is in terms of a common temporal structure that we can identify such moments which are an epiphany of the real.

Eucharistic presence is characterised as temporal fullness, or pleroma of time. That fullness is to be understood against the background of a the-ology of creation which, in biblical tradition, is the 'already-always-there'. As we attempt to comprehend creation, we encounter the impossible para-dox of attempting to conceive what cannot be known – at least not by us – as the 'not-yet'.[9] In Pierre Gibert's terms, 'the beginning is the place that cannot be grasped, a place that is radically impossible to perceive or experi-ence as such a beginning'.[10] That 'beginning' is likewise determined as an 'end', however, in the close intermeshing of redemptive and soteriologi-cal themes with Israel's reflection upon its origins and the origins of God's world. The temporal structure of the Eucharistic presence, then, is one in which the end and the beginning sustain each other; each is in the pos-session of the other. The divine beginning, which encloses the end within itself, cannot be thought of as a sequence of events, which is to say, within our ordinary experience of time, but manifests rather as a fullness of pres-ence, as a way of being in the present moment.

This Eucharistic temporality, which is the unity of beginning and end, destabilises the ordinary sense of time of those who participate in it. In Ecclesiastes the Teacher states that although God has placed within us a sense of long duration (ôlam), we cannot understand 'God's deeds from the

---

9. André LaCocque and Paul Ricoeur, *Thinking Biblically. Exegetical and Hermeneutical Studies* (Chicago and London: University of Chicago Press, 1998), pp. 31–67, especially 54–67.

10. Pierre Gibert, *Bible, mythes et récits de commencement* (Paris: Seuil, 1986), p. 8 (quoted in LaCocque and Ricoeur, *Thinking Biblically*, p. 50).

beginning until the end'.[11] In other words, the eternity or a-temporality of God's actions within history disrupts the ordinary sense of time which is native to us, so that we are frustrated in our attempts to make sense of the world as the place in which God reveals himself to us. For Christians, it is the sacrifice on the Cross, together with the Eucharist which makes that one sacrifice present to us again, which is the place where God's logic of eternity breaks in upon us in the most ostensive way. In that moment the body of Christ is both particular, which is to say temporally located, and is universal, or eternal. Past and future combine in the unity of Eucharistic presence, which shatters the temporality of the world and draws the worshipping community to the threshold of a different kind of time.

There are experiences in life which seem to stand in a limit-relation to the natural attitude of our ordinary living. They are moments when questions of ultimate meaning seem to come into play, and the ordinary temporal structure of our lives is radically called into question, as if intensities of the real bring with them a new kind of – Eucharistic – temporality. In the case of the Eucharist itself, that atemporality is not experienced as disorientation or alienation, since the real manifests here as relatedness and hospitality. We are drawn into Eucharistic presence as into a state of *having been received* which is prior to any act of cognition on our part. The human response to the Eucharistic atemporality, which so restructures our world, is necessarily one of radical trust, as we are called to give ourselves over into the flow and dynamic of elemental reality. Trust and the real are ordered one to the other: the emergence of the real is fostered by trust and an increase in trust follows from our coming-into-relation with the real. Such 'passages of the real' as we encounter in our ordinary living are therefore moments of possibility, when we can experience the world in its depths as a being-in-relation, as a form of bodiliness, which calls forth in us a creative, 'cosmic' trust.

But a total trust of this kind cannot be divorced from hope or joy. Hope is a transcendental condition of the self. It may have a specific cause, coming about on account of particular events in which we reason to the possibility of a positive outcome. But as a transcendental virtue, hope is an expression of our sense of being buoyed up, and sustained, by the deep structure of the world. Hope follows upon trust, and is likewise a modality

---

11. Eccl. 3:11 (NRSV: 'he has put a sense of past and future into their minds, yet they cannot find out what God has done from the beginning to the end').

of being given over to the world, and being received by it. Joy, like hope, can be occasioned by many things, but joy is itself more than delighting in something: it is a deep-seated sense of well-being which is co-extensive with our being in the world. Through the sense of joy, which comes to us spontaneously as a received state of mind rather than one which we ourselves control or manufacture, we again find that we are given over into a structure of transformation which both transcends our individuality and yet is predicated upon it.[12]

Trust, hope and joy are thus transcendental states of mind which are grounded in the ultimate goodness of the world as it contains and transforms us. They follow from our own participation in the divine creativity, in which we enter into the divine compassion as the deep structure of the world. That is a moment which escapes our cognition in itself but which can nevertheless become known to us in a transcendental and unconditioned way. The trust, joy and hope that come upon us are a sign that we are living in the world as true creatures of the creative and compassionate God.

Sense-life

In the intense drama that is each and every human life, there are moments, then, when we are summoned into a more intimate, and trusting, relation with the world around us. Perhaps it is not surprising that one of the chief ways in which we experience the claim of the real is in the intimacy of sexual love. In sexual stimulation, with a life-partner to whom we have made a total and open-ended commitment as in the marriage vows, we find that we are given over to the other in a deep reciprocity of sensation. In this case, the externality of the other is overcome at every stage by the increasing intimacy and inwardness of the sexual sensation. The tactility of love-making leads to an intensity of awareness of sensation as a mutuality between self and other, in an exchange of inwardness and externality. In love-making, the senses become the place in which we know ourselves as given over entirely into the sense-impressions of the other, just as the other enters as new intensive life into our own internal and sensate world. In the exchange of love, the senses are no longer the border that separates self from world, the inward from the external, but become the possibility of a unique translocation, as we become

---

12. Forms of 'enthusiasm' or *Schwärmerei* are parallel states of mind but ones which tend to efface the cognising self rather than affirm the point of relation between self and world.

the sense impressions of the other and they become the life of our own sense-world.

The creativity of the participation of the self in the real through sexual love is mediated in terms both of transformation of life on the part of the couple and of the procreation of children who are the embodiment of their love and mutual commitment. The temporal destabilisation which takes place in the former case comes to the fore in the marriage vows, in which each partner commits themselves to the other for the whole of their lifetime. When we are young, it is impossible to have any real sense of what such a commitment over a period of forty, fifty or sixty years might mean. Binding vows entail the embrace of a significant degree of temporal alienation, therefore, as young people make a grave, personal commitment within a duration of time they cannot possibly understand. The 'creation' of a person entails more than their physical procreation, of course; the personality of the child is moulded and formed by the shared values and world-views of the couple who parent them: that is, by that same relation which is also the life and fruition of their love-making. But that 'creation' of children also entails a degree of temporal alienation, as the parents know that they are only a small part in a chain that will extend far beyond their own lifetimes. The birth of a child is one of the key points in a person's life when they are brought to an understanding of the limit of their own temporal world.

Praying the end

The end of life, like the beginning of life, sets us before the claim of the real. Death encircles our lives, and is the constant limit that shadows our health and our strength. We know in youth that it is the logical and necessary end of our existence but this knowledge takes on a new and existential force as we increase in years and experience the loss of close relatives. In their dying we can observe the way in which death is an overcoming of our bodily life but nevertheless one in which the individual person has their own crucial part to play.[13] As we approach death, we can reject it, as the irremediable rupturing of our temporality, as something entirely senseless within the patterns of our ordinary living. Or alternatively we can give assent to the greater dynamic of living, finding in the ending of our bodily existence traces of the divine compassion, moving forward in trust, hope and joy. Then we shall find that it is potentially a uniquely creative time: we can

---

13. Joel Shuman, *The Body of Compassion* (Boulder, Colo.: Westview Press, 1999), pp. 1–6.

perhaps never play a greater part in the mystery of life, and never possess a greater possibility to shape it, than in its ending.

Art

The twofold character of the real as laying claim to the self, with an invitation to a creative participation on the one hand and as a destabilisation of our ordinary temporality on the other, comes into view also in the case of art and the aesthetic response. Hans-Georg Gadamer has argued that the interpretation of the work of art is a particularly intensive example of the way in which we make sense of the world in general.[14] In other words, rather than standing as an isolated experience, cut off from our ordinary perceptions, the appreciation of the work of art actually stands in close relation to the way in which we experience the world as such. If the world is constituted through its meanings, then it is certainly the case that a major art work possesses a semantic richness of extraordinary density. On each occasion when we read a fine novel or stand before an intriguing painting in a gallery, we open ourselves up to an object which is the compressed and complex expression of a whole range of cultural forces. Indeed, one of the defining qualities of an outstanding work of art is its capacity to lay full claim to our attention, and to demand from us a serious, sustained and open-ended act of interpretation. In line with the other life events discussed above, the encounter with the work of art can be an encounter with the world itself at a heightened level of intensity, and in a way which draws us into itself. In its appreciation, the work of art lays claim to us as someone who is integral to itself. As we struggle to come to terms with its rich complexity, we are ourselves, as interpreters, made part of its meaning.

It is easy to forget that the work of art results from the skills of a particular individual who, in the case of the classic works of art at least, is likely to have been born at a time and place very remote from our own. Art is nevertheless a distinctive form of *address*. We can be powerfully addressed by its compelling complexity and astonishing grace. There are two ways therefore in which the work of art destabilises our temporality. The first is the extent to which it introduces into our own world the voices, insights and imaginations of others who have lived before us. We are exposed in a most intimate and affective way to very different social horizons and times, though in ways that are recognisable. Indeed, a work of

14. Hans-Georg Gadamer, *Truth and Method* (London: Sheed and Ward, 1979), pp. 99–150.

art can convey in a very powerful way the sense of the presence of those – long dead – who are depicted in it. But the sense of the artist's own presence is likewise communicated in the work of art. In the reception of their creativity, we can subtly share with the artist something essential of their own vitality. We can be moved by people we have not known; we can share with them the strangeness of reality. In the appreciation of a work of art, we find that our own time is submerged in the temporality of others. Our lives are relativised; and we are brought before our own temporal limit.

Conclusion

From a Christian perspective, the real at its foundation is expressive of the graciousness of God. In the sacrament of the Eucharist, that graciousness comes into view as the fulfilment of the sign. In the celebration of God's transforming act, at the heart of the world, the structure of the world as *created* is opened up to us and becomes in itself body and food. We encounter it in the Eucharist as body because the real is in its deepest sense God's relatedness with us, and God's self-communication. We receive it as food because the understanding of the real is at the same time a communication in which we ourselves participate as active interpreters of the fulfilled sign who are drawn into the life of God, which is given with it. We are not merely observers from without, therefore, but are an intrinsic part of its self-communication.

Certain limit-experiences in our lives exhibit a structure which approximates them to the Eucharist as a vehicle for the manifestation of the real. Although they do not share the explicit thematisation of reality as the body and blood of Christ, they represent an intensity of engagement with the world which brings with it a powerful invitation to a creative participation. They also call into question the temporality of our natural attitude, not as radically as is the case with the real presence, but in them the limit of our temporal nature becomes manifest in an unmistakable way. Such moments, which I have called 'intensities of the real', offer an invitation to engage with the heart of life and to reject or receive life in the specificity of its address to us.

The Eucharist teaches us that all reality is to be received as the divine body. This cannot be taught in any propositional sense, but only as the inculcation of a new passivity of mind and body which is itself the discovery of a prior dynamic of relatedness, too fundamental and pre-conceptual to be known in any other way than through the slow learning of a new form of – Eucharistic – embodiment in the world.

The Christian account of the real, then, is ultimately one which understands it to be not so much resistance or limit as excess, a wave, a momentum of embrace, which comes to meet us at the root of our perceptions. It is in the Eucharist that we can learn to discern and receive the real: as a divine being-in-relation: as the body of Christ, given for us.

8

Wisdom of the flesh

Osculetur me osculo oris sui
Quia meliora sunt ubera tua uino

May he kiss me with the kiss of his mouth
For your breasts are more delightful than wine
Canticum Canticorum

The primary argument I have presented in this book is that the deep reality which is at the root of the world is as much a divine reality as it is a temporal one and that it can be conceived of as a kind of Primal Text, which is to say a creative, 'externalised' self-communication of God (by analogy with the way that a human author produces a text). The Primal Text of the creation cannot be known in itself but comes into view in its function as a cosmic principle of intertextuality. This means primarily that all the many textualities which inform our existence are grounded in the one Primal Text, or primary text of creation, and receive their form from it. But it means not only that textuality itself is a product of the Primal Text, but also *intertextuality*, or the interaction between the different textualities, which is the structure that enables the emergence of world. This theory of a first, cosmic text plays the same role as that of analogy in medieval theology, which gave an account of how the successive orders of creation were linked through a common cause, in God. It does not presuppose a pre-modern notion of causality, however, as that which entails the replication of the cause in the effect, but looks rather to the organic and expressive relationship of the author to his or her own text.[1]

1. This is to adopt elements from Romantic hermeneutics, which laid a greater stress upon the author–text relation than was the tendency amongst later hermeneutical thinkers (see

I have further argued that it is in the Eucharist that we learn a responsivity to the divine text. Unknowable in itself, it is mediated to us in and through the real presence of the body of Christ. We can say, therefore, that the root of the world as divine body is also made present to us in and with the Eucharistic body of Christ.[2] The structure of that moment is threefold. In the first place, the originary voice of God, whose speaking is the creation, sets up the expectation of a divine body. Voices are produced by bodies; bodies are 'voice-bearing'.[3] For God to have a voice is therefore, by implication, for God to have a body. This sets up a highly dialectical process, since it is unthinkable that the voice of the one whose speaking is the origin of the world should itself be borne by a body, for any material thing can only be the product and not the source of that creative speaking. The body of Jesus, as the man who bears the divine voice, is conceived within this impossible, dialectical space. The Christian belief that creation is through the Second Person, the Word who – in the formula of the Prologue to the Gospel of John – 'became flesh', is also expressive of this same dialectic.[4] The second part of this threefold structure is found in the alienation of the divine voice within the text of the world, as the divine

for instance Schleiermacher's General Introduction in his *Hermeneutics and Criticism*, trans. A. Bowie (Cambridge: Cambridge University Press, 1998), pp. 3–29). In his *Divine Discourse* (Cambridge: Cambridge University Press, 1995) Nicholas Wolterstorff advances a broadly Schleiermacherian account of the nature of texts, including scriptural ones, against the anti-authorial tendencies of Paul Ricoeur and Jacques Derrida's hermeneutics. In contrast, the scriptural hermeneutics that I am proposing here can be seen to represent an intensification of Schleiermacher's authorial model but, since the author concerned is the superabundant divine presence, I argue that the human act of interpretation necessarily takes on some of the characteristics of deconstruction. As an encounter with the divine overwhelming, interpretation becomes partial, mobile and dynamic to the extent that each interpretative act, though possibly full and complete in itself, is rapidly overtaken by the abundance of the divine self-communication. Interpretation thus becomes a constant process of reappraisal and repairal undertaken before the intensity and richness of the divine presence. According to this model, interpretation – though at one level individual – is also grounded in the community and subject to its verification. The character of the divine reality as *embodied*, implies the divine revelation to the 'body' of Israel, or the 'body' of the Church, of which the individual can only ever be a *mediation*.

2. I am writing this within the Catholic tradition. But it seems to me to be the case that the universalised body of Christ is manifest within other modalities, not least in the reading and reception of Scripture itself. See also note 11 below.

3. See the useful discussion of voice in José Gil, *Metamorphoses of the Body* (Minneapolis and London: University of Minnesota Press, 1998), pp. 186–94.

4. There is also an implication here that embodiment – however construed – is a principle which obtains within the Trinity and which prefigures the creation of the world-text and the Incarnation of the Son. It can be argued that the notion of the Son as Word already implies a certain textuality, and thus corporality, and it is this which underlies the tradition, which extends from Origen to Hamann, St Bonaventure and von Balthasar, that the Son 'is the very language of the Father' (Peter Casarella, 'The Expression and Form of the Word: Trinitarian Hermeneutics and the Sacramentality of Language in Hans Urs von Balthasar's Theology', *Renascence* 48.2 (winter 1996), 111–35, here 111). See also Ewart Cousins, 'Bonaventure's

speaking is externalised and made subject to radical interpretation. This calls for a process of repair or healing which is at the same time the repristi-nation of the world. In order for the divine voice to enter correctively into the very fabric of the world-text, it was necessary for the dialectic of the divine body to be worked out within Christ's own body. The realisation of the divine speaking within Jesus led to a moment of sacrificial redemp-tion as his human body – under the weight of the divine voice speaking in him – was broken and poured out, becoming one with the elements, renewing and reanimating the body of the world. This repristination, or redemption, of the world can be summed up in the principle that *the body of Christ is that which mediates between the voice of God the Creator and the world-text that is the issue of God's creative speaking*. The redemptive sacrifice is therefore also the moment when the world is restored back into the unity of God's speaking and when the world becomes in a new sense the body of God. The third stage is the Eucharistic recapitulation or making present of the cosmic sacrificial act. In this chapter I shall focus upon the transformed embodiment which is the appropriate human response to the redemptive self-communication of God mediated through the Eucharist. I shall argue that this new body-sense, formed within the celebratory and compassion-ate community of the Church, who are summoned into unity by the voice of God, is the emergence of radical ecclesiality.

The human body and the Primal Text

The human body is at its core and in its perfection the point of our unity with the Primal Text. It is therefore the point of our greatest vulnerability in the world and greatest receptivity before the creativity of God at work in the world. But we do not in general know our bodies in this way. We only know our body in its self-replications that play through the fields of our sense-perceptions. We know it, for instance, as that which defines us as an entity in the world. Bodies are boundaries, marking a territory of which we are sole sovereign. Such bodies have rights, and require personal space and autonomy. But body is also the domain of relationality; it is in Merleau-Ponty's sense our participation in the element of the 'flesh' which tran-scends any one entity or gathering of entities. It is the 'sea' of touching and being touched in which we move and have our being without ever seeing

Mysticism of Language', in Stephen Katz, ed., *Mysticism and Language* (New York: Oxford University Press, 1992), pp. 236–57.

the possibility of a horizon. Body too is a kind of memory in which is inscribed all our negotiations with the world. As Spinoza suggested, we only come into our own body-sense through other bodies which serve as stimuli to the senses.[5] Each point of stimulus, or sequence of stimuli, mediates to us what is other than us, and yet does so in a way that seems internal to our own bodies and minds. The compacting memory of those touchings or points of contact is the formation of our world as a place in which we share a series of coherent relations with other bodies, known to us in the repeated patterns of the sense stimuli. But the body is also the formation of our own ways of acting in this world, our habitual and generally corporate practices and responses which become ingrained in us and which are themselves a kind of memory of who we are, and of who we have been. As *habitus*, the body is a set of practices which define our existence in the world, as social and relational beings.

Body is further the primary expression of our gendered and sexual nature. It is the domain of intimate response ordered to the body of another in which we gain access to the most intense experiences of mutual indwelling through the senses. In sexual love we discover our own body in new ways through the body of the other, and lovers come to inhabit a new space, neither mine nor yours, but crafted through a sharing in the sense-life of the other. Here again body is reproduced but now as a shared body: a world that is sustained by a shared *habitus* of love-making.

We encounter our own bodies too in the ways that they are mediated to us through culture. Here the paradigms may be so deep as to be almost invisible. The fundamental ways in which we construe our bodies may be governed by the most powerful paradigms that operate in the construction of our world.[6] In modern society, we are dominated, for instance, by sophisticated instrumental, functionalist paradigms of the body which stress chains of causality and which reflect the broader technological mentalities of the age. The body either 'works' or 'breaks down' and where its functions are impaired, these may be taken over by machines. Another

---

5. Benedict de Spinoza, *Ethics*, vol. II, P14–31 (*Benedict de Spinoza, Ethics*, trans. Edwin Curley (Harmondsworth: Penguin Books, 1996), pp. 44–52). On the link between imagination and body in Spinoza, see Moira Gatens and Genevieve Lloyd, *Collective Imaginings. Spinoza Past and Present* (London and New York: Routledge, 1999), pp. 12–18.

6. Dale Martin, for instance, has shown how the church community which Paul was addressing in his First Letter to the Corinthians was one in which two fundamentally distinct paradigms of the body came into conflict. The one was permeable and hierarchical and ordered to an external cosmology, while the other was concerned with pollution and with policing boundaries (Dale B. Martin, *The Corinthian Body*, New Haven and London: Yale University Press, 1995).

paradigm which is powerfully influential in our society is that of the body as a field of performance. We like to watch athletes who perform at the limits of human capacity, but we also like to practice popular leisure sports ourselves. 'Fitness' is the public expression of a person who is in control of their body and world in an athleticism of cultural and social performance. Further, the body is continually replicated as the focus of sexual desire. Direct and indirect pornography and the skills of advertising companies combine to ensure that alluring images of the human body are never far from our view. This is to make the body the object of wish-fulfilment and desire; it is to generate the human body in its representations as itself an aspect of consumerist values and as detachable from the paradigms of social and relational living. In David Le Breton's words, the 'modern body . . . implies the cutting off of the subject from others (a social structure of an individualistic kind), from the cosmos (the primary matter of which the body is composed does not exist elsewhere), from oneself (we have a body rather than are a body)'. The Western body is 'the place of division, the objective frame of the sovereignty of the self'.[7]

The body self-replicates through technology, cultural iconography, sense-memories and the physical reproduction of children, but at its core and in its perfection, it remains hidden from our experience.[8] It is an empty field which takes on the symbolic values of the social imaginary and, as Le Breton argues, the successive cultural images of the body can be seen as an attempt to reduce its 'mystery'.[9] To this extent it is like the Primal Text itself, which is the intensive, pre-conceptual reality that human thought brackets and evades.

Voice, text and body

Texts and bodies have this in common: both are constituted, or even animated, by a circularity of breath which draws the sign away from the materiality of the world into a universe of conceptuality and meaning. It is the unity of texts, which is intrinsic to their formation as a *corpus*, which forms the ground of this higher and more intensive degree of signifying. The individual signs in a text take on a heightened impetus and meaning within the specific borders which frame the text as text: the words

---

7. David Le Breton, *Anthropologie du corps et modernité* (Paris: Presses Universitaires de France, 1990), p. 8.
8. See Le Breton's comments on this (ibid., chapter 1: 'L'insaisissable du corps').
9. Ibid., p. 22.

of a poem resonate with each other and refer forwards and backwards within the poem's overarching unity. The different scenes of a novel co-alesce through memory and anticipation within the text's unfolding narrative. In the case of Scripture, it is the unity of the canon which supports figural and typological meanings, allowing readings which point forward to fulfilment and back to anticipation. It is the unity of the text, then, which can generate complex cycles of free-flowing meanings, as the text as a whole is received by different interpreters, or different acts of interpretation, and as the text is itself set in alignment with other texts and other readings. The 'life' of the text resides precisely in this density of meaning, which is the circulation of semiological possibilities within its own borders. Consequently, it is the *boundaries* of the text which are the text's own unique individuation and which create the possibility of its own extended semiotic life.[10]

The boundaried body, for its part, is the individuation which is intrinsic to the human person. Human flesh is matter which is so permeated with voice and personal presence as to be virtually no longer recognisable as matter. When we look upon material bodies, we see the person themselves: matter saturated with meaning, personality and intent. It is only when we look upon the dead body of a family member or close friend that we see their body for the first time in the starkness of its pure materiality. Every part of the living body is referred to its 'centre' in the personhood of the vital self, which finds its visible analogue in the face and its oral analogue in the voice. The body is animated and held together as a whole on the grounds of the life that circulates within the borders which are its individuating definition.

But the differences between bodies and texts are also profound. We are addressed by texts, but only indirectly so. The original address of the author's voice in the text can seem remote and inconsequential to us, or it can appear to be no longer discernible. But in the case of human bodies, the materiality of the sign is entirely taken up in a form of intensive semiosis which is at the same time personal. We feel the person in the body. We

---

10. Paul S. Fiddes has developed an enormously rich theological reflection upon 'the notion of the canon as bordered space' ('Canon as Space and Place', in John Barton and Michael Wolter, eds., *Die Einheit der Schrift und die Vielfalt des Kanons. The Unity of Scripture and the Plurality of the Canon* (Beihefte zur Zeitschrift für die neutestamentliche Wissenschaft 118; Berlin: Walter de Gruyter, 2003), pp. 127–49). Fiddes sees canon as grounded in a dialectic between 'space' (as openness, hospitality) and 'place' (as particularity and limit) which presents the community of readers with a structure of obligation, encounter and transformation of life. This paradox looks back to the Wisdom tradition of the Old Testament and, for the Christian reader, is finally rooted in the dialectical, eschatological personhood of Jesus Christ.

see the selfhood in the light of the eyes and we hear the distinctive and personal presence in the speaking of the voice. Matter – according to the present governing metaphor of the divine text of the world – is itself the substance of signification; it lends itself to be taken up in innumerable different forms of signification, the interaction of which constitutes our world. The human body is that domain of matter in which the power of signification, which is a potentiality within all matter, becomes *personal* and so densely articulated that it stands as a place of luminosity in the world: a reflex and icon of matter's own power to communicate meaning as world. The living body in this sense is a type of prophetic microcosm: a sign that the world too can become just such a place of address, in which the materiality of the world is filled and transformed by God's Trinitarian self-communication.

Eucharistic flesh

I have maintained throughout this work that the body of Christ of which we speak, which is to say, the body that is broken and poured out for us, is now a universalised body which is, on the one hand, the regeneration of the world as God's body and, on the other, the foundation of the life of discipleship which is the embodied Christian response to that transformation of world. I do not hold that the Catholic Eucharist, upon which I have extensively drawn, is a unique realisation of that body, but rather that it gives access to it in a uniquely sacramental way. The emphasis I have placed upon it in this work is a consequence of its sacramental character; I do not argue that only those who participate in a Catholic Eucharist can know or receive the universalised body of Christ.[11]

But the sacramental character of the Eucharist does foster a particular kind of reflexive engagement with the nature of that body, which is both mysterious in itself and mysterious in its relation to us. After all, we do not receive the body in the way that we might expect: as bread, or body, that is eaten and wine, or blood, that is drunk. Catholic tradition insists that this is a literal eating, though not of bread and wine, nor of body and blood. It is a literal eating that is itself a metaphor of something which has already happened and which exceeds the dynamic symbolic of eating and drinking. Bodies are not eaten and drunk: they are embraced and held. But

---

11. See, for instance, Douglas Farrow, *Ascension and Ecclesia. On the Significance of the Doctrine of the Ascension for Ecclesiology and Christian Cosmology* (Edinburgh: T. & T. Clark, 1999), which specifically links the universalisation of Christ with the ascension.

the holding and embrace of the one whose body is the world is well signified by an act of eating and drinking, for this is being nourished by the
real. Becoming part of and entering into the body of Christ as world, being
entered and incorporated by the unique and universal body that is given
for all, is captured and accomplished in the act of eating and drinking the
Eucharistic body and blood of Christ.[12] At the moment of institution of
the Lord's Supper, when Jesus became Voice-bearing, his body had already
become pure sign, poured out into the elements, distributed through the
material order: shattered, consumed, perfected, universalised. Our reception of that body, under the Eucharistic species, is therefore an embodied
semiotics of radical reception. It is a living within the text of the world
by a self who savours both Christ's body, given for all, and the semiosis
of the world, transformed, en-Spirited, by the sacrificial fragmentation
and pouring out of the body of Christ as the mediating structure between
Trinity and world.

The compassionate body

The Eucharist is the place in which our own bodies are conformed to the
world which has been regenerated through the new fullness of the Spirit as
the universalised body of Christ. The transformation of the human body in
that context is its entry into the corporate and sacramental embodiedness
of the Church. Once again it is the Holy Spirit that animates the people of
God and makes of them a single body, mirroring the body of Christ and
the 'world made body' that is the result of Christ's sacrifice for us and the
new giving of the Spirit at Pentecost. It is in a Pauline sense through the
different charisms of the Spirit, exercised by individuals on behalf of
the Church as a whole, that the individual Christian is integrated into the
life of Church as the body of Christ.

But a further mode of participation is through compassion, as St Paul
develops this theme in the Letter to the Philippians. The term *splanchna*
(verbal form *splanchnizomai*) picks up the Hebrew noun *raḥămîm*, which is
most appropriately translated as 'compassion'. It is cognate with *reḥem*,
meaning 'womb', and denotes a deeply visceral feeling of care and concern.
The words *raḥămîm*, and *raḥam* ('to show compassion') are consistently
used of God's presence with Israel, and are so intimately linked with the

---

12. There is a tradition which can be found in Augustine (*Confessions*, 7.10.16, PL 32:742) and
Bernard of Clairvaux ('Sermons on the Song of Songs' 71.5) which sees in the act of
communion the incorporation of the faithful *into* the body of Christ. I am grateful to Bernard
McGinn for this point.

divine name of Yahweh that the rabbinic tradition records: 'At times I am called El Shaddai, Seba'ot, Elohim and Yahweh. When I judge creatures, I am called Elohim; when I forgive sins, I am called El Shaddai; when I wage war against the wicked, I am called Seba'ot, and when I show compassion for my world, I am called Yahweh.'[13]

In 2 Corinthians and the letter to Philemon, Paul develops this vocabulary in terms of ecclesiological unity. In the former text it appears with the word 'heart' (*kardia*), for instance, and forms part of his appeal to the church at Corinth, to whom he says that he has opened his heart ('Our heart (*kardia*) is wide open to you'), and whose response he seeks: 'There is no restriction in our affections, but only in yours.'[14] The word 'affections' translates *splanchna* here, which can be interpreted as marking our affectivity *in relation with others*. Paul has declared that his 'heart' (*kardia*) has been opened to the Corinthians, and his complaint is that his 'affections' (*splanchna*) are not being reciprocated by them. If the 'heart' denotes the centre of affectivity at this point, then it may be that *splanchna* denotes something more akin to unitive love as the basic Christian disposition. It is *kardia* enriched by the mutual and self-dispossessing love which is most deeply characteristic of the Pauline Church.[15] In the Letter to Philemon Paul again uses *splanchna* in the sense of the emotional centre of 'the saints', which is refreshed through the love of Philemon, their brother.[16] Paul uses the same phrase when he appeals to Philemon on behalf of Onesimus: 'Yes, brother, let me have this benefit from you in the Lord! Refresh my heart in Christ.'[17] The *splanchna* which is again to be refreshed by the mutual love of the Church seems to be a distinctively ecclesial centre of feeling. When Paul refers to his 'child' Onesimus as 'my own heart' (*splanchna*), whom he is now sending back into the care of Philemon, to whom he previously belonged as slave, the intense feelings of relation conveyed by *splanchna* have become hypostasised in the person of the individual concerned.[18]

13. Rabbah on Exodus 3:14 (S. M. Lehrman, *Midrash Rabbah III* (London: The Soncino Press, 1961), p. 64); see also chapter 4, note 27 above (pp. 82–3).
14. 2 Cor. 6:12.
15. The word *splanchna* underlies the NRSV translation of 'heart' at 2 Cor. 7:15, where it refers to Titus' visit to the church at Corinth. Paul writes: 'And his heart (*splanchna*) goes out all the more to you, as he remembers the obedience of all of you, and how you welcomed him with fear and trembling.' This again points to the warmth of Christian mutual love, highlighted at the point of its inception through mission.
16. Philem. 7.
17. Philem. 20.
18. Philem. 12.

Compassion is a virtue that is located within the body sense in a way that is as reminiscent of the passions as it is of the virtues.[19] This is acknowledged in the terms *raḥəmîm* and *splanchna*, as it is in the Latin equivalent *misericordia* ('sorrow of heart'), and the modern *com-passion*. Compassion is something we feel in our own body, on account of the bodily condition of another. We are moved most urgently to compassion by the extreme physical needs of others, and the compassionate response is not merely of the mind but is an orientation of our bodily life, with physical commitments and engagements. It entails the enactments and *practices* of care: feeding, healing, comforting. Compassion, then, is an appropriate expression at the level of human existence of our unity with Christ's body. And in the Letter to the Philippians Paul supplements the ecclesiological character of this terminology with more explicitly Christological and incarnational dimensions. Following the salutation, the letter continues with Paul's prayer for the Church at Philippi, in which he expresses his strong affection and bond of unity with them and states: 'For God is my witness, how I long for all of you with the compassion of Christ Jesus.'[20] The Greek phrase literally means 'in the bowels/compassion of Christ', and it suggests that the *splanchna* which Paul feels for his 'saints in Christ Jesus who are in Philippi', which is powerfully expressive of the mutuality of Christian love, can in fact be defined as a compassionate love not *felt* by Christ but rather *given* by him.[21] It is 'of Christ Jesus' in the sense that it is the condition which marks the change from ordinary human relations to the ecclesial mutuality which takes place *in* Christ.[22]

The inner animation of the embodiment that we call Christian living is therefore this visceral element of being wholly given over into the other through a compassionate care or concern for the well-being of the other in the concrete circumstances of daily living. Following the Pauline model, we can say that it is that movement of caring which establishes our relations as truly *Christian* relations and as our incorporation into the fragmentation and issue of the universalised body of Christ. But that love is characterised also as being universal, turned away from itself, always communicated for and intercepted by a third. Christian love is therefore not the love only for other Christians but is realised most fully as Trinitarian

---

19. Spinoza identifies the corporal basis of compassion in the *Ethics*, vol. III, P27 (*Benedict de Spinoza, Ethics*, trans. Edwin Curley, p. 84).
20. Phil. 1:8.
21. Phil. 1:1.
22. Other important texts which express the role of compassion as *splanchna* in the Christian life are Phil. 2:1–2, 1 Pet. 3:8, Col. 3:12, 1 Jn 3:17 and Eph. 4:32.

love where the other is external to the community of the beloved. This is a generative and creative love, which calls forth and identifies the other as an equal inheritor of this love and hence as one who is called also to give of this love, beyond the beloved, into the community of those who are not yet called. The circulation of this compassionate love is the unfolding of the body of Christ as the element, or environment, in which we live out our lives. It is the animating spirit of the integration of our bodies into the world as Christ's body, and is the fulfilment of our embodied life through the realisation of Christ's body within us.

The dancing body

Dance is not something we are inclined much to do in our church services in the Western world, unlike some other cultures. But there is nevertheless something of great importance in the theme of dance which captures what we might otherwise not easily notice. Dance is the movement of excess. It is what we do in extremes of joy and celebration. As such, it is uniquely suited to be the embodied expression of our Eucharistic sense of being received by and of receiving the divine bodiliness. If Eucharistic semiotics is one of cosmic pleroma and overwhelming, then part of the appropriate human response is the rhythm of dancing: a giving over of the self into an embodied and joyful act of corporate worship.

But there is a further reason why we need to talk about the body of celebration and dance following a discussion of the compassionate body. The compassion of God, in which we participate and to which we are called, is fundamentally also an excess of life. Compassion *is* the divine creativity. It is the outflowing of the inner Trinitarian life in the formation of world. Human compassion is a sacrament or sign of the joyful, life-giving creativity of God. In human compassion we see the divine compassion. We cannot discuss compassion, therefore, without at the same time talking of celebration and joy. The 'raising up' of Jesus which was his crucifixion, according to the Gospel of John, was at the same time his being 'raised into glory'. The one implies the other. Although we cannot see that identity for much of the time in our lives, it nevertheless remains the case that the compassionate body is a dancing body: one overflowing with an excess of life.

Although dancing at the Eucharist may not be something that many Westerners do, it remains a deeply symbolic motif which must find its place here. In 2 Samuel we read of King David who brings the Ark back to Jerusalem, and we are told that he 'danced before the Lord with all his

might' and that he was 'leaping and dancing before the Lord'.[23] Michal re-
buked him for showing his nakedness 'like any vulgar fellow', but David
defends himself in terms which suggest that dancing is a form of humility which disrupts the privileges of social rank and brings equality before
the Lord.

The eschatological body

The ceaselessly generative processes of self-replication, which are the life
of the human body, are intimately connected with the imagination. It is
the imagination which allows us to move from what we already know to
what might be; and human identity is itself incurably nomadic and projec-
tural. We habitually imagine ourselves into new forms of embodied identity and lived contexts of self-realisation. We make judgements on the basis of 'what if . . . ?', and hold the futures of others, and our own futures,
constantly in mind as we deal with present realities. The imagination is in
particular the faculty which betrays our own incompleteness and restless-
ness as the developing personality and life's possibilities interact, in new
permutations of self-realisation.[24]

The imagination is itself generated from within the life of the senses as
we apply remembered sense impressions within new contexts and as we
extend or subvert what we already know of the world around us. There
is therefore a particular difficulty with the operation of the imagination
in the religious sphere, since God is not an object in the world. As we
saw in chapter 1, the pre-modern constructions of the heavenly were effectively extensions of the earthly realm, conceived within the framework
of an Aristotelian account of space and time, and the significant marker
to set that supernal reality off from the empirical world was that of distance itself (the heavens were simply a very long way away). We inherit that
tradition which is encoded in our sacred and spiritual texts, in our religious architecture and even in the liturgy, as a form of metaphor by which
we speak of and conceive the heavenly. It is in particular the metaphors
of light and height that surround our speaking of the transcendental.
But these are at the same time tropes which are so conventional as to
be what Paul Ricoeur calls 'dead metaphors' which lack 'invention' and

---

23. 2 Sam. 6:12 and 16.
24. There is an abundant literature on the imagination; see Garrett Green, *Imagining God:
Theology and the Religious Imagination* (Grand Rapids: Eerdmans, 1989), Richard Kearney, *The
Wake of the Imagination* (London: Routledge, 1998) and Ray L. Hart, *Unfinished Man and the
Imagination* (republished by Louisville, Ky.: Westminster John Knox Press, 2001).

'a new extension of meaning'.[25] They do not 'tell us something new about reality', but function rather as ciphers which simply signal reference to transcendence.[26] It is impossible to construct a renewed scriptural cosmology, as I have sought to do in these pages, without addressing the question of the kind of eschatological imaginary which might derive from this cosmology and which might open up new possibilities for an imaginative reconceptualisation of a redeemed heaven and earth.

Both light and height and their respective semantic fields reflect a sensorium which privileges sight and space. It is within the coordinates of sight and space that we have our ordinary empirical experience of the world. The visible exists as a field around us, showing a world through which we move. One of the principal difficulties with this kind of emphasis in our imagery of heaven and the heavenly is that it is so closely tied to our experience of the empirical world. But we know that heaven cannot be an extension of this world; it cannot be another universe juxtaposed with (or 'above') the one we ordinarily know. Heaven has to be something other which cannot be constructed as another 'somewhere', for that is only to make it a replication of the world of space and time that we ordinarily know. We may well feel also that heaven has to be itself folded within the earth, that is, a dimension not in opposition to the world, but at the world's root. Can there be another way of imagining heaven which does not extrapolate its spatiality from light and the visual, which are so foundational for our experience of the empirical world?

One way in which we might begin to do this is through reflecting again on the role of the divine voice in the creation. Following a series of scriptural texts, I have argued in previous chapters that the world itself, from a biblical perspective, issues from the divine speaking and is the product of divine breath as when a human author writes down their own words in a text. The Word and Spirit of God animate the world, and the Incarnation of the speaking Word is the repristination, or redemption, of the world-text by the divine voice, manifest now as the unity of originary Voice and cosmic text in the sacrificial personhood of Jesus Christ. If we are to follow this theme through, then we may well feel that the great emphasis upon heaven in terms of visibility, space and light in Christian tradition is as much reflective of non-biblical modes of thinking as it is of biblical ones. The proposition that it is the human voice which stands in

---

25. Paul Ricoeur, *Interpretation Theory* (Fort Worth: Texas Christian University Press, 1976), p. 52.
26. Ibid., p. 53.

closest proximity to the originary divine speaking, and thus to the heavenly, would seem to be in stark contrast with most of the traditional modes of imaging the spatiality of heaven. And yet this is the subtle logic of the scriptural cosmology which is proposed here. Human speaking, as I have argued, represents matter that is so saturated with meaning, personhood and address that it is no longer perceptible to us as *sound* but only as *voice*. And voice is always personal, so that we can say that in human speaking matter is transformed into personal presence. I would like to argue that it is here, in the domain of the human voice, that we must look for an alternative account of spatiality and of the heavenly.

Merleau-Ponty has drawn our attention to the way in which music can release a sense of spaciousness which contrasts with the confinement of the auditorium.[27] In the traditions of the Church we find many different kinds of musical space, but it is singing and the human voice which above all give artistic representation in the liturgical life of the Church to its experience of the heavenly. Music is itself the purity of the world. Denys Turner has argued that if poetry foregrounds the materiality of the linguistic sign, then music is the highest stage of purified semiosis: 'at one and the same time absolutely material and all meaning, matter entirely alive with meaning'.[28] Music has a grammar, yet, unlike language, may evoke but cannot refer. Music is language reduced and purified to its most formal characteristics. Thus, in our present terminology, music is the finest text which we can know. It is textuality itself made present in sound that has become 'all meaning'. Perhaps that is why Turner can say with McCabe that 'music is the body trying to become language' or, as he prefers it, 'music is all body but precisely as language'. The text that is body and the text that is music, as sound purified into meaning, stand in a close analogical relation to each other, which again may be why the power of music over us is so physical and why it comes to us with such immediacy. And perhaps there is something of the *angelic* body in musical form: refinement, grace and an immediacy of knowing. This would suggest an absence of location: another kind of spatiality.

Indeed, where the voices are pure, it is easy to describe the choral singing of the Church as 'angelic'. We may have in mind not only the harmony of musical form, but also the words which are sung; for as Thomas Aquinas tells us, angels may not have voices but they do have a kind of

27. Maurice Merleau-Ponty, *Phenomenology of Perception* (London: Routledge and Kegan Paul, 1962), p. 222.
28. 'Faith and Reason' (unpublished paper).

interior speech with which they proclaim the praise of God and teach others, bringing light and understanding.[29] By virtue of the words of proclamation that are sung in the choral traditions of the Church, we can say that the semiotic purity of the world released by musical form is illumined as being both cosmic and grounded in the self-dispossessing unity of the Trinity. In this 'angelic' music, meaning which transforms matter, matter as meaning, 'Eucharistically' (thus also Turner) manifests the ground of the world as a circularity of life, love and meaning.

Perhaps, then, it is here that we can catch the sense of a new spatiality, one which derives not from flat surfaces and plain lines, but from the relationality inherent in the singing voice, intensified through harmonies, antiphons and counterpoint. There may be a kind of architecture of the voice, which carries to us where human beings sing 'angelically' in both form and spirit, in praise and proclamation. That architecture, then, would not be something posited as being over and against the world, still less 'beyond' it. Rather, it would be a spatiality of relation which arises from within the body of the world and which comes to the fore, as a new dimensionality, through 'angelic' singing. Nor would it be a relationality which is constrained by the spatiality of the world. Rather, it would itself constitute a new environment, another spatiality of the Spirit, which grows from the life which exists *between* those who love: as a heavenly space, a Christ-shaped space of love.

Conclusion

In this chapter I have attempted to develop further the cosmic structural dynamic which is given with the idea of author and text, and of their relation. I have suggested that this relation can take the place held by analogy in traditional metaphysics, whereby the relation between God and world was understood in terms of a causality which granted some degree of likeness between the cause and the caused. In the case of the author–text relation, we must speak not of likeness but rather of communicative implication: the author is implicated in his or her text, which seeks to communicate – albeit in terms heavily accented by interpretation – the authorial presence. Texts understood in this way are formed in the will to communicate with another, and the world, taken as a text, becomes a form of divine communication which bodies forth the divine expressivity.

---

29. *ST* I, q. 107, a. 2 corpus and a. 3 corpus.

A second significant idea has been that texts are like bodies. In the first place, they are voice-bearing and extend the reach of the speaker's voice beyond the intimate circle of those who can hear that voice. But they do so of course at the price of transposing the signs from an aural medium to a written and visual one. That movement into the materiality of the written sign signals a further parallel between body and text, for both bodies and texts are material entities in which signification attains such an intensity that the material basis of the sign becomes effectively invisible. We struggle to perceive the materiality of words, and are deeply shocked by the sight of the pure materiality of a dead human body.

This analogical relation between bodies and texts can be extended into the cosmic realm through the metaphor of the Primal Text as the ground of the world which has been developed here. There is accordingly an implication that the world itself, conceived as *text*, somehow replicates or reproduces that divine body. As text, the world bears its Author's voice, which speaks for others, whose speaking indeed is the *creating* of others. The final move, as we have seen, is that the voice-bearing body of Jesus Christ is both that of the Creator and the creation, and becomes in the sacrifice of the Cross truly one with the fabric of the world. The impossible realisation of that dialectic is manifest in the fragmentation and pouring out of his body wholly given for us, and its universalisation, through the resurrection and the ascension, as made one with the world.

But a further point in this chapter has been that that universalisation of the body of Christ sets up further reflexes and transformations through the Eucharistic celebration which affect the formation of our own embodied life in its personal and social manifestations. This is now inwardly shaped by the self-giving of Christ, so that in our ecclesial embodiedness we are compassionate and celebratory. In and through our bodies we enter the radical unity of the Church and relate to the world with care and concern, giving thanks to God in God's creative and regenerating Spirit.

In the final section of this chapter I argue for a new eschatological imagination based not upon the metaphors of sight and space, but upon a Trinitarian spatiality which can come into view in the choral traditions of the Church. This intuits heaven as a potentiality *within* the earthly and not above or beyond it. It appears to offer us a home in which the world itself is wholly conformed to the structure of God's speaking voice, 'heard' at the creation, inscribed as world and as biblical text, and uttered again for us, redemptively, through the Spirit in the death and resurrection of Jesus Christ.

9

Eucharistic reasoning

L'acte de penser ne découle pas d'une simple possibilité naturelle. Il
est, au contraire, la seule creation veritable. La creation, c'est la genèse
de l'acte de penser dans la pensée elle-même … Penser, c'est toujours
interpreter, c'est-à-dire expliquer, développer, déchiffrer, traduire une
signe. Traduire, déchiffrer, développer sont la forme de la création
pure.

The act of thinking does not proceed from a simple natural possibility;
on the contrary, it is the only true creation. Creation is the genesis of
the act of thinking within thought itself. To think is always to
interpret – to explicate, to develop, to decipher, to translate a sign.
Translating, deciphering, developing are the form of pure creation.

Gilles Deleuze, *Proust et Signes*

In the first section of this book we saw that reason itself in the pre-modern
world was understood to be an integral part of the world as created. The
detaching of reason from its matrix in a creation-centred cosmology itself played a crucial role in the evolution of the modern, and has become
a condition of modern living. Theology has struggled to realise its potential from within the parameters laid down by secular reason. It is only with
the rise of Barthianism and its aftermath that alternatives arose, which
wrested theology away from secular reason by denying its purchase in
thinking ordered to the divine freedom. In this final chapter I argue for a
perspective upon reason which is neither modernist nor Barthian in kind,
but which is predicated upon the distinctively Christian semiotics which I
have attempted to outline in the preceding chapters, a semiotics which understands the divine presence to be a cosmic embodiment which manifests
as overwhelming and calling. This is the root of the world and is the mark

of its createdness. This pragmatist semiotic therefore gives expression to a deeply dialectical relation of difference and oneness. We are both one with the world, as part of the created order, and are other than the world, to the extent that we possess knowledge and awareness of the world. Consciousness divides us from that with which we are most intimately one.

This condition of separateness and unity means, therefore, that there is a fissure, ambiguity or intersection at the very centre of thought which can be called the division between subjectivity and objectivity, self and other, cognition and world. This primal place of initiative and response, of receiving and giving, is the finitude of thought itself. Without that pulsation thought cannot be, but with it, thought cannot be anything other than that which is drawn of necessity time and again to inquire into its own limitations and possibilities. The predicament of thought is its own implication in what is other to it, in what we term the real: an implication which repeatedly presents itself to thought but also eludes it. How do we know what is real and what is thought, or the role of thought in the construction of the real? How do we think the distinction between what is real and what appears to be real? How do we think what it is to think? How do we feel, or know, the real?

The bifurcation at the centre of thought is no mere academic conundrum. The ground of human self-awareness and self-possession is determined in its own self-definition, and thus self-realisation, by the way that we seek to answer these questions. Do we control our experiences, or are they in control of us? Are we victims of the world or regents of it? Does that which is other than us in our experience abuse us, threaten us, or enrich us? How firm is our grasp of it? Do we understand and order the otherness which is endemic to thought? Or are we perpetual victims of the surplus which exceeds our capacity to reason and command so that we are always on the point of being swamped by it, as if by a sea in storm? In its history philosophy has never moved far from the fundamental questions spawned by the unity of mind and world. Indeed, in some deep-seated sense philosophy *is* the asking of these kinds of questions, since the inquiry into knowing and knowing of the real is an attempt to clarify the ground of all knowing.

Historical reason

In the preceding chapters I have given an account of the Eucharist as the place in which the pre-conceptual unity of subject and object comes into view as the divine body, the Primal Text, which is the ground of the world. I analysed the response to that disclosure not in terms of objective knowing, but rather as a transformative embodiment: a new, compassionate and celebratory way of being in the world. But questions have to be raised about what kind of reasoning is supported by that changed way of being in the world, and how it relates to some of the major types of reasoning which form part of our historical inheritance. The Eucharistic mind must learn the practice of resting with the difficulty; it must fight its own instincts and deepest practices of slipping away into schemes of knowing which cocoon the fissure so that all becomes recognisable and familiar and susceptible to control. From its earliest days we can see that philosophy itself can in respects become just such an exercise in gaining release from the excess of otherness which is the condition of all thought; and which is the impotence of thought before the unimaginability of the world.

The rationalist spirit

The first evasiveness of thought before the primal otherness of perception is a rationalist one. In his discussion of the ground of demonstration and the nature of human knowing, Aristotle points to the role of prior knowledge in the establishing of any new knowledge about the world. Only by building upon what we already know, with certainty, can we securely progress in our attempt to understand the causes of things, in which alone human science is founded. If an infinite regress is to be avoided, then, we must at some point grasp the truth of the principles which – whether as propositions or terms – form the ground of our reasoning, and we must do so without demonstration or deduction. We must simply comprehend them with immediacy. But in the discussion of *nous*, which is just such a faculty of immediate knowing, we can see what is a primary tension within rationalism. Aristotle's uncertainty as to what exactly *nous* might be and where it comes from and his difficulty in explaining the processes of its operations are matched by his affirmations of the certainty of the knowledge that it delivers.[1] Indeed, the capacity of *nous* to generate certain knowledge is what distinguishes it from scientific knowledge, practical wisdom and philosophic wisdom, all of which deal with matters which could be otherwise.[2] Only the *archai* or 'principles' are unchangeable and only *nous* as

---

1. On the ambiguity of the origins of *nous*, see *De anima*, III, 5 and *De generatione animalium*, III, 5.
2. *Nicomachean Ethics*, VI, 6.

'intuition' or 'comprehension' is the certain grasp of them. It is this kind of certainty which grounds our knowledge of the world, both in terms of a comprehension of prior principles and of the ends that guide our actions.[3]

But if Aristotle is convinced of the general validity of the propositional and definitional reasoning that constitutes our ordinary knowledge of the world and which must therefore be based upon comprehension of the *archai*, then at the same time he is unable to give a satisfactory account of the way in which we grasp the *archai*.[4] In other words, Aristotle's view that there is a general match between mind and world is driven by the conviction that it cannot be otherwise, since that would leave the door open to infinite regress and radical scepticism. Once a feeling of the way things ought to be, predicated perhaps on a general conviction that we do by and large possess authentic knowledge of the world, is allowed to shape our reasonings about perception, then reason itself can rapidly take on a certain subjective and even mythological colour. The long tradition of commentary on Aristotle which proposed the divine origins of the intellect (looking back to texts such as *De anima*, III, 5 and *De generatione animalium*, III, 5), was simply the exploitation of an impulse that was already present in Aristotle's philosophy.[5]

The spirit of rationalism exhibits different characteristics at various points in the philosophical tradition, but its common feature is the supposition that rational methods of ordering and controlling the ground of experience are *given* with experience and have an immediate purchase in reality itself. For Locke it is the 'ideas' which present with an immediacy to the mind from within the world and form the elements of knowing, while for Descartes it is the mind itself, in its own self-possession, which constitutes the unassailably real. In the twentieth century, Frege argued in the Preface to the *Begriffsschrift* that his motivation in developing a logical-numerical system of sequential ordering was to overcome the 'inadequacy of language' and thus to set up a way of conceiving of relations and of the world which was 'independent of the particularity of things'. Only by this means could the chain of reasonings be tested in 'the most reliable way'. Frege intends that his *Begriffsschrift* will fulfil the 'task of

---

3. *Nicomachean Ethics*, VI, 11.
4. *Posterior Analytics*, I, 3.
5. See for instance the statement from the *Protreptikos* B, 110 (quoted in Werner Marx, *Introduction to Aristotle's Theory of Being as Being* (The Hague: Martinus Nijhoff, 1977), p. 10): 'for our intellect is god'.

philosophy' which is 'to break the power of words over the human mind'.[6] What Frege's system represents is the determination that a particular system of thought which offers itself for comprehensive tests of validity shall become the master language for assessing empirical thinking. It becomes the new code which establishes the 'conceptual content' of things. But the fact that a particular logical system enjoys a verificationary transparency and power does not mean that it necessarily accurately reflects the nature of the real. The act of translation from empirical, language-based forms of thinking to logical structures which are 'independent of particulars' may create illusory relations between itself and the real which are as significant as are 'the illusions that through the use of language often almost unavoidably arise concerning the relations of concepts'.[7] Freeing thought 'from the taint of ordinary linguistic means of expression' may in fact be a way of avoiding or eluding the real on account of the failure of the real to match our longing for a fully transparent conceptual scheme.[8] Frege's project embodies something which is integral to the rationalist enterprise, which can be summed up as its foundational presupposition that reality *ought to be* and therefore really *is* susceptible to those systems of reasoning which give the human observer the fullest and most trustworthy sense of being in control. For all its appeal to calm and order, rationalism can sometimes be a heroic mode of thinking.

The romantic sublime

The philosophy of the sublime substantially begins in the Western tradition with the work *Peri Hypsous* (*On the Sublime*) traditionally – though inaccurately – attributed to 'Dionysius or Longinus', or alternatively 'Dionysius Longinus', in the earliest extant manuscript, and dating from some point in the early centuries of the Common Era.[9] With the translation by Boileau in 1674, this work exercised a profound influence on aesthetics and early romantic philosophy across Europe until the mid nineteenth century. The context of the discussion of *hupsos*, or 'height', is the matter of literary style, but the author's focus lies primarily on the *effects* of style. Indeed, there is much in his work that is against *technē* as the acquisition

---

6. Gottlob Frege, *Conceptual Notation and Related Articles* (Oxford: Clarendon Press, 1972), pp. 104–6.

7. Ibid.

8. Ibid.

9. These forms of attribution can be found in the tenth-century codex Parisinus 2036 which is the archetype of all existing manuscripts. See D. A. Russell, ed., *'Longinus' On the Sublime* (Oxford: Oxford University Press, 1964), pp. xxii–xxx.

of specific skills and in favour of the incalculable fertility of 'transcendent genius', which like 'the wonderful' 'always prevails over what is persuasive and pleasant, shattering the heart's composure'.[10] Unlike the careful modulations of technical craft, the effects of genius are of the moment and 'scatter the subjects like a bolt of lightning'.[11] The 'greatness of genius . . . is a gift rather than a thing acquired'.[12] In contrast with rationalism, where the emphasis is upon control, Longinus' text constantly draws out the extent to which the human observer or recipient is *overwhelmed* in the generation of sublime feelings and 'noble passions', since that which is 'wonderful and of great genius . . . exercises domination and irresistibly draws every hearer'.[13] Drawing upon Plato and Stoic sources, Longinus links the nobility of our response to the 'irresistible love of whatever is great and stands to us as the more divine to the less'. We are drawn not to the detailed and small scale, but rather to the 'extraordinary'. And not even 'the whole of the universe' is adequate to the possibilities of our mental scope.[14]

What we find here, therefore, is a privileging of certain kinds of perceptions, which are 'divine' and 'noble' precisely because they possess a disruptive grandeur that escapes our measure. The privileging of what appears 'immoderate' and 'immeasurable' (my terms) is at the same time an aestheticisation of it as the 'sublime': a notion with deep obligations to the realm of formal art but which also resonates powerfully with respect to a general epistemology. There is an alignment here, then, between the real, as that which transcends boundaries, and the extremes of an aesthetic response – as transport and ennobling delight. The real does not address us in the position where we are, or particularise us as its *interpreter*, but rather overwhelms our faculties and, in a sense, reduces our response to that of pure aesthetical transport.

The most articulate and sophisticated advocate of Romantic epistemology is Friedrich Schiller, in whose work *Über das Erhabene* (*On the Sublime*), published in 1801, it takes on its classic outline. Schiller sets out his understanding of nature against the background of determinism as the domain of forces which constrain the human spirit. Humanity can either meet the 'violence' of nature with violence, 'realistically', as in technology and the

---

10. Quotations from Benedict Einarson, trans., *Longinus on the Sublime*, Chicago: Kenaga Press, 1945 (slightly emended), 1.

11. *On the Sublime*, 1.

12. Ibid., 9.

13. Ibid., 1.

14. Ibid., 35.

physical sciences, or it can remove itself from the reach of nature 'idealis-tically' through an act of resignation, parallel to a religious submission to the will of God. What interests Schiller at this point is the capacity of the self to discover within itself a source of transcendental freedom which is its liberation from the dictates of nature and the senses. The emergence of that inner freedom, however, is concomitant with our perception of nature not as a field of constraint but in a quite different way: as the 'sublime'. The sublime represents an intensification of the beautiful and it 'affords us an egress from the sensuous world in which the beautiful would gladly hold us forever captive'.[15] In the perception of the 'sensuous infinite . . . we are able to think what the senses can no longer apprehend and the under-standing can no longer comprehend'.[16] By looking upon the infinite and lawless chaos of nature, which formerly appalled us, in free contempla-tion, we can 'discover in the flood of appearances something abiding in our own being . . . then the savage bulk of nature about us begins to speak quite another language to our heart; and the relative grandeur outside us is the mirror in which we perceive the absolute grandeur within ourselves'.[17] At this point Schiller adopts an emphatically anti-rationalist position in his argument that such a chaotic 'press of appearances' constitutes a 'strik-ing image for pure reason, which finds in just this incoherence of nature the depiction of her own independence of natural conditions'.[18] We should not focus on the *explanation* of nature, therefore, but take 'this incompre-hensibility itself as a principle of judgement'.[19] The highest expression of the sublime in nature, for Schiller, actually occurs in sublime art, which is a free representation of it, or better a representation in freedom. As a vehi-cle of the sublime, the art of genius can operate within human culture as an instrument of education to make available to humanity more broadly its possibilities as a liberated and liberating way of looking upon the world.

Many of the same themes occur in Schiller which were already present in Longinus, though in the German they are intertwined with highly so-phisticated philosophical material arising, in the main, from his reaction to the work of Kant. The controlling power of rationality, for Schiller, is in effect our captivity to the senses and to the field of determinism; but

15. Friedrich Schiller, *Über das Erhabene*, in *Sämtliche Werke*, vol. v (Munich: Winkler Verlag, 1975), p. 222 (quotations, with slight emendations, from Julius A. Elias, *Schiller. Naïve and Sentimental Poetry and On the Sublime* (New York: Frederick Ungar Publ., 1966), here p. 201).
16. *Über das Erhabene*, in Schiller, *Sämtliche Werke*, vol. v, p. 219 (Elias, *Schiller*, p. 199).
17. Ibid., p. 223 (Elias, *Schiller*, p. 203).
18. Ibid., p. 225 (Elias, *Schiller*, p. 206).
19. Ibid., p. 226 (Elias, *Schiller*, p. 207).

where we learn to look upon the immensity of nature and natural forces *with an aesthetic gaze*, we are liberated from them and discover 'the pure daemon within'.[20] This is, however, a freedom which is outside the domain of the world and the senses; that indeed is its defining structure as freedom. The world is not a sign at this point but rather a sign that vanishes under the weight of the immensity of that which it signifies. In *Über naïve und sentimentale Dichtung* (*On Naïve and Sentimental Poetry*), Schiller gives us an account of the structure of his – Romantic – semiotics. It occurs in his discussion of the genius, whose utterances, like 'a single felicitous stroke of the brush', are in stark contrast to the 'understanding of the schools' which 'crucifies the words and concepts [of language] upon the cross of grammar and logic'. If to the schools 'the sign remains forever heterogeneous and alien to the thing signified, to him [the genius] language springs as by some inner necessity out of thought, and is so at one with it that even beneath the corporeal frame the spirit appears as if laid bare. It is precisely this mode of expression in which *the sign disappears completely in the thing signified*, and in which language, while giving expression to a thought, yet leaves it exposed where otherwise it cannot be represented without simultaneously concealing it.'[21]

For all the dramatic differences of values and perspectives, there is something alike in Schiller's 'transcendence' of the sign and Frege's conviction that the inadequacy and illusions of ordinary language have to be replaced by a *Begriffsschrift*. The trajectory of both is to bypass the sign and to establish some direct relation between the self, or mind, and reality: the one through a sublime, aesthetic, quasi-divine vision and the other through the 'trustworthiness' of a transparent, verifiable and, in a sense, 'supernatural' language of reasoning. Both can be characterised as ways of eluding the real, for they leave behind the function of the sign as integral to the communication of the real, while – paradoxically – also recognising the extent to which the sign is ordinarily part of our empirical experience. Both are therefore corrective systems which seek to replace the signifying function of ordinary language use with some other instrument. In the case of Frege, that instrument is a new speech of logical symbols, predicated upon numerical reasoning, which is transparent in its internal validity though less transparent in the validity of its relation to the world.

20. Ibid., p. 229 (Elias, *Schiller*, p. 210).
21. *Über naïve und sentimentale Dichtung*, in *Sämtliche Werke*, vol. v, pp. 444–5 (Elias, *Schiller*, p. 98); my italics.

In the case of Schiller it is a newly constructed sign, which is the product of genius and the creative imagination, and which has so entered in, or has become so expressive of, nature as to be now indistinguishable from it. Indeed, what unites both systems of thinking, despite their apparent polarity, is the fusion of the first element in C. S. Peirce's triad (the self/mind) with the third (the object signified) at the cost of the second (the sign itself). In both cases the sign is refigured in such a way as no longer to be authentically a point of mediation between the mind and its objects, and thus no longer to be an invitation to an act of interpretation, itself constitutive of the condensation of the real, on the part of the human observer.

Transfiguration and reason

The account I gave in chapter 7 of a Eucharistic, or Christian, semiotics, was one which had at its centre a full and equal reciprocity between all three of the Peircean elements. The advent of the 'real presence', or the 'full presence of the real', was not at the cost of the sign but was rather the comprehensive realisation of the sign's own signifying function, which remains integral to the epiphany of presence. That presence was an eschatological one in that it contains within itself a past, both historical and originary, a future made present in the moment and a presence which is itself wholly emptied out into both remembrance and expectation. The three elements of the triad in the transformation of the Eucharistic moment become the elements of a new temporality constructed as future-presence, presence-past and presence which so extends beyond the horizons of the empirical as to be no longer capable of being grasped in any sense through the operations of mind or reason but only received with a responsive and embodied passivity, expressed as worship, praise, thanksgiving and celebration.

In chapter 8, I argued that the Incarnation entails an intensification of the meaning of the world in a new and heightened unity of sign, referent and interpreter. This unity finds expression in the body of Christ which on the one hand is so saturated with meaning as divine presence that it is broken up and poured out into the world, for the sake of the world, and on the other transforms and transfigures the community of the Church as those who encounter the body in the world and, in an intensively sacramental way, in the Eucharistic celebration. The point we come to now is the question as to what kind of reasoning it is that a Christian realism, predicated on a Eucharistic semiotics, supports and sustains.

Two issues need to be clarified before proceeding to address this question, however. The first turns on the nature of 'reason' itself, for it is one of those words which defies close definition, while the second concerns the question of sources: what sources shall we consider for an examination of Christian reasoning? From one perspective, 'reason' is linked with 'meaning', 'understanding' and 'logic', though not necessarily in ways that are consistent and precise. The connotation here is that the proper use of reason gives access to valid knowledge; reason is the cognitive interface between self and world. The right use of 'reason' is the guarantee that the contours of our thinking are both internally consistent and correspond to the way the world appears to be. The failure to take note of the way the world is, is a failure in our reasoning and reflects a descent into an ideological, deluded or simply mistaken frame of mind. Reason in this sense has a proximity to science and to scientific method.

From another perspective, however, 'reason' is intimately linked with 'actions' and 'goals', and with the polemics that follow from these. Reason – the rational analysis of a situation – justifies a course of action within a specific situation, and is the sign that self, action and world form a coherent unity. We can call the former use of reason 'theoretical' and the latter 'practical', and both will have to be borne in mind as we consider the shape of Christian reasoning in a world of God's making.

With respect to sources, I have – throughout this book – wished to argue that the fundamental paradigm of reality which is made manifest in the Eucharist actually belongs more generally to Christian tradition. It is certainly the case, for instance, that the Wisdom tradition also offers rich possibilities for an account of the real and the kind of reasoning that is predicated upon it.[22] But I wish at this point to focus upon the pericope of the transfiguration, as offering a view of reality which is not specifically tied to a Catholic understanding of the Eucharistic transformation of the elements, but which points forward nevertheless to the Passion and resurrection of Christ. The interpretation I shall offer here is one of 'thick' theological description in that I set this event in the lives of Jesus, Peter, James and John in the context of the theme of creation through the Word as we find it in John 1:3, Colossians 1:15–16, 1 Corinthians 8:6 and Hebrews

---

22. See the discussion by Paul S. Fiddes, for instance, in his 'The Quest for a Place which Is "Not a Place": the Hiddenness of God and the Presence of God', in Oliver Davies and Denys Turner, eds., *Silence and the Word: Negative Theology and Incarnation* (Cambridge: Cambridge University Press, 2002), pp. 35–60.

1:2–4, none of which can possibly have been in the mind of the Synoptic writers upon whose accounts we rely.

Theoretical reasoning

The Sinai motif of transfiguring glory is present in the opening phrase 'after six days' which was the length of time that the cloud of glory rested on the mountain, prior to Moses hearing the voice of God.[23] Moses was accompanied by Aaron, Nadab and Abihu, while it is Peter, James and John who accompany Jesus as he climbs the mountain to pray. In Exodus the stress lies upon the singularity of Moses from the outset, who alone 'draws near' God. Jesus is also set apart from his disciples, for he is transfigured before them, but at the same time Moses and Elijah are with him in glory. Their intimate speaking with him recalls Moses' own speaking with God.[24] There is the suggestion here that it is now Jesus who stands in the same relation to Moses (and Elijah) as once did YHWH, the God of creation. But we can note that Moses and Elijah share in the divine glory in a way that was not the case with Moses' companions. It is as if human nature itself has been elevated by the transfer of glory from the Father to the Son, and the foremost prophets of the old dispensation participate in that new reality.

The motif of the light of glory, which points forward to the death and resurrection of Christ, sets Jesus apart from the disciples and presents him in terms of the divine Logos through whom all things were made. We can read the transfiguration, then, as a moment in which, for the disciples, the deep reality of the world, as formed in Christ, comes into view. It is the point at which, however inchoately, Christ is identified with the *truth* of the world as the self-communication of God. And the disciples are perplexed by what they see. The evangelists use different images for communicating their confusion. They are dazzled by the radiant light that encompasses Jesus, as well as Moses and Elijah. The three disciples are 'overshadowed' by a cloud and are terrified at its darkness. Peter, who speaks for the disciples, becomes confused and states: 'Master, it is good for us to be here; let us make three dwellings, one for you, one for Moses

---

23. Matt. 17:1–13; Mk 9:2–8; Lk. 9:28–36. Luke has eight days.

24. The verb used here for 'to speak with' in all three synoptics is συλλαλέω. This is the word that is used in the Septuagint at Exod. 34:35 to translate the Mosaic *dâḇâr bᵊ*. It is also used outside this context (e.g. Isa. 7:6; Jer. 18:20; Lk. 4:36, 22:4; Acts 25:12, generally in the sense of 'confer'), although its use at Prov. 6:22 is also suggestive of the theophany on Sinai.

and one for Elijah'; Luke adds 'not knowing what he said'.[25] To the themes of intense light and darkness, and confusion of intellect in the presence of the divine, we must also add that of 'silence', which the disciples maintained when they descended from the mountain. If the transfiguration can be read as an epiphany of the real, and the discovery on the part of the disciples that the world is at root already realised and fulfilled *as the body of Christ*, then it marks also the point at which the disciples themselves begin to be taken up and transformed in their embodied existence by the embrace of God communicated in and through Christ's body.[26]

What, then, does this reading tell us about a Christian account of theoretical reason, or the way in which we most fundamentally make sense of the world? In the first place, it puts not knowing, rather than knowing, at the centre of human cognition. There is an essential sense in which not knowing is itself foundational to human understanding. Socrates' view, repeated throughout the early dialogues of Plato, is that he is indeed the wisest among men since he alone knows how little he knows. Questioning is only a possibility where our minds are open to receiving new knowledge and understanding. Understanding is dynamic not static and needs constantly to be self-questioning. Platonic dialectic, which is the struggle for a foundational knowledge which will ground right action, is predicated upon a prior recognition of our own failure to grasp in depth the nature of the world. In the modern period, Hans-Georg Gadamer is among those who have most fully articulated this position. In *Truth and Method* he argued that the act of understanding rests upon a fundamental condition of cognitive openness. In particular, he has pointed to the role of 'experience' in shaping understanding, stressing its paramountly 'negative' character. It is integral to the nature of what we 'experience' that we can be arrested and challenged by it. 'Experience' can confirm our convictions, but it can also unsettle and refute them. To be radically open to 'experience' is also to know that our most cherished beliefs can be put thereby at risk. But to shy away from 'experience' is to risk that our thinking will lose its purchase on the world. The experience of the disciples, then, is that the real imposes itself upon them in the transfiguration of Christ with such an intensity that they are forced into a condition of unknowing; nothing of their assumptions about the world is left intact by their encounter with reality.

---

25. Lk. 9:33.
26. The disciples have not yet received the Spirit, however, so they are in an intimate sense excluded from the divine reality which is communicated to them at this point.

The most rigorous form of human knowing, based upon practices of self-questioning and exposure to 'experience', are the experimental sciences. But although these prioritise the value of 'not knowing' and openness to correction, they do not in the main share another important aspect of Christian theoretical reasoning, which is its pragmatism. Scientific understanding is in general a kind of comprehension in which human subjectivity is reduced to the point of virtual eradication. With the exception of certain rare cases, the scientific observer stands outside the domain of what is known. In the transfiguration narrative, however, Peter and the other apostles are not simply expunged by the divine presence nor are they merely external observers of it. Although Peter speaks confusedly, ineptly proposing the building of booths for what are ethereal, glorified figures, he prefaces his remarks with the comment 'Master, it is good for us to be here.' However strange this might seem in the flow of the narrative, it is a powerfully pragmatic statement to the extent that it affirms human participation in the disclosure that is taking place. Human beings, represented by the disciples, belong to the revealing of the divine reality: we are not extraneous to it but are rather integral, as interpreters, to the divine manifestation.[27]

The disclosure of the real, then, which is implicit in the transfiguration, stands in a close relation to the theme not only of a heuristic of not knowing but also to an account of discipleship. In all three Synoptic versions, it is preceded by Peter's confession of Jesus' Messiahship and the teaching that following Christ entails a life of radical self-denial. If we read the transfiguration as a Christian paradigm of the real, which resonates with the 'Socratic ignorance' at the heart of modern scientific method, then we need to add to scientific reasoning the sense of reverence and awe that attends the disclosure of the truth of the world. Scientific knowledge alone may not adequately reflect this model, which entails also a God-centred,

---

27. Indeed, in the light of this, it is possible to regard Peter's subsequent comment about the building of booths as being less incoherent than might first appear. If Peter identifies in the transfigured body of Jesus, and in the prophets who share his glory, the presence of the divine *kabod*, then his remark may spring from the deep Jewish instinct to provide a place of dwelling for God's glory. It was this that motivated the construction of the tent of meeting, the Ark of the Covenant and subsequently the Temple. Perhaps then the 'building of the booths' is another way of affirming the role of human interpretation at this point. To 'build a booth' is to adopt an interpretative stance which has immediate practical consequences of work and labour. But this particular interpretative stance is itself off-centre, so overwhelming is the communication of a divine presence. In this case the *kabod* already has a dwelling place, which is the body of Jesus and which, following the events at Jerusalem, will finally become the world.

human relationship with the real, and it must be complemented with a more complete sense of the human observer, or scientist, as one who works fundamentally within a context of values. There is a case for a deep-seated respect for the nature of the reality that is disclosed, wonder at its complexity, and humility before it. Further, it is important that those who work in scientific research remain aware and self-questioning about the technological developments which may follow from advances in knowledge.

A third corrective element in the paradigm of theoretical reasoning which the transfiguration as a model of reality supports concerns the apophatic or negative moment in Christian theology. The intense light, darkness, confusion of intellect and silence which befall the disciples on the mountain top (Mt Tabor according to tradition) are the common themes of the classical Christian apophatic tradition, which does in fact look back to the Transfiguration as one of its chief texts. The tendency has been for commentators to read this passage as offering a paradigm of the mystical vision of God, which is to say, a radically alternative perception of God to that of the world. The transfiguration need not, however, be seen as marking an ascent away from the world into a knowledge of divine self-communication through the Incarnation. It can be seen rather as an anticipatory insight into the realisation of the divine unity with the world which will come with the resurrection and ascension of Christ. To this extent, therefore, the apophatic motifs can be read as signalling a new kind of perception of the world, as God's body, and therefore a new form of embodied existence in the world on the part of the disciples. This reading of the transfiguration is to correct the tendency for mystical theology to be detached from the world; and it restores the remembrance that Christ is not beyond the world, in some place of transcendence, but is to be found *within* the world, as its divine life and meaning.

Practical reasoning

The experience of Peter, James and John at the transfiguration of Christ tells us also that the foundational human response to reality is one of worship and reverence and a prayerful attentiveness to the way in which reality as a divine self-communication entirely transcends our capacity to make sense of it, enclosing it within purely human categories. Christian reason does not close off the deep enigma of the disclosure of reality but suffers it and realises it within itself, in its fullest form as adoration and love. In other words, Christian fundamental reasoning allows itself to be shaped in its depths by the divine self-communication of the world, however difficult this may be. To say that Christian thought keeps vigil before the immensity of reality is not to say that this is its constant theme but rather that Christians need to turn time and again to this passivity before the real, which is akin to the contemplative prayer of apophatic tradition. Christians must not lose the sense of world as modality of divine presence, and must repeatedly ground their thinking in a prior posture of adoration and prayer.

But pure apophatic prayer is not a state in which many of us can remain for any length of time, and it is important to note also the ways in which ordinary discursive thinking can be structured around the basic Christian experience of reality as the body, self-communication, or overwhelming embrace of God. The pragmatism of Christian practical reasoning means that it should not be divorced from the embodied existence of the person who thinks. There can be a tendency for those who reflect on reason to set rationality apart from its locus in human living. Logic can be presented as a discrete system which stands outside culture and biography; certain kinds of questioning about meaning and truth can appear simply to be located in a domain of pure thought, outside any context and free from subjectivity of any kind.

But in so far as reason engages with the world, it inheres in ways of thinking which are incurably human, social and embodied. As we are required to make rational *judgements* about the world in which we live, personal and therefore historical subjectivity will inevitably come into play. Judgements are based on values, which are the impacted consequences of the kinds of judgements which we have made in the past; especially of course those judgements which have an ethical, or political, orientation. We develop habits of mind, or moral practices, which become our virtues or vices, just as we develop in our bodily life habitual postures or behaviour. Judgements are habit-forming and, over the course of time, are consolidated as values which are already present at every new act of judgement. These are the habituated positionings which manifest as a given within any new set of circumstances and which guide our judgement in the situation to hand. Values are thus, in a very intimate sense, locked in with our *character*, as the unity of values, which forms the bedrock of our mental and physical practices in the world, and thus of our moral disposition. Character in turn is an aspect of our sociality; our character is formed by the kind of education, in the broadest sense, which we receive and the kind of communities of which we are a part. The way we reason is therefore determined by our relations not only with the other people with whom we have formed a close connection in life but also with God through the person of Christ. The human – and divine – relationships that shape us also inform the values by which we arrive at judgements about the world.

Christian values can only be grounded in the community of the Church. As we have seen in preceding chapters, ecclesial life is substantially formed on the twin axes of celebration and compassion. As we think in ways that engage with the world, and make judgements about it, we must do so not only with thanksgiving at our sharing in the real, but also with attention to the suffering other, in whom we discern Christ – himself the face of the real – in a particularly intensive way. But the ecclesial nature of our value formation brings with it a further principle of reasoning. The Church is an antiphonal, or dialogical community. It is pluralistic at its core, and Christian reasoning must therefore be one which is shaped throughout by dialogue with other voices, both within and outside the Church. If the Christian revelation itself is triadic, then the reasoning that is predicated upon it cannot be monological but must itself embody the 'conversational' structure that is given with the Person of Christ. This is not to advocate a dialogical pluralism which undermines the power of reason to compel action, but is a guarantee that when action is decided upon it will be informed as far as possible by the many voices of those who are implicated and involved in the particular issues under discussion.

Ethical choices: a case study
The flow of reason in its Christian form is dialogical and open to the other, as it is pragmatic and embodied. Most fundamentally, it is grounded in an attentiveness before the real, which means that Christian reason must always be open to refiguring and renewal, as the real comes into view in our social and cultural contexts in new ways. For Christians, it is Christ himself, given for us and made one with the world, who most embodies this sense of the real. If Christ is the compassion of God, therefore, then Christian reasoning itself must be at its core compassionate. We must always take the effects upon others carefully into account when we deliberate upon our actions. We must be guided by principles of concern and compassion in the judgements we make about the world and about the practices of living which we shall support and those we wish to reject. In this section I wish to offer an outline of practical Christian reasoning, in which the principles of practical reasoning become manifest, in the context of a specific though by no means extraordinary situation. The character of this situation is one of ethical decision-making which – perhaps

more than any other field of practical decision-making – makes clear the particular contours of practical reasoning.

Many of us today will at some time or other face a particular conundrum as someone close to us approaches death. Advancements in medical care mean that medicine is more and more capable of supporting the bodily functions of individuals to a point beyond the end of their natural life. A particularly difficult decision must be made where the patient faces further invasive medical intervention which is uncertain in its outcome but he or she is no longer able to express, or perhaps even adequately formulate, a view on the desirability or otherwise of the treatment. On such occasions we can see a conflict between different kinds of goal-orientated, value-driven reasonings. In the first place, there is medical reasoning in which the medical staff attending the patient will have been trained. This is a way of thinking which is tuned to the preservation of life. The rationale of that reasoning is therefore one of intervention in order to preserve life as long as possible. Consequent upon that reasoning is a further way of thinking which is based on the legal obligation of medical staff to provide the fullest treatment possible. Where treatment is withheld unreasonably, the medical staff become vulnerable to a legal challenge with possible serious consequences. The medical rationale of providing all possible treatment in order to preserve life is therefore supported by a natural reasoning of self-defence whereby the medical staff may wish to reduce their potential vulnerability in law to the accusation of having failed to care for the patient adequately. It is of course the case that in many instances doctors will be aware that the medical rationale needs to be moderated where the patient is elderly and unlikely to benefit from what may be invasive treatment. But this must be considered a humane recognition of the limits of medical reasoning within particular liminal circumstances, rather than an alternative form of reasoning.

The motivations of the members of the family may also be mixed. On the one hand they may feel sadness and shock at the suffering of their close relative, while on the other they may feel concern at the possible financial and personal cost to themselves of having to care for a chronically ill relative. They may feel that there is no hope for the life of the relative concerned and may wish to see as rapid a conclusion as possible to what may be an intensely draining and traumatic time. Alternatively, they may desperately cling to the hope of a full recovery for the person they love. It is the family, of course, who are most likely to be in a position to know what the wishes of the individual concerned were, or would be likely to be, although this might in turn become a vehicle for an act of deception where there is no supporting evidence.

Friends of the patient constitute a further interest group. They do not carry the same responsibility for the patient as do the family, and are less likely to bear any costs involved or profit from an inheritance. A true friend's concern will, however, be very deep, and a friend or friends are in a good position dispassionately to safeguard the interests of the patient themselves. A further participant may be a hospital chaplain or counsellor. The concern here will be for both the patient and the relatives, but a minister of religion will bring into this situation certain general assumptions based upon a set of spiritual values. These may vary according to the tradition represented but they will tend to focus upon the sanctity of life and upon submission of the individual to the will of God.

In a situation of this kind, therefore, where the patient is not able to make a decision for themselves, diverse points of view, some relational and some professional, may come into conflict with each other. The reason for this fragmentation lies in the collapse of what we may call a more general political consensus regarding the way such decisions are arrived at. The dominant public ideology in our society is that of a Rawlsian libertarianism whereby it is the individuals themselves who hold the power to determine their own fate, within the constraints of the law. It is precisely where this function of the individual is either absent or compromised that ethical reasoning, particularly in the area of bio-ethics, becomes acutely difficult. We cannot leave it to a foetus, or a potential future clone, or indeed to an elderly and incapacitated patient to give definitive expression to their own wishes. In the absence of the conditions which make possible an application of the principles of liberal democracy, the participants will confront a vacuum, in which conventional public reason can find no real purchase. It is at this point that a Christian or other religious approach may have most to offer.

A Christian form of practical reasoning will seek to reflect the principles noted above in a way that is adapted to the situation at hand. Tomasz Okon has drawn a parallel between the situation of the medical staff who attend a dying patient in the normal course of their duties and the pericope from the Synoptic tradition which records how Simon of Cyrene, a 'passer-by', was compelled to carry the cross of Christ.[28] This reflects a truly Christian perception that the suffering of the patient is from the

---

28. Conversation with Tomasz Okon (May 2002).

point of view of the Christian professional also, or more deeply, the suffering of Christ. It also entails the recognition that the professional participants cannot avoid some degree of empathy with the suffering of the patient and of the family. This analogy serves also to locate the suffering patient at the centre of the situation, and pushes to the sidelines any additional concerns. This is consonant with the Christian commitment to place the marginalised – through disability or disadvantage – at the centre of society. It is a reminder that Christian practical reasoning is at its core compassionate, expressing an engagement with and sensitivity to each and every individual who is involved in the situation.

The collective and pluralistic character of Christian reasoning can be expressed in open discussion of what the patient's own wishes would be. Christian values to do with the sanctity of life but also with the naturalness of death need to be informed by the knowledge and judgement of the medical professionals. The opinions of the patient's friends should also be sought so that as far as possible a consensus can emerge among all the participants for whom the interests of the patient are paramount. The compassionate character of Christian reasoning can be expressed in a paramount concern for the patient, at the centre of the situation, as well as a concern for the demands of physical caring for the patient on the part of individual relatives. The needs of all should be addressed as far as possible and practical measures of support taken. But there is a place here too for celebration. Joel Shuman has drawn our attention to the way in which the manner of dying of older relatives can in fact provide invaluable instruction for those who are left behind in terms of their own dying. We learn our basic life skills from those close to us, and, where those close to us are Christians, we learn the practices of Christian living – and dying. Traditionally, the Church has placed the death of martyrs at the centre of remembrance, but for most of us it is in the death of close relatives that we can learn the skills of dying and of living in the face of the certainty of death. As Shuman states, it is important therefore that the dying are not entirely removed from view and cut off from their family and friends.[29] In each and every dying there has to be a place also for celebration, as a sign also for the living. And it would be a natural part of Christian reasoning in the context outlined above to look for ways of exploring the celebratory aspect of living and dying, as sign of the divine creativity which makes us who we are.

29. Joel James Shuman, *The Body of Compassion* (Boulder, Colo.: Westview Press, 1999), pp. 1–6.

Most moral decision-making involves a precarious combination of universal principles of action and the particularities of a specific situation. Ethical reasoning is necessarily contingent and involves feeling our way through a situation in all its irreducible particularity, guided by our Christian principles and values but not released by them from the risks and unpredictable consequences that inhere within any action. If we choose to act, and any proper action entails such a moment of decision, then we do so without any certain knowledge of the consequences which may flow from our actions. Human action is, as Maurice Blondel observed, like the leap of a grasshopper which cannot see where it will land.[30] In ethical actions, this unpredictability becomes particularly difficult, since to act for the good is necessarily to risk the good; it is to embrace the possibility that – however pure our intentions may be – evil may flow (and at a time we do not know) from the actions we take in the belief that we act in accordance with the good.

The unpredictability of the consequences of our action, then, must itself be part of the burden that we assume when we act for the sake of the other. Only when God's reign is fully realised, and the good is all, can we know what the consequences will be of what we do. In the Not-Yet of our current state, we do not have that knowledge and we possess only uncertain judgement. We should not look upon this negatively, however, as an incurable inability to work out what is right in any given situation. Indeed, according to the pragmatic-creationist paradigm developed in this book, we should not think of reason as the faculty by which we calculate the right thing to do against a range of 'wrong' options. This would be dyadic reasoning, whereby a situation in life with a complex ethical structure becomes a 'test' for us to see whether we can discern 'the right answer'. Christian pragmatic reasoning proposes a different kind of ethical horizon. This is the case principally because it presupposes that we are ourselves part of the world that we understand. This sets the act of making a judgement and acting upon it within a different context. The central focus of the ethical now no longer lies in the particular character of the judgements we make in a given situation (whether they are 'right' or 'wrong') – however important these may be to the actual act of ethical decision itself, as expressive of a particular, compassionate-centred, celebratory and Christocentric life-form. When we adopt what we believe to be an ethical position through an act of will, we affirm our place in the

---

30. Maurice Blondel, *L'action (1893)* (Paris: Presses Universitaires de France, 1950), p. 141.

world in terms which derive from our most ideal understandings of the nature of the world. *The very act of genuinely seeking to give expression to the good through positive action in the world is itself ethical, independently of the subsequent consequences of what we do.* Moreover, an intrinsic part of the goodness of that act of positioning resides in the very unpredictability of its consequences. If where we seek to do good, with all due consideration and in all conscience, we actually find that we have acted in a way that brings evil consequences, then our most considered reasoning will have been shown to be empty and futile. In fact, we will prove to have been an agent of evil precisely where we strove to be an agent for good. It is difficult to imagine a more complete humiliation for an individual than the reversal of the relation between our most dearly held values and our actions in the world. In Romans 7:19, St Paul acknowledges the fragility of his will to do the good, but if I will to do the good and find that the consequences are evil, then I am called into question in the most fundamental way, that is, in terms of my capacity to act reasonably as an agent in the world. The very act of ethical positioning, therefore, itself bears the marks of the incarnational moment. If we reason in order to safeguard the coherence between the principles and values we hold dear and our actions in the world, then in our free ethical decision-making we embrace the possibility that our best reasoning will turn out to have the form and structure of unreason. Despite our intentions, we find that our actions mimic those of a deeply irrational, damaged or irresponsible person, who does not coordinate what they believe with how they act in the world and with the way the world is. By freely choosing the good, therefore, we find that we put ourselves at risk *for the sake of the good*. This deficit which lies at the heart of the ethical act is therefore a participation in the incarnational moment and thus shares in the nature of a sacrament; just as – in the transfiguration – the limited particularity of Jesus' human body became the medium for the manifestation of the infinite light of divine glory.

Conclusion

Questions concerning the operation of reason, both theoretical and practical, are necessarily complex ones and are not easily discussed in summary form. The remarks here can serve only as hints of the ways in which a broader and more fundamental discussion of the Christian contexts of reasoning might be developed. But the view outlined above does clearly find its axis in a condition or state of human freedom. It is not only that

we stand as free agents before our ethical choices, but such choices actually bring the necessary freedom of our choosing into play in a particularly
imperative manner. The choosing of the compassionate good, by the argument given here, entails an embrace of the freedom that resides in our
knowing the impossibility of being sure that what we do will have consequences that are consistent with the intentions of our acting. We may
choose to do good, for the sake of the other, only to find that what we do
injures or harms the interests of others in ways that we would not have
wished. Not to take that risk, however, would be a renunciation of our freedom and a failure to pursue the good, as a riskful enterprise of living that
is ordered to the well-being of the other.

This delicate freedom can be assumed under the theme of divine creativity which has been more generally the topic of this volume. The model
of the world as text proposed here implies an interpreter of the text, which
is the human community. That interpretation is not extraneous to the
world-text, however, but embedded within it. From a Christian perspective, it is an interpretation which must be informed by the world-text's
own memory of its origin in the divine breath; it must thus at some level
be a free, intelligent act which is the work of the Spirit. The Spirit is not
coercive; the Spirit indwells the mind and the heart.

From this we can conclude that our brief reflection upon ethical reasoning, formulated in the light of a reading of the pericope of the transfiguration, points us back again to the pragmatic heart of the cosmic theology outlined in this volume. Human beings are created as interpreters
of the creation, in the fullest sense possible. Structured by and within language, we are by our very nature disposed to move from and towards understandings of the world through actions, with their implicit knowledge,
or through reflection. We constantly re-engage with the world by multiple acts of 'reading' the world and our place in the world, in a chang-
ing flux of localities, temporalities, languages, memories and relations.
What these processes of 'reading' lead us to understand, therefore, is that
the world is the domain of a continuing divine creativity which finds expression also within ourselves, in our understandings of and interactions
with the world. The shaping of the world, as Thomas Aquinas once argued
in his concept of a cosmic 'circulation', entails our own contribution and
reshaping by the Spirit: as a pulsation in the world, in ourselves, and in the
movement between the two.

Conclusion
Cosmology and the theological imagination

Asreracht in doman uile leis, uair ro bui aicnedh na ndula uile isin
choluinn arroet Issu ... Ar cach adbar ocus cach duil ocus cach aicned
atcither isin domun conrairceda uile isin coluinn i n-esserract Críst.i. i
colainn cach duine.

All the world rose with him, for the nature of all elements dwelt in the
body which Jesus assumed ... Every kind of matter, every element and
every nature to be seen in the world were all combined in the body in
which Christ rose from the dead, that is, in the body of every human
being.

    The Evernew Tongue

The primary argument in the early chapters of this book was that the classical world-view combined thought, faith and the imagination in ways
that allowed human beings, as the creatures of God, to be at home in a
world that was created and thus, by its very nature, ordered to the divine
Creator. It was the collapse of this synthesis which led to the particular
conditions of the modern intellectual world, with its characteristic emphasis upon the instrumentality of reason, rather than what we might call
its cosmic commitments. The purpose of the book as a whole has been
to give content to the createdness of the world by developing cosmic imagery that is already present in scriptural traditions. This has not been in
any sense a contestation of scientific reason but rather an attempt to recontextualise reasoning within the parameters of a scriptural account of
the world: the image of world as divine body which is the embrace or address of God. I have argued that that scriptural cosmology contests the
ideology of scientism, which derives only remotely from science as such,

and which tends to offer a shallow and materialistic image of the world by which to live.

Of all the texts explored in this book, the one which stands out as communicating seminal insights into the radical transformations of human self-understanding and the place of the human in the world is the essay on Winkelmann by Johann Wolfgang von Goethe. Wilhem von Humboldt, who was the father of the modern German university system which played such a vital role in the cultural and intellectual life of Europe during the nineteenth century, noted in a letter to Goethe that it contained 'passages . . . which are among the greatest ever uttered'.[1] In that piece Goethe was writing about a man (though perhaps more about himself) whose aesthetic vision inaugurated a new understanding of Greek civilisation and a new religion of artistic sensibility. Winkelmann's aesthetic religion resided in the implicit claim that the moral ideals of classicism (as serenity), and the cosmic ideals of medieval Christianity (as the Good, the True and the Beautiful), become accessible to us in a new synthesis through a correctly schooled appreciation of the work of art. Goethe's approval for this position is very specific. In Winkelmann himself, within the contours of his life of aesthetic practice, the different faculties of his nature were united and, for Goethe, a new mutuality of inner and outer, of the human and the cosmic, was brought into being. The two perspectives seem in this text to be related. It is only because Winkelmann learned a new mode of 'seeing' and thus recognised in the work of art the epiphany of reality in all its intrinsic nobility and exaltation that Winkelmann's own faculties, his sense of the inner and outer world, were united. We can take this to be the overcoming or repairal of the divide between subjectivity and objectivity which was consequent upon the Kantian turn. For Winkelmann, in Goethe's reading of him, the alienation of the self – under banishment through the instrumentalisation of the natural order – was healed through the new unity of inner and outer achieved in the appreciation of the work of art. The unity of the faculties (which Kant had divided) becomes possible only with the discovery in the outer world of a profound receptivity to the human self, brought about in the religious intensity of the aesthetic gaze. Goethe's point, then, is that the problematic of the divided and alienated self can only be addressed by a new imaginary *of the*

---

1. Letter of 12 April 1806 (quoted in Henry Hatfield, *Aesthetic Paganism in German Literature* (Cambridge, Mass.: Harvard University Press, 1964), p. 203).

world in all its materiality, of which – albeit under alienation – we remain an integral part.

Viewed from this perspective, Romanticism and its aftermath represented the first attempt by a society to reshape our understanding of the world through constructing a new *vision* of the world, in ways that would restore a place to the human self *in* the world and thus heal the rift, or what Goethe called the 'fragmentation of our faculties', between our reasoning, our senses and their cosmic object. As a society, we still remain strongly influenced by that moment in our cultural history. Two modalities of the religious which are distinctive to the modern are the product of that Romantic age. The first is the rise of art as that which takes the place of religion, by becoming the site in which we encounter the world in a new strangeness and fullness. Art refreshes and heals us, inviting us into new depths of perception, involving our senses, judgements and feeling. The second is religious experience. This represents an intensity of experiencing which stands outside the norm of our empirical perceptions, and in which we find the elements of ultimate disclosure. Both phenomena are deeply embedded in contemporary society, and offer access into the immediacy of the world as an enchanted place. But both do so in ways that bypass the pre-modern principle that our ordinary cognitions and reasoning about the world already contain *in nuce* the possibility of knowledge of the divine Creator by virtue of the world's own state as created. Art reveals to us the powers of a human, and not a divine, creator, while religious experience stands outside our ordinary experience of the world as an exceptional and ineffable state of mind.

It has not been my intention to suggest that the movement from knowing the world to knowing God, or knowing *about* God, of earlier tradition was in any sense a straightforward one. Rather it was characterised by complex systems of dialectical negation. But nevertheless some kind of relation, as between created and Creator, necessarily obtained between the ordinary knowledge of the world and the extraordinary knowledge of its maker, and this cosmic unity became the object, however transcendentally nuanced, which united the faculties of the human creature. God was not just the absolute Other, but was also implied at every point in our perception of the world since this was of God's making and stood *as world* in intimate relation with him. All our faculties, of perception, thinking and feeling, found their centre, and unity, in this relation.

The restoration of a theological account of world is a precarious task which must resist the temptation of falling back into a variation of pre-modern cosmology on the one hand, while understanding the nature of its success on the other. That success flowed in no small part from the integration of the imagination into the ground of religious life. Under the discipline of Christian concepts, rites and practices which ordered the world as a theophanic space, the imagination opened up the domain of ordinary experience to the possibility of encounter with the divine which was neither wholly other than the ordinary world nor reducible to it. The imagination bridged the temporal and the eternal, earthly and celestial, and secured a sense of an ultimate human belonging in the world, whether optimistically configured as heaven and blessing or pessimistically as hell and damnation. Medieval reason functioned within the sheath of the religious imagination.

This volume is an attempt to rediscipline our own contemporary religious imagination as a way of recontextualising our practices of reason. The route I have chosen is the construction of a scriptural cosmology, based on an extended interpretation of significant texts from Genesis and Exodus, looping through the Catholic experience of the Eucharist as the place in which the unity of Christ's body with the world is made present and made known. The notion of body as the site of metaphor, as an underlying, ungraspable reality, generating a plethora of cultural formations, has been central to this view. So too has the understanding that the voice of God, divine speaking, is fundamental to the meaning of Scripture and specifically to the scriptural account of creation and redemption. What has linked the two has been the argument that texts are much like bodies, in that they carry the voice of the one whose speaking is their genesis. The world, then, is like a divine text, made up of signifying matter, and we are the creatures who are hosted at its core, as interpreters animated by the Spirit, and as agents whose own body life has been taken up and shaped by the divine creativity.

The construction of a new imaginary of the world, as divine body – which bears the divine voice, addressing us – is an attempt to bring relationality to the fore in our thinking and experience of the world. That new relation with God, as divine body, reorganises our own body life, setting us within an ecclesial and compassionate embodiment. Without that step of the imagination, the world will remain a field of measurable forces, of quanta (or only that), and our own bodies will remain sophisticated machinery, and not the living bearer of a unique and divinely created voice.

Voice, body, imagination and the text are the elements in this attempt at the development of a new theological account of the nature of the world as world. What unites them is Spirit-breath, which is the animating going forth from God which is at the same time an entering into God and the divine life. Spirit hovers between world and Trinity. Spirit warms us as the living breath of God, and rests as the dynamic remembrance of the Trinity in space and history.

Select bibliography

Abbot Suger on the Abbey Church of St-Denis and its Art Treasures, ed., trans. and annotated by Erwin Panofsky (2nd edn by Gerda Panofsky-Soergel, Princeton: Princeton University Press, 1979).

Aertsen, Jan A., *Medieval Philosophy and the Transcendentals* (Leiden: E. J. Brill, 1996).

Aristotle, *On the Heavens*, trans. W. K. C. Guthrie (Cambridge, Mass.: Harvard University Press, 1960).

 Posterior Analytics, trans. with commentary by Jonathan Barnes (Oxford: Clarendon Press, 1994).

Augustine, St, *Confessions*, trans. Henry Chadwick (Oxford: Oxford University Press, 1998).

 On Music, ed. Martin Jacobsson, *Aurelius Augustinus. De musica liber vi*, Acta Universitatis Stockholmiensis, Studia Latina Stockholmiensia 47 (Stockholm: Almqvist & Wiksell International, 2002).

Bacon, Francis, *Novum Organum*, ed. Lisa Jardine and Michael Silverthorne (Cambridge: Cambridge University Press, 2000).

Bayer, Oswald, *Gott als Autor. Zu einer poietologischer Theologie* (Tübingen: Mohr Siebeck, 1999).

Begbie, Jeremy, *Voicing Creation's Praise. Towards a Theology of the Arts* (Edinburgh: T. & T. Clark, 1991).

 Theology, Music and Time (Cambridge: Cambridge University Press, 2000).

Beiser, Frederick, *The Fate of Reason* (Cambridge, Mass.: Harvard University Press, 1987).

Blondel, Maurice, *L'action (1893)* (Paris: Presses Universitaires de France, 1950).

Blumenberg, Hans, *The Genesis of the Copernican World* (Cambridge, Mass.: MIT Press, 1987).

Brueggemann, Walter, *Theology of the Old Testament: Testimony, Dispute, Advocacy* (Minneapolis: Augsburg Fortress, 1997).

Carson, D. A. and H. G. M. Williamson, eds., *It Is Written. Scripture Citing Scripture* (Cambridge: Cambridge University Press, 1988).

Casarella, Peter, 'The Expression and Form of the Word: Trinitarian Hermeneutics and the Sacramentality of Language in Hans Urs von Balthasar's Theology', *Renascence* 48.2 (winter 1996), 111–35.

Chadwick, Henry, *Boethius. The Consolations of Music, Logic, Theology and Philosophy* (Oxford: Clarendon Press, 1981).

Chamberlain, David S., 'Philosophy of Music in the Consolation of Boethius', *Speculum* 45 (1970), 80–97.

Chauvet, Louis-Marie, *Symbol and Sacrament* (Collegeville, Minn.: The Liturgical Press, 1995).

Coakley, Sarah, ed., *Religion and the Body* (Cambridge: Cambridge University Press, 1997).
Powers and Submissions: Spirituality, Philosophy and Gender (Oxford: Blackwell 2001).

Cousins, Ewart, ed. and trans., *Bonaventure*, The Classics of Western Spirituality (New York: Paulist Press, 1978).
'Bonaventure's Mysticism of Language', in Stephen Katz, ed., *Mysticism and Language* (New York: Oxford University Press, 1992), pp. 236–57.

Crouzel, Henri, *Origen* (Edinburgh: T. & T. Clark, 1989).

Davies, Oliver, *A Theology of Compassion* (London: SCM Press, 2001 and Grand Rapids: Eerdmans, 2003).
'Soundings: towards a Theological Poetics of Silence', in Oliver Davies and Denys Turner, eds, *Silence and the Word* (Cambridge: Cambridge University Press, 2002), pp. 201–22.
'The Sign Redeemed: towards a Christian Fundamental Semiotics', *Modern Theology* 19.2 (April 2003), 219–41.

Davies, Oliver and Denys Turner, eds., *Silence and the Word: Negative Theology and Incarnation* (Cambridge: Cambridge University Press, 2002).

Dawson, John David, *Christian Figural Reading and the Fashioning of Identity* (Berkeley: University of California Press, 2002).

de Certeau, Michel, 'The Black Sun of Language: Foucault', in *idem, Heterologies. Discourse on the Other* (Minneapolis: University of Minnesota Press, 1986), pp. 171–84.

de Vaux, Roland, 'The Revelation of the Divine Name YHWH', in John I. Durham and J. R. Porter, eds., *Proclamation and Presence* (London: SCM Press, 1970), pp. 48–75.

Dickson, Gwen Griffith, *Johann Georg Hamann's Relational Metacriticism* (Berlin: W. de Gruyter, 1995).

Duhem, Pierre, *Le système du monde*, vol. I (Paris: A. Hermann, 1913).

Emerson, Jan Swango and Hugo Feiss, eds., *Imagining Heaven in the Middle Ages: a Body of Essays* (New York and London: Garland Publishing, 2000).

Farrow, Douglas, *Ascension and Ecclesia. On the Significance of the Doctrine of the Ascension for Ecclesiology and Christian Cosmology* (Edinburgh: T. & T. Clark, 1999).

Fiddes, Paul S., *Participating in God. A Pastoral Doctrine of the Trinity* (London: Darton, Longman and Todd, 2000).
'The Canon as Space and Place', in John Barton and Michael Wolter, eds., *Die Einheit der Schrift und die Vielfalt des Kanons. The Unity of Scripture and the Plurality of the Canon* (Beihefte zur Zeitschrift für neutestamentliche Wissenschaft 118; Berlin: Walter de Gruyter, 2003), pp. 127–49.

Ford, David, *Self and Salvation* (Cambridge: Cambridge University Press, 1999).

Frege, Gottlob, *Conceptual Notation and Related Articles* (Oxford: Clarendon Press, 1972).

Funkenstein, Amos, *Theology and the Scientific Imagination: from the Middle Ages to the Seventeenth Century* (Princeton: Princeton University Press, 1986).

Gadamer, Hans-Georg, *Truth and Method* (London: Sheed and Ward, 1979).

Gatens, Moira and Genevieve Lloyd, *Collective Imaginings. Spinoza Past and Present* (London and New York: Routledge, 1999).

Gaukroger, Stephen, *Francis Bacon and the Transformation of Early Modern Philosophy* (Cambridge: Cambridge University Press, 2001).

Gil, José, *Metamorphoses of the Body* (Minneapolis and London: University of Minnesota Press, 1998).

Goethe, Johann Wolfgang von, 'Winkelmann und sein Jahrhundert', in *Goethe, Berliner Ausgabe*, vol. XIX (Berlin: Aufbau Verlag, 1973), pp. 469–520.

Gracia, Jorge J. E., *A Theory of Textuality. The Logic and Epistemology* (New York, Albany: SUNY Press, 1995).

Grant, Edward, *Planets, Stars and Orbs. The Medieval Cosmos, 1200–1687* (Cambridge: Cambridge University Press, 1996).

Gray, G. B., *A Critical and Exegetical Commentary on Numbers* (International Critical Commentary; Edinburgh: T. & T. Clark, 1903).

Green, Garrett, *Imagining God: Theology and the Religious Imagination* (Grand Rapids: Eerdmans, 1989).

Grosz, Elizabeth, *Volatile Bodies: towards a Corporeal Feminism* (Bloomington, Ind.: Indiana University Press, 1994).

Gunton, Colin, *Christ and Creation* (Carlisle: Paternoster Press and Grand Rapids: Eerdmans, 1992).

The Triune Creator (Edinburgh: Edinburgh University Press, 1998).

Gunton, Colin, ed., *The Doctrine of Creation* (Edinburgh: T. & T. Clark, 1997).

Hamann, Johann Georg, *Johann Georg Hamann. Sämtliche Werke*, vols. I–VI, ed. Josef Nadler (Vienna: Herder, 1949–57).

Briefe, ed. Arthur Henkel (Frankfurt am Main: Insel Verlag, 1988).

Londoner Schriften, ed. Oswald Beyer and Bernd Weissenborn (Munich: Verlag C. H. Beck, 1993).

Hardy, Dan, 'Christ and Creation', in *idem, God's Ways with the World* (Edinburgh: T. & T. Clark, 1996), pp. 114–31.

'Creation and Eschatology', in *God's Ways*, pp. 151–70.

Hatfield, Henry, *Aesthetic Paganism in German Literature* (Cambridge. Mass.: Harvard University Press, 1964).

Hildegard of Bingen, *Hildegardis Bingensis Epistolarium, Pars Prima I–XC*, ed. L. van Acker, (Turnholt: Brepols, 1991).

Honnefelder, Ludwig, 'Der zweite Anfang der Metaphysik. Voraussetzungen, Ansätze und Folgen der Wiederbegründung der Metaphysik im 13./14. Jahrhundert', in J. P. Beckmann et al., eds., *Philosophie im Mittelalter. Entwicklungslinien und Paradigmen* (Hamburg: Meiner, 1987), pp. 165–86.

Ihde, Dan, *Listening and Voice: a Phenomenology of Sound* (Athens: Ohio University Press, 1976).

Irwin, T. H., *Aristotle's First Principles* (Oxford: Oxford University Press, 1988).

Jacobi, Friedrich Heinrich, *David Hume über den Glauben, oder Idealismus und Realismus*, ed. Hamilton Beck (New York and London: Garland, 1983) [facsimile reproduction of 1787 edition and the *Vorrede* to the 1815 edition].

The Main Philosophical Writings and the Novel 'Allwill', ed. and trans. George di Giovanni (Montreal and Kingston: McGill-Queen's University Press, 1994).

Jeanrond, Werner, *Theological Hermeneutics* (New York: Crossroad, 1991).

Jenkins, John I., *Knowledge and Faith in Thomas Aquinas* (Cambridge: Cambridge University Press, 1997).

Jenson, Robert W., *Systematic Theology*, vol. I: *The Triune God* (New York and Oxford: Oxford University Press, 1997); vol. II: *The Works of God* (New York and Oxford: Oxford University Press, 1999).

Jeremias, Joachim, *The Eucharistic Words of Jesus* (London: SCM Press, 1966).

Johnson, Aubrey R., *The Vitality of the Individual in the Thought of Ancient Israel* (2nd edn, Cardiff: University of Wales Press, 1964).

Kant, Immanuel, *Critique of Pure Reason*, trans. Norman Kemp Smith (London: Macmillan Press, 1933).

Kearney, Richard, *The Wake of the Imagination* (London: Routledge, 1998).

Koyré, Alexander, *The Astronomical Revolution*, trans. R. E. W. Maddison (Paris: Hermann, 1973).

Kretzmann, N., 'Trinity and Transcendentals', in R. Feenstra and C. Plantinga, eds., *Trinity, Incarnation and Atonement* (Indiana: University of Notre Dame Press, 1989), pp. 79–109.

Kuhn, Thomas S., *The Copernican Revolution* (Cambridge, Mass.: Harvard University Press, 1957).

LaCocque, André and Paul Ricoeur, *Thinking Biblically. Exegetical and Hermeneutical Studies* (Chicago and London: University of Chicago Press, 1998).

Le Breton, David, *Anthropologie du corps et modernité* (Paris: Presses Universitaires de France, 1990).

Lehrman, S. M., *Midrash Rabbah III* (London: The Soncino Press, 1961).

Longinus, *On the Sublime*, ed. D. A. Russell, (Oxford: Oxford University Press, 1964).

Loughlin, Gerard, *Telling God's Story. Bible, Church and Narrative Theology* (Cambridge: Cambridge University Press, 1996).

Marcus, Joel, *The Way of the Lord. Christological Exegesis of the Old Testament in the Gospel of Mark* (Louisville, Ky.: Westminster/John Knox Press, 1992).

Mark 1–8, The Anchor Bible, New York: Doubleday, 1999.

Markus, R. A., *Signs and Meanings* (Liverpool: Liverpool University Press, 1996).

Martin, Dale B., *The Corinthian Body* (New Haven and London: Yale University Press, 1995).

Marx, Werner, *Introduction to Aristotle's Theory of Being as Being* (The Hague: Martinus Nijhoff, 1977).

McDannell, Colleen and Bernard Lang, eds., *Heaven. A History* (2nd edn, New Haven: Yale University Press, 2001).

McDonald, Scott, 'Theory of Knowledge', in Norman Kretzmann and Eleonore Stump, eds., *Cambridge Companion to Aquinas* (Cambridge: Cambridge University Press, 1993), pp. 160–95.

Merleau-Ponty, Maurice, *Phenomenology of Perception* (London: Routledge and Kegan Paul, 1962).

Midgley, Mary, *Science and Poetry* (London: Routledge, 2001).

Milbank, John, *The Word Made Strange. Theology, Language, Culture* (Oxford: Blackwell, 1997).

Being Reconciled. Ontology and Pardon (London and New York: Routledge, 2003).

Moore, Andrew, *Realism and Christian Faith. God, Grammar and Meaning* (Cambridge: Cambridge University Press, 2003).

Morrison, Jeremy, *Winckelmann and the Notion of Aesthetic Education* (Oxford: Clarendon Press, 1996).

Mosès, Stéphane, ' "Je serai qui je serai." La révélation des Noms dans le récit biblique', in Marco M. Olivetti, ed., *Filosofia della Rivelazione* (Padua: Casa Editrice Dott. Antonio Milani, 1994), pp. 565–76.

Moyise, Steve, *The Old Testament in the New Testament. Essays in Honour of J. L. North* (Sheffield: Sheffield University Press, 2000).

Murphy, Nancey, *Theology in the Age of Scientific Reasoning* (Ithaca: Cornell University Press, 1990).

Murphy, Nancey and Ellis, George F. R., *On the Moral Nature of the Universe* (Minneapolis: Fortress Press, 1996).

Noth, Martin, *Numbers. A Commentary* (The Old Testament Library; London: SCM Press, 1968).

Ochs, Peter, 'Three Post-Critical Encounters with the Burning Bush', in Stephen E. Fowl, ed., *The Theological Interpretation of Scripture. Classic and Contemporary Readings* (Oxford: Blackwell, 1997), pp. 129–42.

   Peirce, Pragmatism and the Logic of Scripture (Cambridge: Cambridge University Press, 1998).

Origen, *On First Principles*, trans. G. W. Butterworth, Gloucester, Mass.: Peter Smith, 1973.

   Contra Celsum, trans. Henry Chadwick (Cambridge: Cambridge University Press, 1980)

   Commentary on the Gospel of John, trans. Ronald E. Heine (Washington: Catholic University of America Press, 1989).

Peacocke, A. R., *Creation and the World of Science* (Oxford and New York: Oxford University Press, 1979).

   Paths from Science towards God (Oxford: Oneworld Publications, 2001).

Pérez-Ramos, Antonio, *Francis Bacon's Idea of Science and the Maker's Knowledge Tradition* (Oxford: Clarendon Press; New York: Oxford University Press, 1988).

Pickstock, Catherine, *After Writing: on the Liturgical Consummation of Philosophy* (Oxford: Blackwell, 1998).

Polkinghorne, John, *Science and Providence* (London: SPCK, 1989).

   Reason and Reality (London: SPCK, 1991).

Polkinghorne, John, ed., *The Work of Love. Creation as Kenosis* (London: SPCK, 2001).

Pseudo-Clementine, *Die Pseudoklementinen*, vol. II: *Rekognitionen in Rufins Übersetzung*, ed. Bernhard Rehm (Berlin: Akademie-Verlag, 1965).

Pseudo-Denys, *The Complete Works*, trans. Colm Luibheid (New York: Paulist Press, 1987).

Quine, W. V., *Pursuit of Truth* (Cambridge Mass.: Harvard University Press, 1990).

Rahner, Karl, *The Trinity* (Tunbridge Wells: Burns and Oates, 1970).

Randles, W. G. L., *The Unmaking of the Medieval Christian Cosmos, 1500–1760* (Aldershot: Ashgate, 1999).

Ricoeur, Paul, *Interpretation Theory* (Fort Worth: Texas Christian University Press, 1976).

   'Philosophy and Religious Language', in *idem*, *Figuring the Sacred: Religion, Narrative and the Imagination* (Minneapolis: Fortress Press, 1995), pp. 35–47.

Samuelson, Norbert M., *The First Seven Days. A Philosophical Commentary on the Creation of Genesis* (Atlanta, Ga.: Scholars Press, 1992).

Schiller, Friedrich, *On the Sublime*, in *Sämtliche Werke*, vol. V (Munich: Winkler Verlag, 1975).

Schleiermacher, Friedrich, *Hermeneutics and Criticism and Other Writings*, trans. A. Bowie (Cambridge: Cambridge University Press, 1998).

Schnur, Harald, *Schleiermachers Hermeneutik und Ihre Vorgeschichte im 18. Jahrhundert* (Stuttgart and Weimar: Verlag J. B. Metzler, 1994).

Schrade, Leo, 'Music in the Philosophy of Boethius', *The Musical Quarterly* 33 (1947), 188–200.

Shuman, Joel James, *The Body of Compassion* (Boulder, Colo.: Westview Press, 1999).

Spinoza, Benedict de, *Ethics*, trans. Edwin Curley (Harmondsworth: Penguin Books, 1996).

Stewart, Larry, *The Rise of Public Science: Rhetoric, Technology and Natural Philosophy in Newtonian Britain, 1660–1750* (Cambridge: Cambridge University Press, 1992).

Swartley, William M., *Israel's Scripture Traditions and the Synoptic Gospels* (Peabody, Mass.: Hendrickson Publishers, 1994).

Tanner, Kathryn, *God and Creation in Christian Theology: Tyranny or Empowerment?* (Oxford: Blackwell, 1988).

Thomas Aquinas, St, *Expositio super librum Boethii De trinitate*, in *Opera omnia*, vol. XXVIII (Vivès, 1871–2).

In librum Beati Dionysii De divinis nominibus expositio, in *Opera omnia*, vol. XXIX (Vivès, 1871–2).

Quaestiones disputatae de veritate, in *Opera omnia*, vols. XIV–XV (Vivès, 1871–2).

Summa theologiae, ed. P. Caramello (Rome: Marietti, 1948).

Toulmin, Stephen, *Foresight and Understanding* (New York: Harper and Row, 1963),

The Return to Cosmology: Postmodern Science and the Theology of Nature (Berkeley: University of California Press, 1982).

Cosmopolis; the Hidden Agenda of Modernity (New York: Free Press, 1990)

van Deusen, Nancy, *Theology and Music at the Early University* (Leiden: E. J. Brill, 1995).

van Fleteren, Frederick, 'Augustine's Ascent of the Soul in Book VII of the Confessions: a Reconsideration', *Augustinian Studies* 5 (1974), 29–72.

'Principles of Augustine's Hermeneutic: an Overview', in Frederick van Fleteren and Joseph C. Schnaubelt, eds., *Augustine. Biblical Exegete* (New York: Peter Lang, 2001), pp. 1–32.

von Bingen, Hildegard, *Epistolarium*, ed. L. Van Acker (Turnhoult: Brepols, 1991).

Liber divinorum operum, ed. A. Derolez and P. Dronke (Turnhoult: Brepols, 1996).

Ward, Graham, *Cities of God* (London: Routledge, 2000).

Barth, Derrida and the Language of Theology (Cambridge: Cambridge University Press, 1995).

Williams, Rowan, 'The Deflections of Desire: Negative Theology in Trinitarian Disclosure', in Davies and Turner, eds., *Silence and the Word* (2002), pp. 115–35.

Wilson, Catherine, *The Visible World: Early Modern Philosophy and the Invention of the Microscope* (Princeton: Princeton University Press, 1995).

Winckelmann, Johann Joachim, *Werke* (Berlin: Aufbau-Verlag, 1982).

Wolterstorff, Nicholas, *Divine Discourse* (Cambridge: Cambridge University Press, 1995).

Zimmermann, A., *Ontologie oder Metaphysik? Die Diskussion über den Gegenstand der Metaphysik im 13. und 14. Jahrhundert* (Leiden and Cologne: E. J. Brill, 1965).

Index of biblical citations

General index